An Assembly Collection

An Assembly Collection

Joan Hasler
Headteacher at Dover Grammar School for Girls

LONGMAN GROUP UK LIMITED

Longman House,
Burnt Mill, Harlow, Essex CM20 2JE, England
and Associated Companies throughout the World.

© Longman Group UK Limited 1986
All rights reserved. No part of this publication may be reproduced, stored in a
retrieval system, or transmitted in any form or by any means, electronic, mechanical,
photocopying, recording or otherwise, without the prior written permission of the
Publishers.

First published 1986
ISBN 0 582 36125 7

Set in 11/13 Linotron Plantin

Printed in Great Britain by Mackays of Chatham Ltd.

The author wishes to thank Miss J A Nunn for her help in
preparing the typescript and Jenny Lee for her work in
re-numbering the references in the final stages and correcting the
page proofs. She would also like to record her gratitude to
Longman's editors for their encouragement and optimism.

Contents

Acknowledgements

We are grateful to the following for permission to reproduce
copyright material:

Blandford Books Ltd for an extract from p. 61 *More
Readings for the Senior Assembly* by D. M. Prescott; Calcutta
Diocesan Library at St Paul's Cathedral, Mother Church of the
Calcutta Diocese of the Church of North India for the 'St. Paul's
Cathedral Prayer' by the late Rev. Subir Biswas; Cambridge
University Press for an extract from p. 251 *Baba Kuhi's Vision of
God* by Baba Kuhi of Shiraz, trans. B. A. Nicholson; Jonathan
Cape Ltd on behalf of the Executors of the Laurence Housman
Estate and the Estate of Teresa Hooley for the poems 'Light
Looked Down' by L. Housman from *The Little Plays of St Francis*
and 'Retro Me, Sathanas' by T. Hooley from *Selected Poems*;
author's agents on behalf of the Estate of Rachael Carson for an
extract from *Silent Spring* by Rachael Carson, pub. Hamish
Hamilton Ltd; author's agents for the poem 'Ballad of the
Breadman' by Charles Causley from *Collected Poems*, pub.
Macmillan; Geoffrey Chapman Ltd for adapted prayer 'The
Unity of Christians' from p. 96 *The Unity Book of Prayers* © 1969
Geoffrey Chapman Ltd; author's agents on behalf of Miss D. E.
Collins for 31 lines of verse from *The Good Rich Man* by G. K.
Chesterton; Christian Aid/British Council of Churches for poems
'Statistics' by C. Rajendra and 'The Arithmetic of Poverty' by
P. Appadurai, pp. 42–3, 45 *Other Voices, Other Places* collected by
C. Rajendra; the General Synod of the Church of England for
three collections from pp. 480, 635, 890 *The Alternative Service
Book* 1980, © Central Board of Finance of the Church of
England; Wm. Collins Sons & Co Ltd for extracts from *Mister
God, This is Anna* by Fynn, *A Precocious Biography* by
Y. Yevtushenko, *Surprised by Joy, The Screwtape Letters* and *The
Lion, the Witch and the Wardrobe* by C. S. Lewis; the author,
Murdoch Dahl and St Albans Diocesan Education Committee for
verses from *Words to Share* by Murdoch Dahl; Darton, Longman
& Todd Ltd for poem 'Feed my Little Ones' by C. Day Lewis for
OXFAM from *Assembly Workshop*, Section 7, No. 6 by Ronald
Dingwall; author's agents on behalf of the author for extracts from

Smoke on the Mountain by Joy Davidman; Epworth Press for
extracts from *The Hammer of the Lord* by Colin Morris, *Dreams at
Sunset* by Rev. F. W. Boreham and an extract to Rita Snowden
from Sir Carl Berendsen in *Worship and Wonder*, pub. Stainer &
Bell; Eyre & Spottiswoode, Her Majesty's Printers London for
extracts from the *Book of Common Prayer 1662*, which is Crown
Copyright in England; Faber & Faber Ltd for poem 'Journey of
the Magi', extracts from 'Choruses from "The Rocks" ' by T. S.
Eliot *Collected Poems 1909–1962*, extract from *Murder in the
Cathedral* by T. S. Eliot, poem 'Digging' by Seamus Heaney from
Death of a Naturalist, and an extract from *Ten Principal
Upanishads* by Shree Purobit Swami; Farrar, Straus & Giroux Inc
for extracts from *The Little World of Don Camillo* by Giovanni
Guareschi; author's agents for an extract from *Travelling In* by
Monica Furlong; Gill & Macmillan Ltd for 'Green Blackboards',
'The Brick', 'The Tractor', 'Lord I Have Time' and 'There are
Two Loves Only' from *Prayers of Life* by Michel Quoist; Victor
Gollancz Ltd and the author's Literary Executors for extracts
from *Testament of Youth* by Vera Brittain; Victor Gollancz Ltd for
a prayer by Govind Singh from *God of a Hundred Names* ed.
Barbara Greene and Victor Gollancz; Granada Publishing Ltd for
extracts from 'Christ Looked out at People' by Caryll
Houselander, 'Canoe Story' by Geoffrey Summerfield, 'Boasting
Song' by Margaret Rose from pp. 137, 31, 99 *Folk and Vision*;
author's agents on behalf of the author for the poem 'In the
Wilderness' by Robert Graves from *Collected Poems*; Hodder &
Stoughton Ltd for extracts from *Space Between the Bars* by
Donald Swann, and prayers from pp. 41, 71, 83 *New Parish
Prayers* by Frank Colquhoun; The Hogarth Press and the author
for extracts from *Cider with Rosie* and *A Lion in Winter* by Laurie
Lee; author's agents on behalf of the author, Sir Fred Hoyle, for
an extract from *The Nature of the Universe* © Fred Hoyle 1950;
Lutterworth Press for prayer from *Explorations in Worship* by
Sheila Hobden; Macmillan London & Basingstoke for an extract
from *The Path and the Prize* by C. Astle and a prayer 'Fruit
Gathering' in *Collected Poems and Plays* by Rabindranath
Tagore; the author's agents for an extract from *A Dustbin of
Milligan*, pub. Puffin Books; A. R. Mowbray & Co Ltd for
extracts from *More from Ten to Eight on Radio 4* by Stephen
Hopkinson, *Fireside Talks* by W. H. Elliott (1937), adapted
extracts from *The Story of Taizé* by Balado © A. R. Mowbray &
Co Ltd 1980, *Sundry Times, Sundry Places* by Cuthbert Bardsley,
Bishop of Coventry © A. R. Mowbray & Co Ltd 1962, complete
stories 'The Three Apprentices' by Mary Tayler from *Stories and*

Prayers at Five to Ten © A. R. Mowbray & Co Ltd 1959, and '7 Problems of the Friday Night Youth Club' by John Ward from *Purple Papers* © A. R. Mowbray & Co Ltd 1972; John Murray & Co Ltd for poems 'Harvest Hymn', 'Diary of a Church Mouse' and 36 lines from 'Christmas' from *Collected Poems* by John Betjeman; Navajivan Trust for extracts from *Gandhi, Life and Thoughts of Mahatma Gandhi*, ed. Krishna Kripalani and Mahendra Meghani; the author, Patrick Parry Okeden for an adapted version of his talk 'The Need to be Nasty' from *Pause for Thought*, BBC Publications 1971; Oxford University Press for poems 'Ecce Homo' (omitting verses 10–11) by David Gascoyne from *Collected Poems* © Oxford University Press 1965; Penguin Books Ltd for poems 'Poem of Solitary Delight' by Tachibana Akemi, 'November Third' by Miyazawa Kenji pp. 142–3, 201–2 *The Penguin Book of Japanese Verse*, trans. G. Bownas and A. Thwaite, Copyright © Geoffrey Bownas and Anthony Thwaite, 1964, extracts from pp. 117–8 *The Upanishads*, trans. Juan Mascaro (Penguin Classics 1965) Copyright © Juan Mascaro 1965, and pp. 385–8 from *Mysticism* by F. C. Happold (Pelican rev. edn 1970) Copyright © F. C. Happold 1963, 1964, 1970; the author's agents for poem 'The Donkey's Owner' by Clive Sansom from *The Witnesses*, pub. Methuen; George Sassoon for poem 'The Power and the Glory' by Siegfried Sassoon; SCM Press Ltd for prayers from pp. 14, 18, 20, 23, 25, 29, 30–1, 33, 37–40, 49, 62 (adapted), 67, 73, 83, 87, 91, 94, 99, 103–4, 109 of *A Kind of Praying*, p. 5 (adapted) from *The Cry of the Spirit* by Rex Chapman, prayer (adapted) by Hugh Martin from p. 197 *A Book of Prayers for Schools* ed. Hugh Martin, adapted prayers on pp. 31, 44–5, 48–9, 52–4, 56–8, 60, 68, 111, 113, 125–6, 129 from *Contemporary Prayers for Public Worship* by Coates, Gregory, Micklem, Sewell, Stapleton, Jones and Wren, ed. C. Micklem; author's agents on behalf of Anya Seton for an extract from her *Winthrop Woman*, pub. Hodder & Stoughton Ltd © 1958 by Anya Seton Chase; Sheed & Ward Ltd for extracts for 'God Abides in Men', 'Young Man' from *The Flowering Tree* by Caryll Houselander; Sphere Books Ltd for extracts from *Emma and I* by Sheila Hocken; Stainer & Bell Ltd for prayers from pp. 27, 30 *Word Alive*, ed. Edmund Banyard, p. 23 *Celebration*, ed. Brian Frost & Derek Wensley, © Stainer & Bell Ltd, extracts from *Step into Joy* (1969) by Joan Brockelsby, 'Benedicite' by Canon E. R. Hougham from *Celebration* Book 1, poem 'Happy Christmas' by John Smith in *Worship and Wonder*, ed. Jones, adaptations of 'Can You Tell Me the Way to Bethlehem?' by Canon E. R. Hougham and 'A Child of Our Time' by Derek Wensley from *Celebration*

Book 2; the author, Prof. Iain E. P. Taylor for his article 'A Molecular Genesis' from *Biologist* Journal of the Institute of Biology; United Church of Christ Publications Inc for verse 'Protest in Semantics' by Betty Atkins Fukuyama in *United Church Herald*; the author, Kenneth Walsh for his poems 'Which Half?', 'Life', 'Love', all from *Sometimes I Weep*, pub. SCM Press.

Though every effort has been made to trace the owners of copyright material, in a few cases this has proved impossible, and we take this opportunity to offer our apologies to any copyright holders whose rights may have been unwittingly infringed.

Introduction

There are many assembly books and it seems presumptuous to add yet another, especially at a time when the traditional School Assembly seems nearing its end and especially as there is little that is original or innovative in this offering. However, as one who has spent many hours trying to fit together hymns, readings and prayers in such a way as to present a coherent whole and a valid message, there did seem a great dearth of guides to enable this to be done efficiently. Complaints to publishers' representatives merely drew the usual reply – if you want one, why not produce it? And so, that is what I eventually did.

It is aimed at 11–18 year olds, and if many of the readings seem difficult for the younger end or the less academic, I make no apology. There are others written specifically for both, but in general I am sure we underestimate the intelligence of the young and do them a disservice to read down to them. Where there are particular problems any assembly leader will of course adapt material – but copyright restrictions would make it difficult to do so in print, even if it were desirable. Some adaptations have been made and for permission to make them I am grateful – these, however, are generally made to shorten a passage or to acknowledge a less committed audience rather than to simplify the meaning or the style.

Many of the passages are in other anthologies. I had hoped merely to refer to these and assume that the Assembly Leader would have, for instance, old favourites like Thompson's *Readings*, Elphick's *Faith and Vision*, or *Words for Worship* (Campling and Davis). Preliminary readers, however, objected strongly to this and wanted all passages referred to to be printed, except only Bible passages. So here they are, and I freely acknowledge my debt to previous compilers.

How to Use this Book

1 The most obvious use is to consult the themes which are grouped in sections and listed in the Contents under Readings. Hymns, readings and prayers are suggested in the list of Assemblies at the beginning of each section although the Assembly Leader will often wish to change the particular combination. Hymn numbers can be obtained from the hymn index; the first lines are given. There are references in each section to some prayers and readings in other sections.
2 If a topic is wanted which is not named in the contents it may be in the topic index at the back, with hymns, prayers and readings entered, or there may be some reference to the most appropriate section.
3 If a particular reading or author is wanted the title and author indices should help. Suitable prayers and hymns can be found at the beginning of each section, in the list of Assemblies.

CROSS REFERENCE BETWEEN SECTIONS

Both readings and prayers are numbered consecutively throughout all sections. The numbers within each section are given in the contents so they may be found more readily. The first lines of hymns are given in all sections and the hymn index will be found after this introduction. Suggestions for alternative hymns for each theme can easily be found from the theme suggestions beside each hymn.

The suggestions made are obviously open to much criticism, particularly in the choice of prayers. In many cases the Leader's own prayer would be more appropriate; in many cases, too, the readings will need introduction or adaptation. It is hoped that the Assembly Leader will use the material in whatever way seems most helpful, but that there are enough materials and sufficient suggestions to provide a useful and helpful service.

Hymns

(Carols are not included in this list.)

Index of first lines with reference to possible themes

E.H. – English Hymnal; N.L. – New Life; N.O. – New Orbit; S.P. – Songs of Praise

FIRST LINE	E.H.	N.L.	N.O.	S.P.	POSSIBLE THEMES
1 All creatures of our God and King		43	9	439	Nature, Praise, St Francis
2 All glory laud and honour	622			135	Palm Sunday, Praise
3 All people that on earth do dwell	365	44		433	Praise, Truth
4 All things bright and beautiful	587			444	Nature etc.
5 All who love and serve your city		66			Truth, Values
6 And did those feet in ancient times	656A			446	Community, Remembrance
7 Angels, from the realms of glory				71	Christmas, Epiphany etc.
8 As pants the hart for cooling streams	367			449	Praise
9 As with gladness men of old	39			83	Epiphany, Gifts to God, Light
10 At the name of Jesus	368	136		392	Ascension, Christian unity, Ten Commandments
11 At thy feet O Christ we lay	256			24	Faith, Morning
12 Awake my soul and with the sun	257	47		25	Gifts, Work
13 Away in a manger				353	Christmas (Primary)
14 Be thou my guardian and my guide	369			100	Honesty, Lent, Temptation

FIRST LINE	E.H.	N.L.	N.O.	S.P.	POSSIBLE THEMES
15 Bitter was the night		32			Judas
16 Blest are the pure in heart	370			455	Beatitudes
17 Breathe on me breath of God		86		458	Priorities, Whitsun
18 Bright the vision that delighteth	372			460	Trinity
19 City of God, how broad and far	375			468	Sermon on the Mount
20 Come down, O love divine	152	69		177	God in Man, Whitsun
21 Come ye thankful people, come	289			9	Harvest
22 Dear Lord and Father of Mankind	383	88		481	Family, Good Resolutions, Values
23 Eternal Father strong to save	540			336	Courage
24 Eternal ruler of the ceaseless round	384	70		485	Courage, Fight for Right, God in Man
25 Far round the world thy children sing their song		114		299	Children
26 Father hear the prayer we offer	385	89		487	Courage, Family, Priorities, Remembrance, Truth
27 Fight the good fight with all thy might	389			491	Courage, Fight for Right, Giving, Parable
28 Fill thou my life, O Lord my God		49		492	Gifts, Work
29 For all the Saints who from their labours rest	641			202	Remembrance, Saints
30 For the beauty of the earth	309	50		494	Beauty, Good Resolutions
31 Forth in thy name O Lord I go	259	109		29	Discontent
32 Forty days and forty nights	73			97	Lent- Temptation and Repentance

FIRST LINE	E.H.	N.L.	N.O.	S.P.	POSSIBLE THEMES
33 Give me joy in my heart, keep me praising		63	70		Gifts, Good Resolutions, Love and Joy
34 Glad that I live am I		73		499	Gifts, Joy
35 God be in my head			65	501	Remembrance
36 God is love; His the care		132	34	502	Ascension, Love, Peacemakers, Tolerance, Whitsun
37 God is unique and one		74			God in Man
38 God is working his purpose out as year succeeds to year	548			300	Tolerance
39 God moves in a mysterious way	394			503	Truth
40 God who spoke in the beginning		71			Environment, Genesis, Time
41 God's spirit is in my heart		116			Family, Kingdom of God, Worship
42 Gracious spirit, Holy Ghost	396	133		507	Love, Peacemakers, Tolerance, Values, Whitsun
43 Guide me O thou great Redeemer	397			508	Beatitudes
44 Hail thee, Festival day	630			389	Easter, Ascension, Whitsun
45 He who would valiant be	402			515	Courage
46 Heavenly Father, may thy blessing				516	Community, Honesty, Sermon on the Mount
47 Help us to help each other, Lord				517	Community
48 He's back in the land of the living		35			Easter
49 High o'er the lonely hills				63	Beauty

FIRST LINE	E.H.	N.L.	N.O.	S.P.	POSSIBLE THEMES
50 Hills of the North rejoice		2		64	Advent
51 Holy! Holy! Holy! Lord God Almighty	162			187	Trinity
52 I belong to a family, the biggest on earth		113	10		Brotherhood, Community, Unity
53 I bind unto myself today	212			528	Trinity
54 I danced in the morning		28	54		Death of Christ, Easter, Judas
55 I vow to thee my country, all earthly things above				319	Remembrance
56 If I had a hammer, I'd hammer in the morning		117	11		Peacemakers, Priorities
57 If you are a son of man		38			Easter
58 Immortal, invisible, God only wise	407	77		535	Faith, Light, Trinity
59 In Christ there is no East or West		118	12	537	Christian unity
60 Into the corners of your mind		87			Gifts
61 It was on a Friday morning		34			Easter
62 Jesus shall reign where'er the sun	420	138		545	Kingdom of God
63 Kum ba yah, my Lord, kum ba yah!		103			Children, Suffering
64 Lead us, heavenly Father, lead us	426			555	Family, Sermon on the Mount, Ten Commandments
65 Let us, with a gladsome mind	532			12	Creation, Nature
66 Life could be good and rich and whole		127			Brotherhood, Gifts, International co-operation, Peace
67 Lord bring the day to pass		78	41		Creation, Environment, Gifts

FIRST LINE	E.H.	N.L.	N.O.	S.P.	POSSIBLE THEMES
68 Lord, I love to stamp and shout		94	42		Children
69 Lord of all hopefulness, Lord of all joy		54	39	565	Happiness, Remembrance, Sermon on the Mount
70 Lord, thy word abideth	436			570	Lent-Temptation, Parable-guest
71 Love divine, all loves excelling	437			573	Love, Whitsun
72 Love is something if you give it away		134	14		Love, Tolerance
73 Morning has broken		79		30	Beauty, Joy, Ten Commandments
74 My song is love unknown		135		127	Holy Week, Passion
75 New every morning is the love	260			31	Use of time, Work, Service
76 Now join we, to praise the Creator		41	6		Creator, Gifts, Harvest, International co-operation
77 Now thank we all our God	533	55	33	350	Praise, Worship
78 Now the green blade riseth from the buried grain		36			Easter
79 O brother Man, fold to thy heart thy brother		119		307	Christian unity, Community, Love, Peacemakers
80 O God our help in ages past	450			598	Time
81 O Jesus I have promised	577			255	Parable
82 O praise ye the Lord		56		351	Praise
83 O worship the King	466			618	Creation, Worship, Nature
84 O worship the Lord in the beauty of Holiness	42	57		93	Beatitudes, Holy Week, Parable-vineyards
85 Of the Father's love begotten		30		387	Happiness

FIRST LINE	E.H.	N.L.	N.O.	S.P.	POSSIBLE THEMES
86 On Jordan's bank, the Baptist's cry	9			67	Advent, John the Baptist
87 Once to every man and nation	563			309	Courage, Good and evil, Remembrance
88 One man's hand can't break a prison down		120	84		Freedom
89 Praise my soul the king of heaven	470	58		623	Just for Today, Praise, Ten Commandments
90 Praise the Lord, ye heavens adore Him!	535	59		624	Praise
91 Rejoice! the Lord is king	476			632	Ascension, Happiness
92 Ride on! Ride on in majesty	620			137	Easter, Holy week
93 Said Judas to Mary, now what will you do?		27	49		Judas
94 Show me the prison, show me the jail		105			Temptation
95 Sing we of the modern city		81	71		Values
96 Soldiers of Christ arise	479			641	Courage, Fight for right, Peace
97 Songs of praise the angels sang	481			644	Advent, Creation, Praise
98 Teach me my God and king	485	95		652	Service, Work
99 The bell of creation is swinging for ever		67	2		Beauty, Creation, New Life, Time
100 The church's one foundation	489			249	Christian Unity, Taize
101 The earth, the sky, the oceans		111			Creation, Environment
102 The king (God) of love my shepherd is	490			654 653	Ten Commandments, Praise
103 The sheep's in the meadow, the cow's in the corn		125			Children
104 There is a green hill far away	106			131	Holy Week, Parable

FIRST LINE	E.H.	N.L.	N.O.	S.P.	POSSIBLE THEMES
105 There's a wideness in God's mercy	499			666	Beatitudes, Courage, Sermon on the Mount
106 Thine arm, O Lord, in days of old	526			287	Suffering
107 Thou whose Almighty word	553			303	Light, Trinity
108 Thy kingdom come O Lord		140			Peace
109 Thy kingdom come! On bended knee	504			680	Kingdom of God
110 To everything, turn, turn, turn		129	83		Time
111 Tomorrow is a highway, broad and fair		141			Remembrance, Values
112 Travel on, travel on, there's a river that is flowing		96	60		Peace, Remembrance, Time
113 Was I really once a child		104			Old age, Family
114 Wealthy man you are imprisoned		100			Freedom, Values
115 We ask that we live and we labour in peace		121			Brotherhood, Gifts, Peace, Values
116 We meet you, O Christ		82			Easter, Suffering, Values
117 We plough the fields and scatter	293			14	Harvest
118 When a knight won his spurs in the stories of old			44	377	Courage, Good resolutions
119 When I needed a neighbour, were you there, were you there?		123	13		Community, Love, Unity
120 When I survey the wondrous cross	107			133	Holy Week
121 When in His own image		110			Creation, Freedom, Values
122 When they shouted hosanna, were you there?		40			Easter, Tolerance, Love

FIRST LINE	E.H.	N.L.	N.O.	S.P.	POSSIBLE THEMES
123 Who would true valour see		112	61		Courage

E.H   English Hymnal   O.U.P., 1935
N.L. New Life   Galliard, 1971
N.O. New Orbit   Galliard, 1972
S.P. Songs of Praise   O.U.P., 1931

1 GOD'S WORLD

Assemblies

CREATION

1 Traditional

a) All creatures of our God and King
   Reading: Genesis 1, 1–23
   Prayer **2**

b) All people that on earth do dwell
   Reading: Genesis 1, 24–31
   Prayer **3**

c) God who spoke in the beginning
   Reading **1**: *Creation*, Joan Brockelsby
   Prayer **11**

d) When in His own image
   Reading **1**: *Creation*, Joan Brockelsby
   Prayer **4**

e) The bell of creation is swinging for ever
   Readings: John 1; and **21**: *The Power and the Glory*,
   Siegfried Sassoon
   Prayer **13**

2 Traditions

a) Let us with a gladsome mind
   Readings **1**: *Creation*, Joan Brockelsby; and **15**: *Benedicite*,
   Canon E. R. Hougham
   Prayer **2**

b) O Worship the King
   Reading **4**: *Our Father*, 'Red Indian Myth'
   Prayer **3**

c) Morning has broken
   Readings **2**: *Chaos Before Creation*, Gopal Singh; and **5**:
   The Song of Creation, from *The Rig Veda*
   Prayer **4**

3 *Ancient and Modern*

a)   Praise the Lord, ye heavens adore Him!
     Reading: Genesis 2, 4–14
     Prayer **13**

b)   God who spoke in the beginning
     Reading 7: *A Molecular Genesis*, Iain Taylor
     Prayer **2**

c)   Lord bring the day to pass
     Reading **6**: *Continuous Creation*, Fred Hoyle
     Prayer **3**

d)   When in His own image
     Reading **3**: *God is a Blob*, Betty Atkins Fukuyama
     Prayer **11**

THE ENVIRONMENT

1 *Care of Creation*

a)   The earth, the sky, the oceans
     Reading **10**: *Harvest Hymn*, John Betjeman
     Prayer **4**

b)   All creatures of our God and King
     Readings **11**: *Pollution*, Anon.; and **12**: *A Creed
        of Conservation*, Lyndon B. Johnson
     Prayer **6**

c)   *Benedicite*
     Readings **19**: *A Song of Praise*, from *The Koran*; and Psalm
        66
     Prayers **11** and **12**

2 *Treatment of God's World*

a)   The earth, the sky, the oceans
     Reading **8**: *Silent Spring*, Rachael Carson
     Prayer **4**

b)   Lord, bring the day to pass
     Reading **9**: *Creation in Reverse*, Anon.
     Prayer **4**

   c)   Dear Lord and Father of Mankind
       Reading **10**: *Harvest Hymn*, John Betjeman
       Prayer **5**

HARVEST

1 Benedicite (**15**)

This full-length service can be cut and used in many different ways to form a week's assemblies, and provide both readings and prayers. Suitable hymns, to be fitted to the reading chosen, are:
   Now join we, to praise the Creator
   The earth, the sky, the oceans
   Lord bring the day to pass

2 God and Man

   a)   God who spoke in the beginning
       Readings **14**: *The Allotment*, David Cox; and **16**: *The Tractor*, Michel Quoist
       Prayer **7**

   b)   Now join we, to praise the Creator
       Readings **18**: *The Grain of Wheat*, J. W. Brimer and S. Brimer; and **22**: *The Potato*, Murdoch Dahl
       Prayer **13**

   c)   Lord bring the day to pass
       Reading **8**: *Silent Spring*, Rachael Carson
       Prayer **4**

3 Harvest praise

   a)   We plough the fields and scatter
       Readings **18**: *The Grain of Wheat*, J. W. Brimer and S. Brimer; and **22**: *The Potato*, Murdoch Dahl
       Prayers **6** and **7**

   b)   For the beauty of the earth
       Readings **26**: *Pied Beauty*, Gerard Manley Hopkins; and Psalm 65, 9–13
       Prayer **11**

   c)   O worship the King
       Readings **19**: *A Song of Praise*, from *The Koran*; and **20**: from *Murder in the Cathedral*, T. S. Eliot
       Prayers **9** and **11**

Other useful readings or assemblies can be found under e.g. Nature, Worship etc. Some could be used in combination with part of the *Benedicite* series, e.g., **13** and **16**.

NATURE

1 Unity in Praise

a) All creatures of our God and King/Let us with a gladsome mind
    Readings **17**: *Song of the Sun*, St Francis of Assisi; and **20**: from *Murder in the Cathedral*, T. S. Eliot
    Prayer **12**

b) Immortal, invisible, God only wise
    Reading **27**: *Varuna, the All-knowing God*, from *The Rig Veda*
    Prayer **9**

c) For the beauty of the earth
    Reading **19**: *A Song of Praise*, from *The Koran*
    Prayer **13**

d) Praise the Lord, ye heavens adore Him!
    Reading: Psalm 148
    Prayer **11**

e) Morning has broken
    Readings **110**: *Happiness and Vision*, William Blake; and **21**: *The Power and the Glory*, Siegfried Sassoon
    Prayers **1** and **3**

2 Beauty

a) We plough the fields and scatter/Glad that I live am I
    Reading **24**: *Autumn*, Forrest Reid
    Prayer **11**

b) Morning has broken
    Reading **25**: *God's Grandeur*, Gerard Manley Hopkins
    Prayer **12**

c) For the beauty of the earth
    Reading **26**: *Pied Beauty*, Gerard Manley Hopkins
    Prayer **13**

d)   Glad that I live am I
Reading **113**: *Solitary Delights*, Tachibana Akemi
Prayers **9** and **10**

3 *The Miracle*

See also Section 6, no. 1, c)–d)
a)   God moves in a mysterious way
Readings **22**: *The Potato*, Murdoch Dahl; and **28**: *It is Thou*,
Tadhg Óg Ó Huiginn
Prayers **10** and **13**

4 *Delight in Nature*

a)   For the beauty of the earth
Reading **111**: *Canoe Story*, Geoffrey Summerfield
Prayer **11**

b)   Morning has broken
Reading **112**: *On a Bicycle*, Yevgeny Yevtushenko
Prayer **12**

c)   Glad that I live am I
Reading **113**: *Solitary Delights*, Tachibana Akemi
Prayers **9** and **10**

Prayers

CREATION

1 I thank thee, my Creator and Lord, that thou hast given me these
joys in thy creation, this ecstasy over the works of thy hands. I
have made known the glory of thy works to men as far as my finite
spirit was able to comprehend thy infinity. If I have said anything
wholly unworthy of thee, or have aspired after my own glory,
graciously forgive me.

*Johann Kepler 1571–1630, the famous astronomer, who was crippled
in his hands and had poor eyesight*

2 We thank you, Lord our God, for creating the world and for
preserving it,
We thank you for the regular return of day and night, and of the
seasons,
And for the dependability of nature and of time.
We pray that we and all men may respect your world and use it
wisely.

Contemporary Prayers for Public Worship (*adapted*)

3 Thou, Lord, in the beginning hast laid the foundation of the
earth; and the heavens are the work of thy hands. They shall
perish, but thou shalt endure: they all shall wax old as doth a
garment. They shall be changed: but thou art the same, and thy
years shall not fail. Thou art from everlasting to everlasting, the
creator and upholder of all things, the source of all things, the
source of life and light; for thy wisdom, thy majesty and thy
beauty, we worship thee. Praise be to thy glorious name.

New Every Morning (*adapted*)

THE ENVIRONMENT

4 Father, we acknowledge that the world and its resources are not ours but yours, and that you have put us in charge as your trustees. Help us to exercise responsibly the authority you give us in your world. Give us reverence for life and beauty, and help us to look after all creation for Jesus' sake.

C.P.P.W. (*adapted*)

5 Still the earth needs to be loved
And the animals to be cared for;
Don't let the tractors
Turn our hearts into pumps,
Don't let the machines
Mechanise our minds.
We take our place in creation
With the fish and the beasts and the birds.
God gave us dominion
That we might enjoy and not destroy.
That we might explore creation's limits,
O God how wonderful are Thy works,
Thy glory shall endure for ever.

Celebration 1, Benedicite

HARVEST

6 Almighty and everlasting God, we offer you our hearty thanks for your fatherly goodness and care in giving us the fruits of the earth in their seasons. Give us grace to use them rightly, to your glory, for our own well-being, and for the relief of those in need; through Jesus Christ our Lord.

Alternative Service Book

7 Let us remember with thankfulness all those on whom we all depend for food and drink and for all the harvest of the land and sea: the fishermen and sailors; the farmers and miners; scientists and processors; packagers and distributors; roundsmen and shopkeepers. And let us pray that all resources may be used wisely and shared widely, for the sake of Jesus Christ, our Lord.

NATURE

8 O heavenly Father, protect and bless all things that have breath:
guard them from all evil and let them sleep in peace.

Albert Schweitzer when a child

9 Has thou not seen how all in the Heavens and in the Earth
uttereth the praise of God? – the very birds as they spread their
wings? Every creature knoweth its prayer and its praise, and God
knoweth what they do.

The Koran

10 Almighty One, in the woods I am blessed. Happy everyone in the
woods. Every tree speaks through thee. O God! What glory in the
woodland! On the heights is peace – peace to serve Him.

Ludwig van Beethoven

11 O God, we thank thee for this universe, our great home; for its
vastness and its riches, and for the manifold life which teems upon
it and of which we are part. We praise thee for the sky and winds,
for the driving clouds and the constellations on high. We praise
thee for the salt sea and the running water, for the everlasting
hills, for the trees and for the grass under our feet. We thank thee
for our senses by which we can see the splendour of the morning,
and hear the songs of birds, and enjoy the smells of the spring
time. Grant us, we pray thee, a heart wide open to all this joy and
beauty, and save our souls from being so steeped in care or so
darkened by passion that we pass heedless and unseeing when
even the thorn-bush by the wayside is aflame with the glory of
God.

Walter Rauschenbusch

12 We praise thy Name O Father for the beauty of the seasons, the
glory of the sky by day and night, the healthful wind and
quickening rain. We thank thee for the bloom and fragrance of the
flowers, the songs of birds, the joyousness of every living thing. In
all that thou hast made may we see the wonder of thy wisdom and
thy care, who clothest the grass of the field and takest thought for
the sparrows. Help us to trust thy never-failing goodness, the love
which is beyond our understanding and surrounds our lives with
blessing; for thy Name's sake.

School Worship

13 Blessed be the God of Heaven and Earth for the glory of nature. We offer you praise, Heavenly Father, for the growth of seed, the blossom and fruit, the cleansing frosts of winter, for the earth's rebirth in spring, and the harvest of your gifts. All the earth worships its Creator; your law and power are everywhere. Praised be your name.

A. G. Bullivant

See also under Section 5, Worship; some extracts from Psalms are also suitable (e.g. 8, 66, 104); and some readings (e.g. *Song of the Sun*, 18).

Readings

CREATION

1 Creation

'Today,' said God,
And in that word, created time,
'Today, I will create.'
So from that high Heaven where He dwelt,
He seized a ball of light so incandescent bright
Only His eyes could bear it,
And rolled it in His hands
Till with His light it shone;
Then he hurled it forth into that outer darkness
That for eternity had lodged
Outside the gate of Heaven.
And so created Night.

But see, where His ball of light
Burst in the darkness
Scattering its brilliant fragments
To race by million, million years through space,
Making it bright by even so many stars and suns.
So God created darkness and light,
Rhythm, pattern, pace,
As with related course, they circled one another.
Then walking through His new-made fields of light
He chose one little sun,
Its own small heavens peopled with stars and planets,
And from those planets yet again chose one,
(One average, medium by heat, by light, by speed.)
'This for experiment,' He said.

And from the speeding neutrons and electrons,
Hydrogen atoms racing through light and time,
The ball of earth rolled clear, within its skin of air,
And in its wake, came night and day.

And still the atoms moved and met,
Protons, electrons holding hands in endless patterns,
Patterns always moving towards variation, towards the new,
So that the crust of earth crackled and cracked and hardened,
Layer upon layer in ceaseless sort and kind.
While water, drop by drop, trickled out of the chemistry of rock
Into stream, into river, into sea,
Until lo, 'Let there be earth and sea,' said God.

Then as the atoms ceaselessly chained themselves
In endless variations, yet all unliving,
Suddenly came the new, the different,
The incredible, the cell that lived,
A cell that moved of its own volition,
'Let there be life,' said God.

Came many cells that lived, then one divided,
Self-reproduction had begun, the chain
Ever towards the new continual creation,
'Be fruitful, multiply,' said God.
And from the microscopic small, the single cell,
The amoebas, hydras, early fathers of our race,
Grew with incredible patient grace,
Then each in its time, the astounding complexity of living
    creatures,
The small fathering the immensely great,
Until giant creatures moved with clumsy tread to early doom,
For always to the changing, the unadaptable gave room.

So the earth brought forth grass, herb, flower, tree, all living green,
And the sea, great whales, shark, dolphin, herring,
And those too small to be seen,
Birds, animals of every shape, colour, size,
Cunning, foolish, beautiful, comic, gross and graceful,
And last of all, the ape who began to be wise.

Then came a day an ape rose on his haunches
And turned to God,
'Enough,' said God, 'Let there be man.'

In the green cradle of the world that He had made,
God brought him forth,
A mind like His, in His own image,
Brought He forth His creature, His especial creature,

Born to perceive his maker,
To think His thoughts, to follow after,
In the paths that He had brought Him,
To know His world.

And that world was a garden of delight,
Fashioned for the joy of creation,
For the joy of man and God.

And Adam walked with God in the cool of the evening.
'So God created man in His own image,
In the image of God created He him,
Male and female created He them.'

Then came a day when Adam said,
'I will think my thoughts, not yours alone,'
'You shall, for I have made you free,
But beware, Adam, the fatal Tree.'
'I will do what I want,' said Adam,
And in that moment fell,
Blind to the sight of God.

Surely the Sun had dipped her glory,
The stars, the galaxies shuddered within that moment,
The earth herself gave forth a groan,
And each small creature in his own place, covered his eyes and
    hid.

But Adam heard the voice of God,
As from the garden of unshadowed joy, they stumbled,
And said, 'All life will be a longing memory of this,
We shall hunger, and thirst, know all manner of suffering and
    want
But we shall remember what was here,
To walk with God.'

And Adam wept, with Eve, his wife.
Then came the voice of God,
'In the suffering, in the loneliness,
In the sin, in the darkness, the death,
I am with you.
By trying to hide you from my sight,
You have pulled down gross darkness upon you.
But what I have planned I will accomplish,

What I have made I will redeem,
By the tree you fell, by the tree you shall be saved.'

The Pool of God, reflecting His face,
Has received the stone of Adam's disobedience,
And now the pattern must work itself out,
In ever-widening circles of redemption,
The lost shall be saved.

Stand back you heavens, bow down you farthest star,
Let every proton, neutron, electron hold its changing moment:
Almighty God goes forth to war
For the eternal soul of man,
And Victory is His name.

Joan Brockelsby, from **Step into Joy**

2 Chaos Before Creation

For aeons of years, there was chaos upon chaos.
Neither earth there was, nor the sky; only
God's infinite Will was.
Neither was their night nor day; neither the sun,
nor the moon; and God was seated
in His Absolute Trance,
Neither air there was, nor water; neither birth,
nor death; neither coming nor going; neither
divisions of the world, nor the underworld; neither
the seas nor the rivulets; neither the sky, nor
the stars; neither time nor space; neither heaven
nor hell. Neither woman there was, nor man;
nor pain. Neither creeds were there, nor garbs;
nor the manifold ways. And there was no one
to utter: 'Lo, there is also another.'

Gopal Singh, from **Religion of the Sikhs**

3 God is a Blob

God is a blob
        an amoeba-like blob
    elongating
  fissioning
        stretching

extending in limitless space.
Far from the confines
   of earth and its peoples,
aeons away from the man on the street –
from the thousands of men on the street –
   billions of light years removed from us all,
how could he fashion the soul so small?
In his infinite process of changing and growing,
   what does he know of our little knowing?
How could he care for the tears of our caring?
      or answer with love the love we are daring?
Exploding atoms in galaxy form
  star distance away
   move the god who is gone.
Yet mysteries baffle the mind left behind
 and I who am so strongly I
 feel warmly encroached upon.

Betty Atkins Fukuyama, from **Protest in Semantics**

4 Our Father

What it was our father lay on when he came to consciousness we
do not know. He moved his right arm and then his left arm, his
right leg and then his left leg. He began to think of what he should
do; and finally he began to cry and tears began to flow from his
eyes and fall down below him. After a while, he looked down
below him and saw something bright. The bright objects were his
tears that had flowed below and formed the present waters . . .
Earthmaker began to think again. He thought: 'It is thus; if I wish
anything it will become just as I wish, just as my tears have
become seas.' Thus he thought.

So he wished for light and it became light. Then he thought: 'It
is as I supposed; the things that I have wished for have come into
existence as I desired.' Then he thought again, and wished for the
earth and the earth came into existence . . . Then he began to
talk for the first time. He said, 'As things are just as I wish them I
shall make one being like myself.' So he took a piece of earth and
made it like himself.

Then he talked to what he had created, but it did not answer.
He looked upon it and he saw that it had no mind or thought. So
he made a mind for it. Again he talked to it, but it did not answer.
So he looked upon it again and saw that it had no tongue. Then he
made it a tongue. Then he talked to it again but it did not answer.

So he looked upon it again and saw that it had no soul. So he made it a soul. He talked to it again and it very nearly said something. But it did not make itself understood. So Earthmaker breathed into its mouth and talked to it and it answered.

'*Red Indian Myth*', *quoted in M. Eliade, from* **Primitives to Zen**

5 The Song of Creation

There was not then what is nor what is not. There was no sky, and no heaven beyond the sky. What power was there? Where? Who was that power? Was there an abyss of fathomless waters?

There was neither death nor immortality then. No signs were there of night or day. The ONE was breathing by its own power, in deep peace. Only the ONE was: there was nothing beyond.

Darkness was hidden in darkness. The all was fluid and formless. Therein, in the void, by the fire of fervour arose the ONE.

And in the ONE arose love. Love the first seed of soul. The truth of this the sages found in their hearts; seeking in their hearts with wisdom, the sages found that bond of union between being and non-being.

Who knows in truth? Who can tell us whence and how arose this universe? The gods are later than its beginning: who knows therefore whence comes this creation?

Only that god who sees in highest heaven: he only knows whence comes this universe, and whether it was made or uncreated. He only knows, or perhaps he knows not.

From **The Rig Veda**, *translated from the Sanskrit by Juan Mascaró under the title* **Lamps of Fire**

6 Continuous Creation

Although I think there is no doubt that every galaxy we now observe to be receding from us will in about 10,000,000,000 years have passed entirely beyond the limit of vision of an observer in our galaxy, yet I think that such an observer would still be able to see about the same number of galaxies as we do now. By this I mean that new galaxies will have condensed out of the background material at just about the rate necessary to compensate for those that are being lost as a consequence of their passing beyond our observable universe. At first sight it might be thought that this could not go on indefinitely because the material forming the background would ultimately become exhausted. But again I do not believe that this is so, for it seems likely that new material is constantly being created so as to maintain a constant density in the background material. So we have a situation in which the loss of galaxies, through the expansion of the Universe, is compensated by the condensation of new galaxies, and this can continue indefinitely.

The idea that matter is created continuously . . . in itself is not new. I know of references to the continuous creation of matter that go back more than twenty years, and I have no doubt that a close enquiry would show that the idea, in its vaguest form, goes back very much further than that . . .

From time to time people ask where the created material comes from. Well, it does not come from anywhere. Material simply appears – it is created. At one time the various atoms composing the material do not exist and at a later time they do. This may seem a very strange idea and I agree that it is, but in science it does not matter how strange an idea may seem so long as it works – that is to say, so long as the idea can be expressed in a precise form and so long as its consequences are found to be in agreement with observation. In any case, the whole idea of creation is queer. In the older theories all the material in the Universe is supposed to have appeared at one instant of time, the whole creation process taking the form of one big bang. For myself I find this idea very much queerer than continuous creation.

Fred Hoyle, **The Nature of the Universe**

7 A Molecular Genesis

This is from the magazine of the Institute of Biologists. It is entirely accurate – so was Hoyle. Both leave the question unanswered – where did the beginning come from? This reading is difficult except for VI form biologists – but we can get the general idea.

In the beginning was the Word, and the Word was Hydrogen, and Hydrogen was the only Word.

And the Word consisted of one positive particle, a proton, and one negative particle, an electron. And the electron rotated about the proton, and together they were Hydrogen which was the Word.

And the Word said: 'Let us create other words in our own image. Let us put ourself together in many ways and many forms, but let us adhere to the simplest laws.'

And the Word created another body, with the mass of one proton and one electron, but the electron rotated not about the proton. This neutral body called He the neutron.

And the Word saw that it was good, and the morning and the evening were the first 15 billion years.

And the Word said: 'Let us now combine protons, neutrons and electrons in as many ways as are possible. Let the protons and neutrons form the nucleus and let the electrons spin around the nucleus, each to its appropriate orbit. Let the stable orbits be filled to capacity in series from the most reactive to the inert.' And the stable entities called He atoms.

And the Word said: 'Let the atoms combine and recombine in infinite ways, and let them come together as solids and liquids and gases, and let the natural laws control the behaviour of all atoms, and let the universe evolve according to those laws.'

And the Word saw that it was good. And the morning and the evening were the next 500 million years.

And the Word said: 'Let there be suns and, by their natural explosions, let them disintegrate and give forth planets. Let each planet make its own orbit around its sun. As the planets leave their suns, so may they cool and may their elements combine to form gas clouds, and liquids and solids.'

Many compounds were unstable and others were stable. Some stable compounds contained cations and anions, and others contained carbon, oxygen, nitrogen, and the Word, which was Hydrogen.

And the Word saw that it was good and the morning and the evening were many millennia.

And the Word saw many planets that were made of many compounds. One planet in the Milky Way called He Earth. Earth was made of molten rocks and was surrounded by reducing atmosphere. Carbon dioxide, methane, ammonia and water were therein.

And the Word caused mighty lightning storms to rage about the Earth, and the mighty storms caused the gases to interact. Amino acids, sugars, bases, and fatty acids were they formed. These interacted one with another, and with one another did they form many bonds.

And some bases did condense with sugar and with phosphate to form nucleotides. Many molecules tended to associate one with another, with water, and with inorganic cations and anions. And when associated they drew unto themselves other substances.

And each association formed interface with the surrounding medium which was water. . . . And the Word called the associations coacervates, and the complex interfaces around them called He membranes.

Within the coacervates the molecules continued to interact, and the heat of the sun catalysed some reactions, and when the darkness came the coacervates did cool.

Nucleotides did condense one with another and formed linear chains. By complementary pairing could they interact forming DNA and they could reproduce their structure.

And the Word saw that it was good. And He said: 'Let the coacervates reproduce themselves and rejuvenate their form lest they lose control of their processes, and let them pass information from one generation to another. They have membranes to protect themselves and through which to select their chemicals. They have catalysts to control their chemistry and polynucleotides to pass information from one generation unto the next. Let the coacervates respond to environment and grow. Let them multiply and colonize all the corners of the Earth.

'Let each coacervate be called a cell.'

And the Word saw that it was good. And the morning and the evening were many millennia.

And the Word said: 'Let there be Life', and there was Life.

Iain Taylor

THE ENVIRONMENT

8 Silent Spring

There was once a town in the heart of America where all life seemed to live in harmony with its surroundings. The town lay in the midst of a chequerboard of prosperous farms, with fields of grain and hillsides of orchards. In autumn, oak and maple and birch set up a blaze of colour. Then foxes barked in the hills and deer silently crossed the fields.

Along the roads, laurel, viburnum and alder, great ferns and wild flowers delighted the traveller's eye through much of the year. Even in winter the roadsides were places of beauty, where countless birds came to feed on the berries. The countryside was, in fact, famous for the abundance and variety of its bird life; people travelled from great distances to observe them. Others came to fish the streams which flowed clear and cold out of the hills and contained shady pools where trout lay. So it had been from the days many years ago when the first settlers raised their houses, sank their wells and built their barns.

Then a strange blight crept over the area and everything began to change. Some evil spell had settled on the community: mysterious maladies swept the flocks of chickens; the cattle and sheep sickened and died. Everywhere was a shadow of death. The farmers spoke of much illness among their families. In the town the doctors had become more and more puzzled by new kinds of sickness appearing among their patients. There had been several sudden and unexplained deaths, not only among adults but even among children, who would be stricken suddenly while at play and die within a few hours.

There was a strange stillness. The birds, for example – where had they gone? Many people spoke of them, puzzled and disturbed. The feeding stations in the backyards were deserted. The few birds seen anywhere were moribund; they trembled violently and could not fly. It was a spring without voices. On the mornings that had once throbbed with the dawn chorus of scores of bird voices there was now no sound; only silence lay over the fields and woods and marsh.

On the farms the hens brooded, but no chicks hatched. The farmers complained that they were unable to raise any pigs – the litters were small and the young survived only a few days. The apple trees were coming into bloom but no bees droned among the blossoms, so there was no pollination and there would be no fruit.

The roadsides, once so attractive, were now lined with browned and withered vegetation as though swept by fire. These, too, were silent, deserted by all living things. Even the streams were now lifeless. Anglers no longer visited them, for all the fish had died.

In the gutters under the eaves and between the shingles of the roofs, a white granular powder still showed a few patches; some weeks before it had fallen like snow upon the roofs and the lawns, the fields and streams.

No witchcraft, no enemy action had silenced the rebirth of new life in this stricken world. The people had done it themselves.

This town does not actually exist. Yet every one of these disasters has actually happened somewhere, and many real communities have already suffered a substantial number of them. A grim spectre has crept upon us almost unnoticed, and this imagined tragedy may easily become a stark reality we all shall know.

Rachael Carson

9 Creation in Reverse

In the end, man destroyed the heaven that had been called earth. For the earth had been beautiful and happy until the destructive spirit of men moved upon it. This was the seventh day before the end.

For man said, 'Let me have power in the earth,' and he saw that power seemed good, and he called those who sought power 'great leaders', and those who sought only to serve others and bring reconciliation 'weaklings', 'compromisers', 'appeasers'. And this was the sixth day before the end.

And man said, 'Let there be a division among all people, and divide the nations which are for me from the nations which are against me.' And this was the fifth day before the end.

And man said, 'Let us gather our resources in one place and create more instruments of power to defend ourselves; the radio to control men's minds, conscription to control men's bodies; uniforms and symbols of power to win men's souls.' And this was the fourth day before the end.

And man said, 'Let there be censorship to divide the propaganda from the truth.' And he made two great censorship bureaux to control the thoughts of men; one to tell only the truth he wishes known at home, and the other to tell only the truth that he wishes known abroad. And this was the third day before the end.

And man said, 'Let us create weapons which can kill vast numbers, even millions and hundreds of millions, at a distance.' And so he perfected germ warfare and deadly underwater arsenals, guided missiles, great fleets of war planes and destructive power to the extent of tens of thousands of millions of tons of T.N.T. And it was the second day before the end.

And man said, 'Let us make God in our own image. Let us say God does as we do, thinks as we think, wills as we will, and kills as we kill.' So man found ways to kill with atomic power and dust, even those as yet unborn. And he said 'This is necessary. There is no alternative. This is God's will.'

And on the last day, there was a great noise upon the face of the earth, and man and all his doings were no more, and the ravished earth rested on the seventh day . . .

Anon.

10 Harvest Hymn

We spray the fields and scatter
   The poison on the ground
So that no wicked wild flowers
   Upon our farm be found.
We like whatever helps us
   To line our purse with pence;
The twenty-four-hour broiler-house
   And neat electric fence.

All concrete sheds around us
   And Jaguars in the yard,
The telly lounge and deep-freeze
   Are ours from working hard.

We fire the fields for harvest,
   The hedges swell the flame,
The oak trees and the cottages
   From which our fathers came,
We give no compensation,
   The earth is ours today,
And if we lose on arable,
   Then bungalows will pay.

All concrete sheds . . . etc.

John Betjeman

11 Pollution

'Mummy, Oh Mummy, what's this pollution
That everyone's talking about?'
'Pollution's the mess that the country is in,
That we'd all be far better without.
It's factories belching their fumes in the air,
And the beaches all covered with tar,
Now throw all those sweet papers into the bushes
Before we get back in the car.'

'Mummy, Oh Mummy, who makes pollution,
And why don't they stop if it's bad?'
"Cos people like that just don't think about others,
They don't think at all, I might add.

They spray all the crops and they poison the flowers,
And wipe out the birds and the bees,
Now there's a good place we could dump that old mattress
Right out of sight in the trees.'

'Mummy, Oh Mummy, what's going to happen
If all the pollution goes on?'
'Well the world will end up like a second-hand junk-yard,
With all of its treasures quite gone.
The fields will be littered with plastics and tins,
The streams will be covered with foam,
Now throw those two pop bottles over the hedge,
Save us from carting them home.'

'But Mummy, Oh Mummy, if I throw the bottles,
Won't that be polluting the wood?'
'Nonsense! That isn't the same thing at all,
You just shut up and be good.
If you're going to start getting silly ideas
I'm taking you home right away,
'Cos pollution is something that other folk do,
We're just enjoying our day.'

Anon.

12 A Creed of Conservation

Let us proclaim a creed to preserve our natural heritage with right
   and the duties to respect those rights:
   The right to clean water – and the duty not to pollute it.
   The right to clean air – and the duty not to befoul it.
   The right to surroundings reasonably free from man-made
      ugliness – and the duty not to blight.
The right to easy access to places of beauty and tranquillity where
   every family can find recreation and refreshment – and the duty
   to preserve such places clean and unspoiled.
The right to enjoy plants and animals in their natural habitats –
   and the duty not to eliminate them from the face of the earth.

Lyndon B. Johnson, former American President

HARVEST

13 Diary of a Church Mouse

(Lines, written to order on a set subject, to be spoken on the wireless.)

Here among long-discarded cassocks,
Damp stools, and half-split open hassocks,
Here where the Vicar never looks
I nibble through old service books.
Lean and alone I spend my days
Behind this Church of England baize.
I share my dark forgotten room
With two oil-lamps and half a broom.
The cleaner never bothers me,
So here I eat my frugal tea.
My bread is sawdust mixed with straw;
My jam is polish for the floor.
    Christmas and Easter may be feasts
For congregations and for priests,
And so may Whitsun. All the same,
They do not fill my meagre frame.
For me the only feast at all
Is Autumn's Harvest Festival,
When I can satisfy my want
With ears of corn around the font.
I climb the eagle's brazen head
To burrow through a loaf of bread.
I scramble up the pulpit stair
And gnaw the marrows hanging there.
    It is enjoyable to taste
These items ere they go to waste,
But how annoying when one finds
That other mice with pagan minds
Come into church my food to share
Who have no proper business there.
Two field mice who have no desire
To be baptized, invade the choir.
A large and most unfriendly rat
Comes in to see what we are at.
He says he thinks there is no God
And yet he comes . . . it's rather odd.

This year he stole a sheaf of wheat
(It screened our special preacher's seat),
And prosperous mice from fields away
Come in to hear the organ play,
And under cover of its notes
Ate through the altar's sheaf of oats.
A Low Church mouse, who thinks that I
Am too papistical and High.
Yet somehow doesn't think it wrong
To munch through Harvest Evensong,
While I, who starve the whole year through,
Must share my food with rodents who
Except at this time of the year
Not once inside the church appear.
   Within the human world I know
Such goings on could not be so.
For human beings only do
What their religion tells them do.
They read the Bible every day
And always, night and morning, pray,
And just like me, the good church mouse,
Worship each week in God's own house.
   But all the same it's strange to me
How very full the Church can be
With people I don't see at all
Except at Harvest Festival.

John Betjeman

14 The Allotment

We do not think that there ever was a beautiful garden called 'the Garden of Eden' and that two people called Adam and Eve lived in it, but we do believe that this picture gives a true idea of the place of man in the world. Man does have power over God's world, and he does change and alter it just as a gardener changes and alters a garden by digging new flowerbeds, planting new trees and so on. There is a story told of an old man who begged a farmer for the corner of a field which the plough did not reach. This bit of the field was growing wild with brambles and thistles, and the old man got to work and turned it into an allotment. He was looking after his bit of ground with his beans and his peas looking neat and tidy in their rows when the parish priest came by. The

clergyman leant on the gate and exchanged a few words, and then
he looked at the man's work and said, 'Well, George, you and the
Almighty have made a good job of that, haven't you?' The old
man looked up, spat on the ground and said, 'You should have
seen it when the Almighty had it to himself.' This story brings out
very well the fact that man has a part to play in God's world: God
did not make the world to run itself, he made man in the world to
run it.

David Cox, **What Christians Believe**

15 Benedicite

Methods of use: as a series of Assemblies on the theme of *Harvest*,
either for one reader, as a dialogue or with a group of readers; as a
Creation story from 'God made the world' to 'thought them very
good'; as the story of the *Flood* from 'And he ordered his servant
Noah' to 'One more river to cross' and 'And when the ark' to 'all
over again'; for *Interdependence* for food from 'O all ye
producers' to 'for your joy and health'; for *Christian aid, Third
World* etc., from 'It would be well to remember' to the end.

3 O all ye works of the Lord, bless ye the Lord,
2 Praise him and magnify him for ever
1 This is a song of creation
   And of creation's delight
   In its creator.
   We are part of that creation
   And we should rejoice in it,
   We should be able to sing
   With the stars and the winds,
   With the dews and the frosts.
   But our hearts are heavy
   And our tongues are tied.
   We are no longer children,
   The springtime is over,
   The days are dying,
   The lights are fading
   And we have no home.
   We have wandered the world,
   We have climbed the mountains
   And tunnelled in the earth.
   We have searched the scriptures

And listened to the wise,
And yet we remain
The lost delinquents
Of the Eternal.

2 This is man's adolescence.
No longer child
With only brief intimations
Of responsible maturity.
Too proud to worship,
Too clever to believe,
Too exalted to seek forgiveness.
Too high minded
In a low minded way.

3 We have mastered our dimensions,
We have analysed the earth.
We have perfected our artificials,
We have pursued every grub and insect,
Every weed and wild flower
With our carefully selected selectives.
We are the masters,
To us surely is the power and glory.
We are the reapers and sowers,
We have made our magnificent machines.
To master the harvest,
To sow and reap,
To bind and store,
To dry and keep.
We are the breadwinners of creation,
We are the lords of all the earth.

1 But can we untangle the constellations?
Can we delicately balance Pleiades?
Or give orders to Orion?
Or hobble Taurus?
Or caution Cassiopeia?

2 Can we light sister Sun,
Or burnish brother Moon?
Can we operate the thermostats
Of Autumn, Winter, Summer, Spring?

3 Can we manufacture the life germ
In cabbage and cauliflower,
In wheat and barley,
In brussel sprout
And rumbling radish?

3 Yet we must sow
  And we must reap
  If we would eat.
2 When the world was young
  Men sang Benedicite.
  Their song echoed, they believed,
  In the vaulted rafters
  Of the courts of heaven.
  Caught up and amplified
  By the endless praise
  Of angels and archangels
  Delighting the Eternal God
  And they delighting in him.
  And childlike
  They brought their harvest gifts
  As if to say,
  Lord, look how clever we have been
  Look how wisely we have used
  Your earth and rain and sun and sky,
  Lord most high.

1 O ye servants of the Lord, bless ye the Lord.
2 What is man that thou art mindful of him?
3 When you come home in the evening
  And snugly stable the car,
  When you've eaten your fill
  And packed your pipe
  And tucked yourself in for television,
  Drooping soon in your armchair
  From an overdose of old movies,
  Or from seeing the same clue,
  Or hearing the same cliché
  For the 10th, 20th or 30th time;
  You relieve your infuriated tension
  By stretching for your whisky and water
  Or perhaps for your Benger's and biscuit.
  In an uncomfortable way you are comfortable,
  Not concerned about this or that
  Feeling quite certain
  That you've earned
  Your lack-lustre leisure
  And that you are doing yourself good
  In spite of your irritated droopings.

1 Are you the crowning glory
Of the long evolutionary processes?
Is it for this life stirred
In the primeval slimes?
And that God rested
After his six hard days
Of creating heaven and earth?

2 I have my books,
I play my golf,
I have salted away
My savings
In banks and unit trusts.
I am insured against
Rain and fire, torrent and terror.
I have taken so many precautions
That I am now sick with caution,
So cautious that I dare not die.

3 Lost in the labyrinths
Of marvellous mechanisation
With a sinking heart
And a drooping spirit
And a mind fearful,
The lost fruit
Of the world's harvest.

2 I sit in my chair in the evening
And in the brief silences
I wonder about life and death,
About birth and being.
In my lazy half-hearted way
I try to see the sense of it.
To you it looks as if
I am lazing away my leisure
And you would ask the question
'Are you crowning glory
Of the long evolutionary processes?'
And I would answer 'Yes I am'
Take me or leave me,
Ridicule or torture me,
Curse me or kill me.
I am what it is all about.
I look from my swaying house
Of bones and muscles,
Of flesh sanctified by blood,

I search the skies
And cultivate the earth.
I know that I am not alone,
I have intimate fellowship
With mists and mountains
With beasts and birds and trees.
I from the depths of my
Television chair still try to sing
Benedicite.

1 O ye works of men, bless ye the Lord
2 O ye mechanical devices, bless ye the Lord
3 O warm, well-fed, insurance-covered man, bless ye the Lord
   Praise him and magnify him forever.

1 O ye whales, bless ye the Lord.
2 O ye fowls of the air, bless ye the Lord.
3 O ye beasts and cattle, bless ye the Lord.
2 Praise him and magnify him for ever.
1 God made the world
   And loved the world
   And generously lavished this love
   On all created things.
   Light and colour,
   Colour massed,
   Colour gently shading,
   Reds and blues,
   Greens and yellows,
   Fusing together subtly.
   Shades subduing
   And light intensifying
   The colour climate of creation.
2 Singing and laughter,
   Rhythm and syncopation,
   The dancing delight
   Of the happy heart
   Echoing the ten thousand songs
   Of creation.
3 And God said 'Let the earth bring forth the living
   creature after his kind, cattle and creeping thing,
   the beasts of the earth after his kind', and it was so.
2 He made them long and tall and fair,
   He made them round and fat and stubby,
   He made some gentle and some fierce.
   And some were mean and short and grubby.

1 God made great beasts,
  God made great whales
  and winged fowls,
  Cattle and creeping things.
3 But the ancient story tells
  of tempter, serpent, devil,
  Corrupting creation,
  And it made the Lord God angry
  When he saw all the wickedness
  That was great upon the face of the earth.
1 And God said, I will destroy it all
  And start all over again.
2 He decided to rip open
  The firmament of heaven
  And to cause the deep wells
  To burst forth
  And to make floods dark and deep
  On the face of the earth.
3 For the Lord was sorry that he had made it all.
  But he loved faithful Noah
  And all his ingenious animals.
1 He loved the animals
  The fishes and the birds
  That he had given to man
  For his pleasure
  And for his food.
2 God loved the patient animals,
  He loved the roaring beasts.
  God saw them all
  And thought them very good.
3 And he ordered his servant Noah
  To make a great ship
  And to store in it
  Seed and grain,
  Birds and beasts,
  Sons and daughters,
  So that he might think again
  And replenish the earth.
2 Old Noah he did build the ark
  There's one more river to cross
  He patched it up with hickory bark
  There's one more river to cross
  There's one more river
  And that's the river of Jordan

There's one more river
There's one more river to cross.

1 And Noah and Shem
And Ham and Japheth
And Mrs Noah and Mrs Shem
And Mrs Ham and Mrs Japheth
Organised the animals
Into long, long lines
And told them to be on their best behaviour
And keep still
To be ready
To run and hop and skip
Up the gang planks
When the rain began
And the waters started to rise.

3 The animals went in one by one
The elephant chewing a caraway bun.

2 And when the weather forecast said
Rain and more rain.
Rain for ever and ever
Stormy conditions
And fearful floods
In many places.
The animals speeded up.

1 The animals went in two by two
The rhinoceros and the kangeroo. (*pause*)

2 The animals went in four by four
The great hippopotamus stuck in the door. (*pause*)

3 The animals went in six by six
The hyena laughed at the monkey's tricks,
There's one more river.
And that's the river of Jordan
There's one more river
One more river to cross.

1 So when we come to
Harvest home,
Remember your friends,
The animals
That suffer so much
And bear so much
That men like us
Might live.

2 Without them you would not have made it.
You would have never survived

The dangerous paths
Of dubious evolution
If they had not been there
To feed and sustain you,
If they had not
Carried your burdens
And drawn your ploughs.

3 But we don't need them now
We are mechanised
And with our Massey Fergusons
We can plough and reap and sow.

1 But still the earth needs to be loved
And the animals to be cared for.
Don't let the tractors
Turn our hearts into pumps,
Don't let the machines
Mechanise our minds
We take our place in creation
With the fish and the beasts and the birds.

2 And God gave us dominion
That we might enjoy and not destroy.
That we might explore creation's limits.
O God how wonderful are thy works
Thy glory shall endure for ever.

1 And when the ark
Came safe to shore
God said to Noah and his crew
Open the hatches,
Free the animals,
Get digging organised.
The seeds planted
For we are starting
All over again.

1 O all ye producers of food, bless ye the Lord
2 O all ye butchers and bakers, bless ye the Lord
3 O all ye roundsmen and milkmen, bless ye the Lord
1 O all ye canners and farmers, bless ye the Lord
2 O all ye managers and shop assistants, bless ye the Lord.
3 Praise him and magnify him for ever.
1 Let us turn the supermarket
Into the church
And the church into
The supermarket.

Let us pull out the pews
And wheel in the goods.
Line by line,
Cage by cage,
Cold store,
Deep freeze,
All living things,
All edible forms
From mousse to macaroni.

2 Let us take the pews
And the pulpit
And the choir
And fit them somehow
Into the supermarket.

3 Let us turn
The market into the church
And the church into the market,

1 Moving down the aisles
With your plastic perambulator,
Let your eyes wander
From left to right
Even if you resist
The temptation
To tumble what you see
Into your personal pram.
Consider the marshalled products
Of earth and sea and sky,
Hygienically packed
In contemporary wrappings.
Untouched by human hands,
Unloved by human hearts.

2 But the harvests of the earth
Are here for your choosing.
Here in the supermarket.
In the village store,
Or the little shop on the corner,
Or the allotment patch,
Or in the kitchen garden.
So much for so many
Just move your hand
And all the harvests of the earth
Drop into your basket.

3 Moving down the shelving
On your left and right,

Tea and corn and crumpets
All for your delight.
Fish from foreign oceans,
Fruit from distant lands,
Peaches and bananas,
Oranges and yams.

2 Marmalade and pickles,
Bacon and spiced ham.
Biscuits plain and fancy,
Sandwiches and jam.
Butter from New Zealand,
Cheeses from the dales,
Cockles, whelks and mussels.
Bottled beers and ales.

1 Bread in many guises,
Soft and crispy rolls.
Slimming foods for diet,
Frozen cod and soles,
Sugar from Jamaica,
Oranges from Spain,
Coffee from Mombasa,
Canada for grain.

2 Ships across the ocean
Laded low with food,
Railway and road haulage,
Oil refined and crude.
Mechanised and mighty,
Signs of weal and wealth,
Harvests home and foreign
For your joy and health.

3 But before we get too pleased
And satisfied,
It would be well to remember
Another side of the story.
Why spoil Benedicite
To remind us
Of our privilege
Or our affluence?
We who so often complain
Of the hardness of our lot,
Of the high level of taxation,
Of the smallness of profits
And the cost of insurance stamps.

Do we or dare we forget
Millions of our fellows,
Refugees, victims of war,
Children in despair,
Living, if they live at all,
At subsistence level.
Poverty in plenty
And we stand knee deep in plenty.

2 Give us this day
Our meagre ration
Of rice or meal
Of dried or processed milk.
Just a few calories,
Some of your despised
And unwanted carbohydrates.
Give us this day
What you give to the pigs
Or to your poodles.
Give us this day.
Your rubbish and your waste.
Give us this day.
Your mercy and compassion.

3 Give us this day
Sufficient bread
To let our feeble bodies
Move for another day
And rest fretfully
For another night.

1 Let us turn the supermarket
Into the church
And the church
Into the supermarket.

2 Let the mercy and compassion
Of the Lord Christ
Mould us and move us
Now and forever.

1 Benedicite.

2 Bless ye the Lord.

1 Benedicite omnia opera.
O all ye works of the Lord
Bless ye the Lord.

E. R. Hougham, from **Celebration Galliard Book 1**, *ed. Frost and*
Wensley

16 The Tractor

Machines are a means of progress if, by greatly increasing man's strength, they serve him. Unfortunately, too often man is a slave to their rhythmic beat and power. Machines are the servants of profit, but man is the servant of machines. We must struggle to re-establish a balance. As man extends himself and becomes more powerful through machines he should also develop his spirit, rise above his mechanical work, master it and offer it to God.

Whatever you are doing, whether you speak or act, do everything in the name of the Lord Jesus, giving thanks to God the father through him. (Col. 3, 17)

I don't like tractors, Lord.
I saw one in a field a while ago,
And I loathed it.

Tractors are conceited.
They crush man with all their strength.
They never look at him, they just move forward,
But when they move forward, they crawl, and *that* pleases me.

They are ugly,
They move clumsily, shaking their heavy frames.
Their silly noses upturned, panting
Coughing their deep, measured, mechanical cough.
But they are stronger than man, Lord.
Regularly, imperturbably, they pull their load;
They pull what a hundred human arms could not move,
They carry what a hundred human hands could not lift.
A tractor is ugly, yet it is strong, and I need it.
But it needs me, it needs man.

It needs man to exist, it is man who made it.
It needs man to move, it is man who starts it going.
It needs man to go forward, it is man who steers it.
It needs man, especially, that it may be consecrated.
For a tractor has no soul, Lord, and it is man who must lend it his
    own.

Michel Quoist

17 Song of the Sun

Be Thou praised, my Lord, with all Thy creatures,
   above all Brother Sun,
   who gives the day and lightens us therewith.

And he is beautiful and radiant with great splendour,
   of Thee, Most High, he bears similitude.

Be Thou praised, my Lord, of Sister Moon and the stars,
   in the heaven hast Thou formed them, clear and precious and
      comely . . .

Be Thou praised, my Lord, of Sister Water,
   which is much useful and humble and precious and pure.

Be Thou praised, my Lord, of Brother Fire,
   by which Thou hast lightened the night,
   and he is beautiful and joyful and robust and strong.

Be Thou praised, my Lord, of our Sister Mother Earth,
   which sustains and hath us in rule,
   and produces divers fruits with coloured flowers and herbs . . .

Praise ye and bless my Lord, and give Him thanks,
   and serve Him with great humility.

St Francis of Assisi

18 The Grain of Wheat

Some years ago the Reverend Clifton Robinson, an American
minister, decided to plant a matchboxful of wheat – about 360
grains – and take note of the harvest.

When the crop was ready to be gathered he set the seed aside
for sowing the next year. He did this for six years and by that time
the 360 grains had developed into a harvest field covering 2,666
acres. What an amazing increase! That year the harvest brought in
66,560 bushels of corn. It was estimated that when turned into
flour there would be sufficient to make 2,282,000 loaves of bread.
If these loaves could have been placed side by side they would
have stretched for a distance of 150 miles – all that from a
matchboxful of seed. But the minister had to plant the seed: it

would not have been any use leaving it in the box. God can only do His part if man does his.

Reading

The Reverend Clifton Robinson planted his wheat because he was inspired by some words found in Saint John's gospel:

> Jesus said: In truth, in very truth I tell you, a grain of wheat remains a solitary grain unless it falls into the ground and dies; but if it dies it bears a rich harvest. (John 12, 24 *New English Bible*)

J. W. Brimer and S. Brimer

NATURE

19 A Song of Praise

In the Name of Allah, the Compassionate, the Merciful. The judgement of Allah will surely come to pass: do not seek to hurry it on. Glory to him! Exalted be he above their idols!

By his will he sends down the angels with the Spirit to those of his servants whom he chooses, bidding them proclaim: 'There is no god but me: therefore fear me.'

He created the heavens and the earth to manifest the truth. Exalted be he above their idols!

He created man from a little germ: yet man openly disputes his judgement.

He created the beasts which provide you with warm clothing, food and other benefits. How pleasant they look when you bring them home and when you lead them out to pasture! They carry your burdens to far-off lands, which you could not otherwise reach except with painful toil. Compassionate is your Lord, and merciful.

He has given you horses, mules, and donkeys, which you may ride or use as ornaments; and he has created other things beyond your knowledge.

It is he who sends down water from the sky, which provides drink for you and brings forth the crops on which your cattle feed. And thereby he brings up corn and olives, dates and grapes and other fruit. Surely in this there is a sign for thinking men.

He has forced the night and the day, and the sun and the moon, into your service: the stars also serve you by his leave. Surely in this there are signs for men of understanding.

On the earth he has fashioned for you objects of various hues: surely in this there is a sign for prudent men.

It is he who has subjected to you the ocean, so that you may eat of its fresh fish and bring up from it ornaments with which to adorn your persons. Behold the ships ploughing their course through it. All this he has created, that you may seek his bounty and render thanks to him.

The Koran

20 Murder in the Cathedral (extract)

We praise Thee, O God, for Thy glory displayed in all the
    creatures of the earth,
In the snow, in the rain, in the wind, in the storm; in all of
    Thy creatures, both the hunters and the hunted.
For all things exist only as seen by Thee, only as known by
    Thee, all things exist
Only in Thy light, and Thy glory is declared even in that
    which denies Thee; the darkness declares the glory of light.
Those who deny Thee could not deny, if Thou didst not
    exist; and their denial is never complete, for if it were so, they
    would not exist.
They affirm Thee in living; all things affirm Thee in living;
    the bird in the air, both the hawk and the finch; the beast on the
    earth, both the wolf and the lamb; the worm in the soil and the
    worm in the belly.
Therefore man, whom Thou hast made to be conscious of
    Thee, must consciously praise Thee, in thought and in word
    and in deed.
Even with the hand to the broom, the back bent in laying
    the fire, the knee bent in cleaning the hearth, we, the scrubbers
    and sweepers of Canterbury,
The back bent under toil, the knee bent under sin, the hands to
    the face under fear, the head bent under grief,
Even in us the voices of seasons, the snuffle of winter, the song of
    spring, the drone of summer, the voices of beasts and of birds,
    praise Thee.

T. S. Eliot

21 The Power and the Glory

Let there be life, said God. And what He wrought
Went past in myriad marching lives, and brought
This hour, this quiet room, and my small thought
Holding invisble vastness in its hands.

Let there be God, said I. And what I've done
Goes onward like the splendour of the sun
And rises up in rapture and is one
With the white power of conscience that commands.

Let life be God . . . What wail of fiend or wraith
Dare mock my glorious angel where he stands
To fill my dark with fire, my heart with faith?

Siegfried Sassoon

22 The Potato

This dirty old brown potato,
Muddy and earthy,
Dug out of the damp soil and clay –
A funny object.
A 'tater', the Cockney would call it,
I wash off the mud and there it is –
Knobbly and irregular,
Pitted with eyes – like scabs.
If I peel it or cut it
I see it is just a lump of wet starch!
Yet if I place it in the ground
Things happen;
A whole chemical factory gets to work;
The eyes sprout strange seeking white fingers,
Reaching down, down,
Sucking in nourishment through tiny hairs;
One or two shoot up, split, spread, get pink
Then green, into light,
Grow leaves, become a plant
Flowering in sunlight.
The soppy lump of starch gets slimy and black,
Dying in its own life –
Come tubers, lots of little potatoes,

Swell, grow,
Provide food and wealth!
What a miracle, Lord,
In this dirty old brown potato!

Murdoch Dahl

23 Miracles

Why, who makes much of a miracle?
As to me I know of nothing else but miracles,
Whether I walk in the streets of Manhattan,
Or dart my sight over the roofs of houses towards the sky,
Or wade with naked feet along the beach just in the edge of the
    water,
Or stand under trees in the woods,
Or talk by day with anyone I love,
Or sit at table at dinner with the rest,
Or look at strangers riding opposite me in the car,
Or watch honey-bees busy around the hive of a summer
    fore-noon,
Or animals feeding in the fields,
Or birds, or the wonderfulness of insects in the air,
Or the wonderfulness of the sundown, or of stars shining so quiet
    and bright,
Or the exquisite delicate thin curve of the new moon in spring;
These with the rest, one and all, are to me miracles . . .

Walt Whitman

24 Autumn

Slowly, one by one,
Through the damp-smelling, misty air of autumn the delicate
    leaves drop down,
Covering the grass like a carpet –
A carpet woven in gold and silver –
And the sun,
Shining through the bare black trees,
Turns to a glory of gold these dying woods.
Ah! if any poet
Could stay that brief splendid vision,
Gather these autumn glories into his song,

What joy were his!
Let the winds scatter
The broken scarlet web of autumn wide over the world!
Soft with sleep,
Let the delicate air sigh through the naked branches,
That still preserve their beauty,
Though a barer, a more austere beauty than the green beauty of
    summer.
Now the sap of life runs low:
All that we did in life's spring-time and summer seems far away.
Faint as a dream, and quiet, the sports of those days – the shouts
    and the laughter.
Sad enough they seem
Now that we know well how brief and how fragile they were.
Gone, gone, is their merriment. Only a echo remains while the
    curtain of night is descending;
But how lovely that echo! —
Lovelier far than the shouts and the laughter, the songs and the
    childish play –
Lovely as autumn.

Forrest Reid

25 God's Grandeur

The earth is charged with the grandeur of God.
   It will flame out, like shining from shook foil;
   It gathers to a greatness, like the ooze of oil
Crushed. Why do men then not reck His rod?
Generations have trod, have trod, have trod;
   And all is seared with trade; bleared, smeared with toil;
   And wears men's smudges and shares men's smell; the soil
Is bare now, nor can foot feel, being shod.
And for all this, nature is never spent.
   There lives the dearest freshness deep down things;
And though the last lights off the black West went
   Oh, morning, at the brown brink eastward, springs –
Because the Holy Ghost over the bent
   World broods with warm breast and with ah! bright wings.

Gerard Manley Hopkins

26 Pied Beauty

Glory be to God for dappled things –
    For skies of couple-colour as a brinded cow;
    For rose-moles all in stipple upon trout that swim;
Fresh-firecoal chestnut falls; finches' wings;
    Landscape plotted and pieced – fold, fallow and plough;
    And all trades, their gear and tackle and trim.
All things counter, original, spare, strange;
    Whatever is fickle, freckled (who knows how?)
    With swift, slow; sweet, sour; adazzle, dim;
He fathers-forth whose beauty is past change:
    Praise him.

Gerard Manley Hopkins

27 Varuna, the All-knowing God

He knows the path of birds that fly through heaven, and, sovereign
    of the sea,
He knows the ships that are thereon.
True to his holy law, he knows the twelve moons with their
    progeny:
He knows the pathway of the wind, the spreading, high and
    mighty wind;
He knows the gods who dwell above.
Varuna, true to holy law, sits down among his people; he,
Most wise, sits there to govern all.
From thence perceiving he beholds all wondrous things, both
    what hath been,
And what hereafter will be done.

The Rig Veda

28 It is Thou

It is Thou who givest the bright sun, together with the ice; it is
Thou who createdst the rivers and the salmon in the river.

That the nut-tree should be flowering, O Christ, it is a rare
craft; through Thy skill too comes the kernel, Thou fair ear of our
wheat.

Though the children of Eve ill deserve the bird-flocks and the
salmon, it was the Immortal One on the cross who made both the
salmon and birds.

It is He who makes the flower of the sloe grow through the bark of the blackthorn, and the nut-flower on the trees; beside this, what miracle is greater?

Tadhg Óg Ó Huiginn, sixteenth-century Irish poet

2 THE CHRISTIAN YEAR

Assemblies

ADVENT

1 Prophecy

a) Thy kindom come! on bended knee
Reading: Isaiah 9, 2–7
Prayer **14**

b) O come, O come, Emmanuel!
Reading: Isaiah 11, 1–9
Prayer **15**

c) Hills of the North rejoice
Reading: Isaiah 35, 1–10; or Isaiah 40, 1–8
Prayer **26**

2 The Way to Bethlehem

Three extracts are given (**30**) from *Can You Tell Me the Way to Bethlehem?* in *Celebration*, Advent to Epiphany, publ. Galliard. Songs/hymns/carols recommended are:
O little town of Bethlehem
Sing high with the holly
or How far is it to Bethlehem?
Angels from the realm of glory.

CHRISTMAS

1 The Story

a) Hark the herald angels sing
Reading: Luke 1, 26–35
Prayers **15** and **19**

b) While shepherds watched their flocks by night
Reading: Luke 2, 1–20
Prayer **17**

c) At the name of Jesus
    Readings **36**: *Light Looked Down*, Laurence Housman; and
       37: *At Christmas*, Fra Giovanni; or **36** and John 1, 1–14;
       or Philippians 2, 1–11
    Prayers **16** and **18**

2 Carol Singing

a) and b) Two extracts from *Cider with Rosie* by Laurie Lee (**32**).
It is effective to have a small group of 'carol singers' who should
include 'While shepherds watched' in a) and 'As Joseph was
a-walking' in b), as these are referred to in the text.

c) O little town of Bethlehem
    Reading **33**: *Carols in Seville*, Laurie Lee
    Prayers **17–22**

3 Christmas Poems

a) Born in the night
    Reading **34**: *Towards Bethlehem*, John Smith
    Prayer **20**

b) Hark the herald angels sing *or* Sing high with the holly
    (N.L. 18)
    Reading **35**: *Christmas*, John Betjeman
    Prayer **19**

c) Thy kingdom come! On bended knee
    Reading **38**: *A Week to Christmas*, Louis MacNeice
    Prayers **21** and **22**

4 Christmas for Today

a) Born in the night *or* Away in a manger
    Reading **31**: *A Child of Our Time*, Derek Wensley
    Prayers **17** and **20**

b) It came upon the midnight clear
    Reading **29**: *The Word Became Flesh*, Rex Chapman
    The prayer is incorporated in the reading.

EPIPHANY

a)   As with gladness men of old
Reading: Matthew 2, 1–12
Prayer **23**

b)   O worship the Lord in the beauty of Holiness
Reading **39**: *Journey of the Magi*, T. S. Eliot
Prayer **25**

c)   As with gladness men of old *or* He who would
valiant be *or* When I needed a neighbour, were
you there, were you there?
Reading **40**: *The Fourth Wise Man*, Henry Van Dyke
Prayers **23**, **71** and **80** (two instalments)

LENT

1   Christ in the Wilderness

a)   Forty days and forty nights
Reading: Matthew 4, 1–11
Prayer **28**

b)   Be thou my guardian and my guide
Reading **42**: *In the Wilderness*, Robert Graves
Prayers **27** and **28**

c)   Dear Lord and Father of Mankind
Reading **41**: *Retro Me, Sathanas*, Teresa Hooley
Prayer **29**

2   Temptation

a)   God who spoke in the beginning
Reading: Genesis 3, 1–7
Prayer **27**

b)   Guide me O thou great Redeemer
Reading **44**: *Temptation*, Anon.
Prayer **70**

c)   Be thou my guardian and my guide
Reading **43**: *The Three Apprentices*, Mary Tayler
Prayer **29**

3 *Temptation – Twentieth Century*

Material provided by the Health Education Council on smoking and alcohol can be used. There is much additional material on drugs available, including Brooks and Cockett, *Assemblies for Seniors*, quoting *Man in Black*, Johnny Cash (Hodder and Stoughton); David Kossoff, 'Words for Paul', in *You have a Minute Lord* (Kossoff's younger son died of drugs in 1976). See also David Wilkerson, *The Cross and the Switchblade*.

HOLY WEEK

Bible Readings

a) All glory, laud and honour
   Readings **45**: *Into Jerusalem with Palms*, Rex Chapman; and
      Matthew 21, 1–12
   Prayer included; or **31**

b) Ride on! Ride on in majesty
   Reading: Matthew 26, 1–30, or **46**: *The Donkey's Owner*,
      Clive Sansom
   Prayer **36**

c) My song is love unknown
   Reading: Matthew 26, 35–37
   Prayer **37**

EASTER

1 The Witnesses: Bible and Rex Chapman

a) Bitter was the night
   Reading **49**: *Judas*
   Prayer included

b) Bitter was the night/O Jesus I have promised
   Reading **48**: *Peter's Problem*
   Prayer **33**

c) He's back in the land of the living
   Reading **47**: *On the Cross*
   Prayer included

2 The Lion, the Witch and the Wardrobe, C. S. Lewis (*Three Readings*)

a)   Ride on! Ride on in majesty
     Reading **57a**
     Prayer **34**

b)   I danced in the morning
     Reading **57b**
     Prayer **35**

c)   He's back in the land of the living
     Reading **57c**
     Prayer **38**

3 Readings for Easter

a)   Ride on! Ride on in majesty
     Reading **46**: *The Donkey's Owner*, Clive Sansom
     Prayer **30**

b)   I danced in the morning
     Reading **51**: *Father to the Man*, John Knight
     Prayer **39**

c)   We meet you, O Christ
     Reading **56**: *Ballad of the Bread Man*, Charles Causley
     Prayer **37**

4 Easter Today

a)   He's back in the land of the living
     Reading **52**: *Ecce Homo*, David Gascoyne
     Prayer **42**

b)   When they shouted hosanna, were you there
     Reading **50**: *Indifference*, G. A. Studdert Kennedy
     Prayer **39**

c)   He's back in the land of the living/Now the green blade
         riseth from the buried grain
     Readings **53**: *Christ is Risen*, Leslie Newbigin; **54**: *Calvary*,
         Peter Casey; and **55**: *It is Accomplished*, William Temple
     Prayers **38** and **40**

5 *Ascension*

a) At the name of Jesus
Reading: Acts 1, 1–11
Prayer **43**

b) God is love: his the care
Readings: Ephesians 1, 19–21; and Romans 8, 33–39
Prayer **44**

6 *Whitsun/Pentecost*

a) Breathe on me, breath of God
Readings: Genesis 11, 1–9; and Acts, 2, 1–4
Prayer **45**

b) Come down, O love divine
Reading: 1 Corinthians 12; or John 14, 15–27
Prayer **77**

Prayers

ADVENT

14 Almighty Father, you have come to us in the past; you have
spoken to us in the law of Israel; you have challenged us in the
works of the prophets; you have shown us in Jesus what you are
really like. Help us, Father, to realise that you still come to us
now through other people and their love and concern for us and
through those who need our help. Help us to recognise and to
welcome you.

C. P. P. W. (much adapted)

15 O Father, who hast declared thy love to men by the birth of the
Holy Child at Bethlehem: help us to welcome him with gladness
and to make room for him in our daily life; so that we may live at
peace with one another and in goodwill with all thy family;
through thy Son, Jesus Christ, our Lord.

A Devotional Diary

16   Lord, when you came to the world you brought us hope,
When you came to our darkness you brought us light,
When you came to our strife you brought us peace.
Now, as Christmas approaches we again think of your coming.
Help us to turn the hope, the light and the peace which you
brought us into reality in today's world.

*Hobden, **Explorations in Worship***

CHRISTMAS

17 Father, our complex industrial society looks for a word from you,
and finds this simple pastoral scene of shepherds and a stable. We
love it, of course. But teach us, O Lord, that your Son is here as
well as there. Remind us that the Gospel is in the fact of Christ,

not in his setting: and that the story of his birth is part of the story of his life, his claims, his death and his resurrection.

C. P. P. W. (*much adapted*)

18 O God, our Father, who by the glorious birth of thy Son didst enlighten the darkness of the world, we pray that the light of his presence may shine more and more in the lives of men, that, being filled with his spirit of love, we may inherit that gift of peace which he came to bring.

Hugh Martin (*adapted*)

19 O God, whose love has been shown to us in the birth of Jesus our Saviour, help us this Christmas to find time to let your love speak to us; that we may respond to it and open our hearts to receive your joy and peace, through Jesus Christ our Lord.

20 Lord, we know the Christmas story so well. Help us to understand it better. Make it more real to us, so that with Mary and Joseph we may journey in faith to Bethlehem, with the shepherds we may hear again the good tidings of a Saviour's birth, and with the angels we may glorify your holy name. So give us new joy in our Christmas worship, and fill our hearts with wonder, love and praise.

Frank Colquhoun, **N. P. P.**

21 Lord, let us not be so busy at Christmas time that we lose sight of the meaning behind it all. Help us to find true joy in all the moments these exciting days of Christmas bring to us. And though we think of joy and goodwill especially at this time, help us to know that your spirit is with us always, and to live our lives in that spirit.

Hobden, **Explorations in Worship**

22 Help us rightly to remember the birth of Jesus, that we may share in the song of the Angels, the gladness of the shepherds, and the worship of the Wise Men. Close the door of hate and open the door of love all over the world. Let kindness come with every greeting.

Deliver us from evil by the blessing that Christ brings, and teach us to be merry with clear hearts. May the Christmas morning make us happy to be Thy children and the Christmas evening bring us to our beds with grateful thoughts, forgiving and forgiven, for Jesus' sake. Amen.

Robert Louis Stevenson

EPIPHANY

23 We have read, O Lord, about the wise men of the East who were guided to you by a star and who brought generous gifts of gold, frankincense and myrrh; give us the wisdom to seek you, light to guide us to you and generosity to lay whatever gifts we have before you, to your praise and glory.

C. R. C. (*adapted*)

24 Almighty God, who by the light of a star led wise men to Jesus: by the light of your Word lead us and all men to him, the Saviour of the world; that together we may bring him our best gifts, and pay homage to him as our King.

N. P. P.

25 Eternal God, who by the shining of a star led the wise men to the worship of your Son: guide by his light the nations of the earth, that the whole world may behold your glory; through Jesus Christ our Lord.

A. S. B.

ST PAUL (CONVERSION, JAN. 25)

26 O God, who, through the teaching of the blessed Apostle Saint Paul, hast caused the light of the Gospel to shine throughout the world: grant, we beseech thee, that we, having his wonderful conversion in remembrance, may show forth our thankfulness unto thee for the same, by following the holy doctrine which he taught, through Jesus Christ our Lord.

Book of Common Prayer

LENT

27 Heavenly Father, we confess how often we disobey what we know
to be your will; how often we forget you and leave you out of our
lives; how often we are too blind to know our sins, too proud to
admit them, too indifferent to make amends. We confess how
half-hearted and unworthy we are as members of your Church and
as your witnesses before men. In your mercy, O Lord, forgive
us our sins, and give us honest, humble and penitent hearts, for
the sake of our Saviour Jesus Christ.

After William Temple, **N. P. P.**

28 Almighty God, whose Son Jesus Christ fasted forty days in the
wilderness, and was tempted as we are, yet without sin: Give us
grace to control ourselves in obedience to your Spirit; and, as you
know our weakness, so may we know your power to save; through
Jesus Christ our Lord.

Common Prayer (*adapted*)

29 O Lord, who knowest our temptations, help us by thy Holy Spirit
to fight against them. Give us grace never to approve what our
consciences tell us is wrong. Strengthen each of us against the sins
to which we are most prone, through Jesus Christ, Our Lord.

Uppingham School (*adapted*)

HOLY WEEK

30 We praise you, Almighty God, for the acts of love by which you
have redeemed us through your Son Jesus Christ our Lord. On
this day he entered the holy city of Jerusalem in triumph, and was
proclaimed as King by those who spread their garments and
branches of palm along his way. Let these branches be for us signs
of his victory; and grant that we who bear them in his name may
ever hail him as our king, and follow him in the way that leads to
eternal life.

Episcopal Church, U.S.A.

31 Deliver me, Lord, from blind obedience, unthinking response,
from being immersed in a crowd that cheers or jeers without

knowing why. Make me think, Lord. Make me use my mind.
Keep my eyes open across that leap of faith in you 'who come in
the name of the Lord'.

Rex Chapman (adapted)

32 Lord, strengthen those in despair and in trouble. Strengthen us to
come to terms with ourselves and our actions in the light of your
death, your resurrection, and your forgiveness.

Rex Chapman (adapted), on Judas

33 Lord, Peter stands as witness to the power of your forgiveness.
We confess our faith daily, Lord, and yet we disown you. Thank
you, Lord, for the life and witness of Peter. His problem is our
encouragement.

Rex Chapman

34 Lord Jesus, in the Olive garden you faced in prayer the devil's last
and greatest temptation: to take the easy way, the sensible
solution, that was not the will of your Father. Give us grace, Lord,
to listen to your voice and not simply to take the easy way.

John Kingsnorth (adapted)

35 Our inhumanity to each other is frightening, Lord. You were
made to stand where millions have also stood.
And we talk so glibly about involvement, incarnation.
Forgive us, Lord. Words fail.

Rex Chapman

36 Almighty God, whose Son, our Saviour Jesus Christ, was received
and honoured as a king by those who soon were to ask for his
death; grant that we may never seek the praise nor fear the blame
of men, but may always have the courage to do what we know to
be right.

W. E. Scudamore, **A Book of Prayers for Schools**

(Also Palm Sunday)

37 Lord, I have betrayed you in following my own way;
I have denied you in fearing to follow yours;
And I have mocked you in my pride and my selfishness.
Lest I be utterly lost, meet me with your forgiveness,

Hold me in your strength and renew me with your life.
Lord, you died that I might live, live in me and with me,
For without you I cannot be saved from the evil that would stifle
  me.

Edmund Banyard

EASTER

38 Almighty God, who through your only Son Jesus Christ overcame
death, and opened to us the gate of everlasting life: grant that we,
who celebrate with joy his glorious resurrection, may be risen with
him, and seek the things that are above, where he lives and reigns
with you and the Holy Spirit, one God, for ever and ever.

A revision of the 1662 **Easter Collect** *by Frank Colquhoun*

39 Lord Jesus Christ, forgive us our slowness in believing and our
difficulties in understanding the mystery of Easter. Accept our
faith and help us where faith falls short. Forgive us the way we
still think of you locked in the past. Help us to grasp that you are
permanently risen; so that remembering you as you were we may
worship you as you are.

C. P. P. W

40 Lord Jesus, we greet you, risen from the dead.
We thought that your way of love was a dead end,
  leading only to a cross:
  now we see that it is the way to life.
We thought that your whole life was wasted:
  now we know that it was gloriously worthwhile.
We thought that your suffering was pointless:
  now we can see God's purpose in it.
We thought that death was the end of you:
  now we know that your life was too great to be ended by death.
Lord Jesus, we adore you, risen from the dead.

C. P. P. W.

41 Lord, help us to know joy as a spring always welling up within us
and give us the power to dance through life, not as those who are
blind to sorrow, misery or shame, but as those who know your
victory over death and who cannot but rejoice.

Edmund Banyard, **Word Alive**

42 Lord, come alive within our experience, within our sorrows and disappointments and doubts, within the ordinary moments of our lives. Come alive as the peace and joy and assurance that is stronger than the locked doors within, with which we try to shut out life. Come alive as the peace and joy and assurance that nothing in life or death can kill

Rex Chapman (adapted)

ASCENSION

43 Lord Jesus Christ, you found a way through life's maze and won through to the centre of things. You blazed a trail through all the confusing tangles of life and opened up a path for us. You were the first to struggle through to perfection: Lead us along the path to God and bring us through all our struggles to the love you have shown us, for your Name's sake.

C. P. P. W. (*much adapted*)

44 Once, Lord, you lived a human life subject to the limitations of time:
   now you are the same yesterday, today and for ever.
Once you were limited to one particular place:
   now you are present wherever men turn to you.
Once only those who met you face to face knew you:
   now your divine love extends through all the world.
Help us, O Lord, to recognise and to receive you.

C. P. P. W. (*much adapted*)

WHITSUN/PENTECOST

45 Almighty God, who at this time taught the hearts of your faithful people by sending to them the light of your Holy Spirit: grant us by the same Spirit to have a right judgement in all things, and evermore to rejoice in his holy comfort: through the merits of Christ Jesus our Saviour, who is alive and reigns with you in the unity of the Spirit, one God, now and for ever.

A. S. B.

46 Lord Jesus, we thank you that you have fulfilled your promise
and given us your Spirit to abide with us for ever: grant us to
know his presence in all its divine fullness.

*Botting, **N. P. P.** (part only)*

47 'The fruits of the Spirit are love, joy, peace, patience, kindness,
goodness, fidelity, gentleness and self-control.' The Spirit is the
source of life. Lord give us life.

*Rex Chapman, **The Cry of the Spirit**.*

48 O Lord God, Father Almighty, we give you thanks for making
yourself known to us through Jesus, your Son, and for sending
your Holy Spirit to be with us always. Grant that we may
recognise and receive you in our lives, Father, Son and Holy
Spirit, one God, world without end.

49 (Use can possibly be made of part of St Patrick's Breastplate,
particularly in conjunction with the hymn and possibly the
reading of the whole.)

> I bind unto myself the name,
>   The strong name of the Trinity,
> By incarnation of the same,
>   The Three in One and One in Three,
> Of whom all nature hath creation,
>   Eternal Father, Spirit, Word.
> Praise to the Lord of my Salvation:
>   Salvation is of Christ the Lord.

St Patrick

Readings

ADVENT

29 The Word Became Flesh

Matthew 2, 1–12; Luke 2, 1–20; John 1, 1–14

The children were keen, once again, to act the Christmas story.
They kept asking as Christmas drew near.
Can I be Joseph?
Can I be Mary?
Can I be Herod?
Can I be an angel?
Their parents came to watch, eyes fixed firmly on their own.
Lord, the stories abound.
Embryonic drama is enacted.
A good time is had by all.
There is a sixpence in the pudding.
The cake is cut.
You become flesh in the enjoyment of children.
You become flesh in the forces that draw families together.
You become flesh in the selfish world of men, who force you to
    be born at the edge of a crowded inn.
I do not much mind whether there were angels and a manger,
    shepherds and eastern astrologers.
These stories form a cocoon around you.
Once you have burst forth, they no longer matter.
How many of those children, Lord, will ever see beyond the
    cocoon?
How many parents ever see beyond the superficialities
    surrounding our lives?
Within this life of mine, within the years that lie ahead,
Lord, become flesh within me.

Rex Chapman

30 Can You Tell Me the Way to Bethlehem?

Three extracts are given. The original forms a complete service for
Narrator, 3 Voices, Congregation and Choir.

1 Take the first way to Bethlehem.
 Go to Cooks and book a seat
 On a Skymaster or a VC10
 This will take you to Tel Aviv
 There with permission from the Israeli Security Forces
 You may be able to get a seat in a bus
 That will take you to Bethlehem
 [Remember that Bethlehem was formerly in Arab Occupied
   Territory].

 This is the little guide
 To the little town.
 Six miles SSW of Jerusalem
 Situated on a grey limestone ridge
 Altitude 2,550 feet above sea level
 Hills are terraced and sweep in graceful curves . . .
 There is one main street
 Occupied by shops and workshops
 And the great Church of the Nativity.
 The main industries
 Apart from agriculture
 The manufacture and sale
 Of souvenirs.

 Pause at the roadside stall
 For a Coca Cola (iced)
 And climb refreshed
 To the Church of the Holy Nativity.
 Come inside
 Watch and listen
 The guide will lead you
 To the spot and say . . .
 Here Christ was born.

 And on that night
 In the crowded village streets
 Of the little town
 Men drank wine
 And women kneaded dough

And children laughed and danced
And early went to bed.
The hungry, tired and sick
Wept till their eyes were red,
Silent policemen
Wandered up and down
And Herod's guards
Cast anxious eyes around.
For in the little town
In the shabby inn
In the dark stable of
That INN.
A boy child was cradled
In a cattle feeding bin.
And the street crowd
Knew nothing of it
And cared less.
Busy with the brightness
Of their own business
How could they know?
How could they understand
That the mind and heart
Of the universe
Was cradled incarnate
In a cow crib?

O you good people
Who listen here tonight
How much do you care?
How much do you understand?

2 The second way to Bethlehem is a different way
Bethlehem means – House of Bread
Why it was called a House of Bread
Nobody knows
But the name foreshadows strangely
Our Eucharistic Bethlehem
For the church is the inn
The altar is the crib
In this our parish Bethelehem.

Christ present in the Bread and Wine
Our Bethlehem today . . .
Here at the altar is the crib

Here your incarnate Lord
Move from your seat
And fold your hands
Kneel as the shepherds
Knelt of old
Give of your heart
Give of your gold
Accept the bread
And taste the wine
See in this sacrament divine
Your Christ
Your Bethlehem.

3 The third way to Bethlehem is the hardest.
No need for plane or car
You can reach it in your summer garden
Or in your winter chair
Turn off the radio and television
And you are there.

It's in your heart
Held in the stable of your mind
And cribbed in the manger of your love.
The kingdom is within you
You carry it about wherever you go
And it is either a joy or a burden.
Perhaps sometimes a joy
Sometimes a burden.
You can't cut it out and throw it away
You won't find it any mass X-ray
It is your life
Life pulsing through the senses
Life delighting in colour and in light
Life struggling for truth and understanding
Man made in the image of God.
This is your life
The power and the glory
The shame and the suffering
This is the Christ within you
And with him in His Bethlehem.

Switch off your distraction
Put down your knitting
Close your book

Take the telephone off the hook . . .
Relax your mind and warm your heart
And move into this Bethlehem of your spirit
Where Christ is born in you.

For unto us a child in born
To us a son is given
And on his shoulder ever rests
All power in earth and heaven.

E. R. Hougham, from **Celebration**

31 A Child of Our Time

Extract from a service of modern readings and carols (adapted).

My friend is what is known as 'Artistic' you know, been to an art school, studied embroidery, does clay-modelling, makes glove puppets, that sort of thing. Very good at arranging flowers, often does the Harvest Festival decorating in our church. Anyway, a year or so ago she was asked to do a Christmas crib for a church. 'You're just the person', they said, 'so artistic'. Which now we've come to think about it, should have warned us . . .

We argued the toss for hours, but eventually decided that we'd really try to bring the Christian story right slap bang up to date; Mary and Joseph would be West Indian immigrants – negroes anyway . . . and, truth's truth, but they're not the most popular people in some parts of the world, are they?

There'd be so little room for them in our inn ('What – not another pregnant West Indian? Don't they know any better?') that Mary has to have the baby as best she can in a garage – a shed at least – which, after all is the modern equivalent of a stable.

The shepherds would be a few old age pensioners and a couple of meths drinkers, come into the place for a warm and a brew-up, and the three wise men bringing their gifts would be a scientist, a doctor, and a . . . an engineer with the tools of his trade to represent his skill.

Anyway we all worked hard and, if we'd argued for hours, we certainly worked some: we built, about quarter size, the interior of an old shed being used as a garage: with a view of London by night outside the window at the back . . . an old car up on jacks, work bench along the side, a few rubber tyres, and a pile of greasy sacking where Mary has had the baby.

We modelled and dressed the figures: the old age pensioners

leaving their tiny fire in a dented tin, the meths drinkers turning
from their crude still in the corner, a prostitute who's there to see
what all the fuss is about (she was an afterthought, first as a
contrast to the innocence and purity of Mary and then as
representing the sinners Christ has come to save) and the young
negress and her husband proudly showing off their baby to the
scientist (he had a microscope and a map of the stars with, of
course, the star plainly marked). The doctor (stethoscope and
hypodermic), and the engineer (you know, spanners and
such) . . . we lit it all with a weak bulb, had a model dog and a cat
with kittens to represent the animals – and then allowed them in
to see what we had done. There was a long silence. 'Well', they
said, 'It's certainly very artistic but, er, . . . '

We went to see the Crib they did use: cardboard stable, handful
of real straw and a standard plastic set of the holy family, complete
with silver-paper star, two angels cut from a religious colouring
book, and a photograph of a donkey pinned against the
background.

Anybody want an idea for a Christmas Crib? Or are His own
still receiving him not?

Derek Wensley, from **Celebration 2**

32 The Week Before Christmas

a) The week before Christmas, when snow seemed to lie thickest, was
the moment for carol-singing; and when I think back to those
nights it is to the crunch of snow and to the lights of the lanterns
on it.

So as soon as the wood had been stacked in the oven to dry for
the morning fire, we put on our scarves and went out through the
streets, calling loudly between our hands, till the various boys who
knew the signal ran out from their houses to join us.

One by one they came stumbling over the snow, swinging their
lanterns around their heads, shouting and coughing horribly.
'Coming carol-barking then?'

We were the Church Choir, so no answer was necessary. For a
year we had praised the Lord out of key, and as a reward for this
service – on top of the Outing – we now had the right to visit all
the big houses, to sing our carols and collect our tribute.

To work them all in meant a five-mile journey over wild and
generally snowed-up country . . . Our first call as usual was the
house of the Squire, and we trouped nervously down his drive.
For light we had candles in marmalade-jars suspended on loops of

string, and they threw pale gleams on the towering snowdrifts that stood on each side of the drive. A blizzard was blowing, but we were well wrapped up, with Army puttees on our legs, woollen hats on our heads, and several scarves around our ears.

As we approached the Big House across its white silent lawns, we too grew respectfully silent. The lake near by was stiff and black, the waterfall frozen and still. We arranged ourselves shuffling around the big front door, then knocked and announced the Choir.

A maid bore the tidings of our arrival away into the echoing distances of the house, and while we waited we cleared our throats noisily. Then she came back, and the door was left ajar for us, and we were bidden to begin. We brought no music, the carols were in our heads. 'Let's give 'em "Wild Shepherds" ' said Jack. We began in confusion, plunging into a wreckage of keys, of different words and tempo; but we gathered our strength; he who sang loudest took the rest of us with him, and the carol took shape if not sweetness . . . As we sang we craned our necks, gaping into that lamplit hall which we had never entered; staring at the muskets and untenanted chairs, the great tapestries furred by dust – until suddenly, on the stairs, we saw the old Squire himself standing and listening with his head on one side.

He didn't move until we'd finished; then slowly he tottered towards us, dropped two coins in our box with a trembling hand, scratched his name in the book we carried, gave us each a long look with his moist blind eyes, then turned away in silence.

As though released from a spell, we took a few sedate steps, then broke into a run for the gate. We didn't stop till we were out of the grounds. Impatient, at least, to discover the extent of his bounty, we squatted by the cowsheds, held our lanterns over the book, and saw that he had written 'Two shillings'. This was quite a good start. No-one of any worth in the district would dare to give less than the Squire.

b) Mile after mile we went, fighting against the wind, falling into snowdrifts, and navigating by the lights of the houses. And yet we never saw our audience. We called at house after house; we sang in courtyards and porches, outside windows, or in the damp gloom of hallways; we heard voices from hidden rooms; we smelt rich clothes and strange hot food; we saw maids bearing in dishes or carrying away coffee cups, we received nuts, cakes, figs, preserved ginger, dates, cough-drops, and money; but we never once saw our patrons. We sang as it were at the castle walls, and

apart from the Squire, who had shown himself to prove that he
was still alive, we never expected it otherwise . . .

We approached our last house high up on the hill, the place of
Joseph the farmer. For him we had chosen a special carol, which
was about the other Joseph, so that we always felt that singing it
added a spicy cheek to the the night. The last stretch of country to
reach his farm was perhaps the most difficult of all. In these rough
bare lanes, open to all winds, sheep were buried and wagons lost.
Huddled together, we tramped in one another's footsteps,
powdered snow blew into our screwed-up eyes, the candles burnt
low, some blew out altogether, and we talked loudly above the gale.

Crossing at last the frozen mill-stream – whose wheel in
summer still turned a barren mechanism – we climbed up to
Joseph's farm. Sheltered by trees, warm on its bed of snow, it
seemed always to be like this. As always it was late; as always this
was our final call. The snow had a fine crust upon it, and the old
trees sparkled like tinsel.

We grouped ourselves round the farmhouse porch. The sky
cleared, and broad streams of stars ran down over the valley and
away to Wales. On Slad's white slopes, seen through the black
sticks of the woods, some red lamps still burned in the windows.

Everything was quiet; everywhere there was the faint crackling
silence of the winter night. We started singing, and we were all
moved by the words and the sudden trueness of our voices. Pure,
very clear, and breathless, we sang:

> As Joseph was a walking
> He heard an angel sing:
> This night shall be the birth-time
> Of Christ the Heavenly King.
>
> He neither shall be borned
> In Housen nor in hall
> Nor in a place of paradise
> But in an ox's stall . . .

And two thousand Christmases became real to us then; the
houses, the halls, the places of paradise had all been visited; the
stars were bright to guide the Kings though the snow; and across
the farmyard we could hear the beasts in their stalls. We were
given roast apples and hot mince-pies, in our nostrils were spices
like myrrh, and in our wooden box, as we headed back for the
village, there were golden gifts for all.

*Laurie Lee, **Cider with Rosie***

33 Carols in Seville

Our last nights in Seville now moved timeless, unsorted, gliding gently one into the other . . . These were nights turning towards Christmas, fresh, cold, with glittering pendulous stars . . .

It was the time [now] when the streets were full of [such] children, when the ragged half-naked urchins from the hovels of Triana came out in force and filled the town with carols. In busy gangs they roamed about, carrying a host of home-made instruments – tambourines, castanets, drumskins, and tins which they scraped with their sticks. At a word they would surround one and sing a whole concert for a penny. They were of all ages from four to fourteen, and they threw back their heads and sang with the ease and eagerness of angels, striking clear cool harmonies, and beating out the most subtle rhythms on their assorted instruments. Some blew into water-jars, making deep bass notes; some rattled dried peas in boxes; others shook loose tin-lids threaded on a stick. I never tired of listening to them, for I had never heard or seen anything like them before. Their singing was as precise as though they had rehearsed for months, yet naturally spontaneous and barbaric, as though the tidings they brought were new, the joy still fresh.

The night before we left Seville I walked late in the streets alone. It was past midnight; men were repairing an empty road and there was a wet moon over the Cathedral. As I headed at last for home I ran suddenly into another of these gangs. They were sitting in an alley, warming their bare feet round a fire of burning paper. When I called out they came crowding around me, squealing like starlings, grinning and arranging themselves in order. Their leader, a boy of ten, muttered a few instructions. Then they sang me five ecstatic carols, their smiles wiped away, their faces set in a kind of soft unconscious rapture. Here again, as in the others I had heard, was the same order, expertness and love. A girl of five took solo, singing through the short tangles of her hair in a voice of such hoarse sweetness one felt shriven of all one's sins. As she sang, the others watched her with solemn eyes, their lips pursed ready for the chorus. In this shabby street, lit by the lamp above, their bronze heads seemed disembodied, like Botticelli spirits, floating and singing in the air. They sang of a star in the sky; of Christ and the Virgin; of Triana (across the river); and of Bethlehem (across the hill). And looking and listening to this ragged lot, I believed all their bright songs told me. For they lived near the heart of things, and knew what it was to sleep on straw in stables.

Laurie Lee, **A Rose for Winter**

CHRISTMAS

34 Towards Bethlehem

It is so far, Mary said: oh how many hundred miles
Have we laboured, arguing over and over, it is too far?
the child with its low wail is angry and eager for life;
Though if it knew what a death this life is it might turn back
Even now in a miraculous retraction and unbind us
From the stark terror, the dull ache of this journey.
If we had asked to be blessed thus I should say:
'We will find a birthplace though a sea burst out before us.'
But, as it is, surely some village we passed would have sufficed?
We could have rested there. One more sin, Joseph, on your head,
Would not count much in the long run; you've sinned enough
   already.
So the long trek went on; always the storm
Hung over their heads. The petty bickering that broke out
At every turn in the road frayed the narrow rope
of reason and good will. At last they separated
And tramped in merciful silence, sullenly apart,
With Mary weeping under the too fierce sun.
Toward evening of a day they came to the place. The story is well
   known how, beaten at last, they crawled into a stable
And slept among the straw; after all the pain there was nothing
To ease the agony or bring a little joy to their side.
Joseph, bitter at first, found comfort after the birth.
The miracle, flowering under his eyes, warmed his chill heart.
And Mary? Well perhaps the delirium, the hot fever,
That racked and twisted her face to an old woman's face,
Opened a little door hidden at the back of the mind
And let a little happiness creep in
With the sound of Angels singing, and a glimpse of God.

John Smith, from **Happy Christmas** *compiled by Seymour and Smith*

35 Christmas

The bells of waiting Advent ring,
The Tortoise stove is lit again
And lamp-oil light across the night
Has caught the streaks of winter rain
In many a stained-glass window sheen
From Crimson Lake to Hooker's Green.

The holly in the windy hedge
And round the manor house the yew
Will soon be stripped to deck the ledge,
The altar, font and arch and pew,
So that the villagers can say
'The church looks nice' on Christmas Day.

And London shops on Christmas Eve
Are strung with silver bells and flowers
As hurrying clerks the City leave
To pigeon-haunted classic towers,
And marbled clouds go scudding by
The many-steepled London sky.

And is it true? And is it true,
This most tremendous tale of all,
Seen in a stained-glass window's hue,
A Baby in an ox's stall?
The Maker of the stars and sea
Become a Child on earth for me?

And is it true? For if it is,
No loving fingers tying strings
Around those tissued fripperies,
The sweet and silly Christmas things,
Bath salts and inexpensive scent
And hideous tie so kindly meant,

No love that in a family dwells,
No carolling in frosty air,
Nor all the steeple-shaking bells
Can with this single Truth compare –
That God was Man in Palestine
And lives today in Bread and Wine.

John Betjeman (abridged)

36 Light Looked Down

Light looked down and beheld darkness,
Thither will I go, said Light.
Peace looked down and beheld War,
Thither will I go, said Peace.
Love looked down and beheld Hatred,

Thither will I go, said Love.
So came Light and shone;
So came Peace and gave rest:
So came Love and brought Life.
And the Word was made Flesh and dwelt among us.

Laurence Housman

37 At Christmas

I salute you. There is nothing I can give you which you have not;
  but there is much that, while I cannot give you, you can take.
No Heaven can come to us unless our hearts find rest in it today:
                    Take Heaven.
No peace lies in the future which is not hidden in the present:
                    Take Peace.
The gloom of the world is but a shadow; behind it, yet within our
  reach is joy:
                    Take joy.
And so at this Christmas time I greet you, with the prayer that for
  you, now and forever, the day breaks and the shadows flee
  away.

From the writings of Fra Giovanni, A.D. 1513

38 A Week to Christmas

A week to Christmas, cards and snow and holly,
  Gimcracks in the shops,
Wishes and memories wrapped in tissue paper,
  Trinkets, gadgets and lollipops
And as if through coloured glasses
  We remember our childhood's thrill
Waking in the morning to the rustling of paper,
  The eiderdown heaped in a hill
Of wogs and dogs and bears and brick and apples
  And the feeling that Christmas Day
Was a coral island in time where we land and eat our lotus
  But where we can never stay.
There was a star in the East, the magi in their turbans
  Brought their luxury toys
In homage to a child born to capsize their values
  And wreck their equipoise.

A smell of hay like peace in the dark stable –
   Not peace however but a sword
To cut the Gordian knot of logical self-interest,
   The fool-proof golden cord;
For Christ walked in where no philosopher treads
   But armed with more than folly,
Making the smooth place rough and knocking the heads
   Of Church and State together.
In honour of whom we have taken over the pagan
   Saturnalia for our annual treat
Letting the belly have its say, ignoring
   The spirit while we eat.
And Conscience still goes crying through the desert
   With sackcloth round his loins:
A week to Christmas – hark the herald angels
   Beg for copper coins.

Louis MacNeice, from **Autumn Journal**

EPIPHANY

39 Journey of the Magi

'A cold coming we had of it,
Just the worst time of year
For a journey, and such a long journey.
The ways deep and the weather sharp,
The very dead of winter.'
And the camels galled, sore-footed, refractory,
Lying down in the melting snow.
There were times we regretted
The summer palaces on slopes, the terraces,
And the silken girls bringing sherbet.
Then the camel men cursing and grumbling
And running away, and wanting their liquor and women,
And the night-fires going out, and the lack of shelters,
And the cities hostile and the towns unfriendly
And the villages dirty and charging high prices:
A hard time we had of it.
At the end we preferred to travel all night,
Sleeping in snatches,
With the voices singing in our ears, saying
That this was all folly.

Then at dawn we came down to a temperate valley,
Wet, below the snow line, smelling of vegetation;
With a running stream and a water-mill beating the darkness,
And three trees on the low sky,
And an old white horse galloped away in the meadow.
Then we came to a tavern with vine-leaves over the lintel,
Six hands at an open door dicing for pieces of silver,
And feet kicking the empty wine-skins.
But there was no information, and so we continued
And arrived at evening, not a moment too soon
Finding the place; it was (you may say) satisfactory.

All this was a long time ago, I remember,
And I would do it again, but set down
This set down
This: were we led all that way for
Birth or Death? There was a Birth, certainly,
We had evidence and no doubt, I had seen birth and death,
But had thought they were different; this Birth was
Hard and bitter agony for us, like Death, our death.
We returned to our places, these Kingdoms,
But no longer at ease here, in the old dispensation,
With an alien people clutching their gods.
I should be glad of another death.

T. S. Eliot

40 The Fourth Wise Man

a) We have all heard of the three Wise men who visited Jesus at
Bethlehem. However one legend speaks of a fourth man, Artaban,
who had arranged to meet the other three and travel with them.
Artaban sold all his possessions to buy three jewels to take as a gift
to the king, and he set off in good time to meet his friends. As he
neared the meeting place, however, he came across a poor
traveller, very ill with a fever at the side of the road. He could not
leave him there to die, so stayed with him for several hours and
helped him to reach shelter.

Because of the delay Artaban missed his friends who had gone
ahead leaving a message that he should follow. Artaban had no
more food or supplies and his horse was exhausted. He had to sell
one of the jewels to get himself equipped for the next stage of the
journey.

Artaban reached Bethlehem only three days after his friends had visited the baby, but he found that he was too late. The manger was empty and the innkeeper told him that the little family had left – for Egypt, it was said – soon after the rich visitors had been. The village itself seemed very quiet as Artaban rode through it, for there had been rumours that the soldiers were coming to tax the people and so the men had driven the herds to the hills for safety. In fact as Artaban was chatting to a group of women there was the noise of marching soldiers, the whinnying of horses and the sound of gruff commands. Soldiers ran through the streets, entering each house, and as they moved up the road, from behind them could be heard the screams and cries of young women, some holding red stained bundles.

When they came up to the tall, well dressed foreigner the soldiers hesitated. One of the women in the group with Artaban had a newly born baby and the officer demanded that she hand him over. The panic stricken mother looked at Artaban who took from his pouch the second of the three jewels and offered it to the officer for the boy's life. He accepted it, and the soldiers moved on up the street to continue the slaughter of the babes as King Herod had commanded. The woman, hugging her child, fled to safety. Artaban now had only one jewel left as a gift for Jesus.

b) For many years Artaban searched for the new king so that he could present his gift. He travelled throughout the Roman empire, beginning in Egypt, looking among the rich and powerful at first and then, after talking to a Jewish scholar, among the poor, the sick and the oppressed. As he travelled he helped those whom he questioned, but he kept the remaining jewel, a precious pearl, for the king.

Some thirty years later as he travelled, still searching, towards Jerusalem, he heard strange stories of a Jewish teacher who had claimed to be the Son of God, and had spoken of his kingdom. Artaban felt a thrill of excitement, for with every story of this man Jesus' life, his miracles and his teaching, Artaban felt more and more certain that he was indeed the king for whom he had been searching. As he hurried into Jerusalem he was caught up in the crowds and he heard that this Jesus was to be crucified. He decided to offer his last jewel as a ransom, and made for the palace of Pilate, the Roman governor. Suddenly, however, a young girl, speaking his own language, called to him from a group of soldiers, pleading desperately for help. When he went up to her she said she was to be sold as a slave to pay for her father's debts. She begged him for the money. Artaban could not refuse her, but all

he had of sufficient value to give her was his last gift, the pearl.
Taking it from his pouch he gave it to her.

At this moment there was a loud noise and an earthquake shook
the city. A piece of flying debris hit Artaban on the head and he
fell to the ground, dying. And as the girl bent over him she heard
him whisper 'I have no gift, my Lord. . . . When did I see you
hungry or thirsty, sick or in prison?' And for the rest of her life
she remembered the joy and wonder on his face and seemed to
hear the faint reply: 'In as much as you have done it unto one of
the least of these my brothers, you have done it unto me.'
Artaban's search was finished. He had found his king.

Adapted from a story by Henry Van Dyke

LENT

41 Retro Me, Sathanas

How strange of the Devil
With his unerring aptitude for putting the wrong thing in the right
    place,
To try to tempt Christ
With all the kingdoms of the world and the glory thereof.

He might have guessed
That a soul so ancient,
Treading the echoing corridors of the past to its last goal of
    simplicity, lowliness and degradation,
Would in its journey,
Have worn the purple of kings,
The scarlet of conquerors,
Would have known all pride, pomp, wealth and dominion,
Weighing them less, in its final immense cumulative wisdom,
Than the feather of a sparrow or the petal of a poppy in the corn.
He might have been sure
That it is no use bribing God with unrealities.

He should have offered Him
A quiet cottage in Nazareth,
A little child listening to the birds,
And a patch of field flowers.

Teresa Hooley

42 In the Wilderness

Christ of His gentleness
Thirsting and hungering,
Walked in the wilderness;
Soft words of grace He spoke
Unto lost desert-folk
That listened wondering.
He heard the bitterns call
From ruined palace-wall,
Answered them brotherly
He held communion
With the she-pelican
Of lonely piety.
Basilisk, cockatrice,
Flocked to His homilies,
With mail of dread device,
With monstrous barbèd stings,
With eager dragon-eyes;
Great bats on leather wings,
And poor blind broken things,
Foul in their miseries.
And ever with Him went,
Of all His wanderings
Comrade, with ragged coat,
Gaunt ribs – poor innocent –
Bleeding foot, burning throat,
The guileless old scape-goat;
For forty days and nights
Followed in Jesus' ways,
Sure guard behind Him kept,
Tears like a lover wept.

Robert Graves

43 The Three Apprentices

Three apprentice devils, fully trained and ready for their first job, were being interviewed by their master.

'You'll find,' he told them, 'that it's easier to *lead* men into evil than to *push* them into it. You'll have to be very crafty.'

He looked the three devils over.

'Have you any ideas?' he asked.

Number one devil was arrogant.

'Oh yes, I shall tell men that there is no God,' he answered, full of confidence.

Satan looked doubtful.

'Well,' he said, 'you can try it, but most men know, even if they won't admit it, that God is real.'

Number two devil looked craftily at his master.

'I shall tell men that there is no Hell.'

Satan did not think much of this idea, either.

'You won't find that much good. You'll soon discover that most men have been there already. Man knows all about Hell.'

The third devil was quite unlike his companions. There was an easy, indulgent look about him, and Satan turned to him for his plan of campaign.

Number three devil bowed low.

'I shall tell man that God is real, that He is good and all-powerful, and I shall assure them of the reality of Hell, but I shall also tell them that there's plenty of time, and there's no need to hurry.'

Satan was delighted.

'Off you go,' he shouted, 'you'll do more damage in a day than these two'll do in a month.'

*Mary Tayler, in **Stories and Prayers at Five to Ten***

44 Temptation

One day two friends Jack and Harry, were grumbling about how hard life was. Jack blamed Adam and Eve for all their troubles. Had Adam not eaten the apple, he said, we should all still be in the Garden of Eden, free from sin and unhappiness. Harry agreed but said they had no right to reproach Adam since anyone would have done the same. 'Not me,' replied Jack, 'I have always kept my word, and always would.'

Not long afterwards Harry invited Jack up to his house for a meal. The table was attractively set out with all the guest's favourite foods. Harry, however, said he had unexpectedly to go out but Jack should help himself to anything except what was in one small covered dish, and that he was not to touch. Jack agreed and helped himself to a fine meal. As his appetite was satisfied, however, he began to wonder what was in the dish. 'It can't do any harm to peep,' he thought, and gently lifted the lid. Immediately out jumped a mouse and it began running around the table. Just then, in came Harry, took one look and laughed. 'So much for being better than Adam,' he said. 'It's easy to criticise when we're not put to the test.' Jack had to laugh, but Harry noticed he was much more cautious in his judgements in the future.

Anon.

HOLY WEEK

45 Into Jerusalem with Palms

Mark 11, 1–10

It is an odd tale, Lord, full of symbolism, full of pointers to Old
   Testament ideas.
It is an odd tale indeed.
Those secret passwords, an unridden colt, the pomp of palms.
You meant so much to your disciples.
You were the centre of their hopes, the focus of their aspirations.
They wanted to call you King.
And so do I, Lord
But deliver me from blind obedience, unthinking response, from
   being immersed in a crowd that cheers or jeers without
   knowing why.
Crowds are frightening in the way they convert, cajole, pressurize
   into agreement.
They throw palms and cheer.
They throw stones and shout crucify.
Make me think, Lord.
Make me use my mind.
Keep my eyes open across that leap of faith in you 'who come in
   the name of the Lord'.

Rex Chapman

46 The Donkey's Owner

Snaffled my donkey, he did – good luck to him! –
Rode him astride, feet dangling, near scraping the ground.
Gave me the laugh of my life when I first see them,
Remembering yesterday – you know, how Pilate come
Bouncing along the same road, only that horse of his
Big as a bloody house and the armour shining

And half Rome trotting behind. Tight-mouthed he was,
Looking he owned the world.

Then today,

Him and my little donkey! Ha – laugh? –
I thought I'd kill myself when he first started.
So did the rest of them. Gave him a cheer
Like he was Caesar himself, only more hearty:
Tore off some palm-twigs and followed shouting,
Whacking the donkey's behind . . . Then suddenly
We see his face.
The smile had gone, and somehow the way he sat
Was different – like he was much older – you know –
Didn't want to laugh no more.

Clive Sansom

EASTER

47 On the Cross

Mark 15, 22–39

Proof.
We always want proof.
'Come down and we shall believe.'
Mankind was quite happy, thank you.
Without proof there is nothing more to be said.
This was it.
The end.
The absolute end.

And that would have been that if certain things had not followed.
But how could you know then that there was more to follow?
'My God, my God, why have you forsaken me?'
It is impossible to penetrate the darkness that surrounds you.

Our inhumanity to each other is frightening, Lord.
You were made to stand where millions have also stood.
And we talk so glibly about involvement, incarnation.
Forgive us, Lord.
Words fail.

Rex Chapman

48 Peter's Problem

Mark 14, 26–42, 66–72

He was an impetuous man, Lord,
As loyal to you as any of your disciples.
He would never dream of disowning his friendship.
A born leader,
A man of enthusiasm and zeal.
Worn out in Gethsemane,
Not really understanding the crisis that was upon you,
He slept.
When he awoke he saw you arrested, and was startled into those
    denials.

He, the firm follower, the rock, the man who had said that very
    day: 'Even if I must die with you, I will never disown you.'
Much later, they say, he was to die for you.
But then, at that moment of darkness, his sense of guilt was
    acute. . . .
Yet Peter's weakness, Lord, is a source of encouragement to your
    church.
He regained his balance.
He was able to accept your forgiveness and so forgive himself.
He stands as witness to the power of your forgiveness. . . .
His problem is my encouragement.

Rex Chapman

49 Judas

Mark 14, 10–11, 18–21, 43–6; Matthew 27, 3–5

He could not live with himself.
His regrets were too great to be borne.
He committed suicide.
I find myself sympathizing with Judas, Lord.
Had he wanted to force your hand?
Had he heard you talk so much about God's Kingdom that he
    wanted some divine vindication?
Did he feel that by putting you on the spot God in you would be
    bound to act decisively, dramatically?
Perhaps he had even prayed about it and thought about it, only to
    see his whole scheme backfire in his face.

You were not able to produce the spectacular Judas may have
   wanted.
You just died – painfully.
And Judas was left to live with what he had done.
Only he could not.
Judas, Lord, is everyman in large letters.
He is everyman who has to live or die with his past.
The tragic irony of Judas, Lord, is that the cross and resurrection
   – the very things which he had helped to bring about – contain a
   gospel of hope that enables a man to pick himself up from the
   floor.
He impetuously took his life when forgiveness was so near.
Lord, strengthen those in despair.
Strengthen me to come to terms with myself and my actions in the
   light of your death and your resurrection.

Rex Chapman

50 Indifference

When Jesus came to Golgotha they hanged Him on a tree,
They drave great nails through hands and feet, and made a
   Calvary;
They crowned Him with a crown of thorns, red were His wounds
   and deep,
For those were crude and cruel days, and human flesh was cheap.

When Jesus came to Birmingham they simply passed Him by,
They never hurt a hair of Him, they only let Him die;
For men had grown more tender, and they would not give Him
   pain.
They only just passed down the street, and left Him in the rain.

Still Jesus cried, 'Forgive them, for they know not what they do,'
And still it rained the wintry rain that drenched Him through and
   through;
The crowds went home and left the streets without a soul to see,
And Jesus crouched against a wall and cried for Calvary.

G. A. Studdert Kennedy

51 Father to the Man

I warned the parents, you know,
when he was a child. I said

This boy must really not be allowed
to argue about the law with lawyers and about God
with theologians. And he seems, I said,
to fancy himself as a doctor, too. At this rate
we shall have him, perhaps, giving water
to a feverish patient. Little thinking
he'd do just that; and was lucky
the lad recovered.

It will come to no good, I said.
But one gets no thanks.

And so it went on
until, later, we lost touch;
for he was away for some years,
no one knew where.

Afterwards, I admit, I was half convinced. More than half,
I suppose I should say.

When he preached – and I shall hear no such sermons again –
it seemed that immutable right and wrong –
no, it was not that their boundaries changed. But somehow
acts and facts seemed with a shake of a word
to fall – I saw such a toy once, of foolish beads –
in a different pattern. What was done was the same,
and right and wrong were the same, and yet
not the same, being done in a different world.

There was a wedding, for instance,
with, in plain Aramaic, too much drink,
and you know the country customs –
I fear the old Gods are by no means dead.
Well, he was there, and he preached on the sabbath,
and spoke, just in passing, about the wedding;
and, you know, these junketings (to call them no worse)
seemed transformed, seemed a part
(like David's dancing in the Temple)
of our holy religion; and,

what was stranger, our religion
seemed to have grown, and to be our life.

Well, you see, it has come to no good,
as I told his parents, children
must listen, and lawful authority speak.

. . . and yet
this is the saddest news . . . and I
am nearer to death.

John Knight, from **Let There be God**

52 Ecce Homo

Whose is this horrifying face,
This putrid flesh, discoloured, flayed,
Fed on by flies, scorched by the sun?
Whose are those hollow red-filmed eyes
And thorn-spiked head and spear-struck side?
Behold the Man: He is Man's Son.

Forget the legend, tear the decent veil
That cowardice or interest devised
To make their mortal enemy a friend,
To hide the bitter truth all His wounds tell.
Let the great scandal be no more disguised:
He is in agony till the world's end,

And we must never sleep during that time!
He is suspended on the cross-tree now
And we are onlookers at the crime,
Callous contemporaries of the slow
Torture of God. Here is the hill
Made ghastly by His spattered blood

Whereon He hangs and suffers still:
See, the centurions wear riding-boots,
Black shirts and badges and peaked caps,
Greet one another with raised-arm salutes;
They have cold eyes, unsmiling lips;
Yet these his brothers know not what they do.

And on his either side hang dead
A labourer and a factory hand,
Or one is maybe a lynched Jew
And one a Negro or a Red,
Coolie or Ethiopian, Irishman,
Spaniard or German democrat.

Behind His lolling head the sky
Glares like a fiery cataract
Red with the murders of two thousand years
Committed in His name and by
Crusaders, Christian warriors
Defending faith and property.

Amid the plain beneath His transfixed hands,
Exuding darkness as indelible
As guilty stains, fanned by funereal
And lurid airs, besieged by drifting sands
And clefted landslides our about-to-be
Bombed and abandoned cities stand.

He who wept for Jerusalem
Now sees His prophecy extend
Across the greatest cities of the world,
A guilty panic reason cannot stem
Rising to raze them all as He foretold;
And He must watch this drama to the end.

Though often named, He is unknown
To the dark kingdoms at His feet
Where everything disparages His words,
And each man bears the common guilt alone
And goes blindfolded to his fate,
And fear and greed are sovereign lords.

The turning point of history
Must come. Yet the complacent and the proud
And who exploit and kill, may be denied –
Christ of Revolution and of Poetry –
The resurrection and the life
Wrought by your spirit's blood.

Involved in their own sophistry
The black priest and the upright man

Faced by subversive truth shall be struck dumb,
Christ of Revolution and of Poetry,
While the rejected and condemned become
Agents of the divine.

Not from a monstrance silver-wrought
But from the tree of human pain
Redeem our sterile misery,
Christ of Revolution and of Poetry,
That man's long journey through the night
May not have been in vain.

David Gascoyne

53 Christ is Risen

In the early 1920's, Bukharin was sent from Moscow to Kiev to
address a vast anti-God rally. For one hour he brought to bear all
the artillery of argument, abuse, and ridicule upon the Christian
faith till it seemed as if the whole ancient structure of belief was in
ruins. At the end there was a silence. Questions were invited. A
man rose and asked leave to speak, a priest of the Orthodox
Church. He stood beside Bukharin, faced the people and gave
them the ancient liturgical Easter greeting. 'Christ is risen.'
Instantly the whole vast assembly rose to its feet, and the reply
came back like the crash of breakers against the cliff: 'He is risen
indeed.' There was no reply; there could not be. When all
argument is ended, there remains a fact, the total fact of Jesus
Christ, who requires no authority to commend him, but who
places every man in the position where an answer has to be given
one way or the other to the question that he asks.

Leslie Newbigin, **A Faith for this One World**

54 Calvary

What is it like, Lord, to die
In pain on Calvary's hill,
And know that those who condemn you
Thought they were doing God's will?

What is it like, Lord, to walk
Through streets where no-one cares,
And see the people all passing,
Wrapped up in private affairs?

What is it like, Lord, to starve,
With barren fields all around.
And know that somewhere else, farmers
Plough food back into the ground?

What is it like, Lord, to burn,
Consumed by napalm's flame,
And know that those who dropped it
Did so in liberty's name?

What is it like, Lord, to die
In pain each day again?
For still you're crucified daily,
Living and dying with men.

Peter Casey

55 It is Accomplished

The conflict of Light with Darkness is finished. For a moment
darkness seemed to prevail. But the fight was fought and the
victory won. The date of the triumph of love is Good Friday, not
Easter Day. What remains is not to win a victory, but to gather
its fruits.

William Temple, **Readings in St John's Gospel**

56 Ballad of the Bread Man

Mary stood in the kitchen
Baking a loaf of bread.
An angel flew in through the window,
We've a job for you, he said.

God in his big gold heaven,
Sitting in his big blue chair,
Wanted a mother for his little son.
Suddenly saw you there.

Mary shook and trembled,
It isn't true what you say.
Don't say that, said the angel.
The baby's on its way.

Joseph was in the workshop
Planing a piece of wood.
The old man's past it, the neighbours said.
That girl's been up to no good.

And who was that elegant feller,
They said, in the shiny gear?
The things they said about Gabriel
Were hardly fit to hear.

Mary never answered,
Mary never replied.
She kept the information,
Like the baby, safe inside.

It was election winter.
They went to vote in town.
When Mary found her time had come
The hotels let her down.

The baby was born in an annex
Next to the local pub.
At midnight a delegation
Turned up from the Farmers' Club.

They talked about an explosion
That cracked a hole in the sky,
Said they'd been sent to the Lamb & Flag
To see god come down from on high.

A few days later a bishop
And a five-star general were seen
With the head of an African country
In a bullet-proof limousine.

We've come, they said, with tokens
For the little boy to choose.
Told the tale about war and peace
In the television news.

After them came the soldiers
With rifle and bomb and gun,
Looking for enemies of the state.
The family had packed and gone.

When they got back to the village
The neighbours said to a man,
That boy will never be one of us,
Though he does what he blessed well can.

He went round to all the people
A paper crown on his head.
Here is some bread from my father.
Take, eat, he said.

Nobody seemed very hungry.
Nobody seemed to care.
Nobody saw the god in himself
Quietly standing there.

He finished up in the papers.
He came to a very bad end.
He was charged with bringing the living to life.
No man was that prisoner's friend.

There's only one kind of punishment
To fit that kind of crime.
They rigged a trial and shot him dead.
They were only just in time.

They lifted the young man by the leg,
They lifted him by the arm,
They locked him in a cathedral
In case he came to harm.

They stored him safe as water
Under seven rocks.
One Sunday morning he burst out
Like a jack-in-the-box.

Through the town he went walking.
He showed them the holes in his head.
Now do you want any loaves? he cried,
Not today, they said.

Charles Causley

57 The Lion, the Witch and the Wardrobe

a) A great crowd of people were standing all round the Stone Table and though the moon was shining many of them carried torches which burned with evil-looking red flames and black smoke. Ogres with monstrous teeth, and wolves, and bull-headed men; spirits of evil trees and poisonous plants; and other creatures whom I won't describe because if I did the grown-ups would probably not let you read this book. And right in the middle, standing by the Table, was the Witch herself.

A howl and a gibber of dismay went up from the creatures when they first saw the great Lion pacing towards them, and for a moment even the Witch seemed to be struck with fear. Then she recovered herself and gave a wild fierce laugh.

'The fool!' she cried. 'The fool has come. Bind him fast.'

Lucy and Susan held their breaths waiting for Aslan's roar and his spring upon his enemies. But it never came. Four Hags, grinning and leering, yet also (at first) hanging back and half afraid of what they had to do, had approached him. 'Bind him, I say' repeated the White Witch. The Hags made a dart at him and shrieked with triumph when they found that he made no resistance at all. Then others – evil dwarfs and apes – rushed in to help them, and between them they rolled the huge Lion over on his back and tied all his four paws together, shouting and cheering as if they had done something brave, though, had the Lion chosen, one of those paws could have been the death of all of them. But he made no noise, even when his enemies, straining and tugging, pulled the cords so tight that they cut into his flesh. Then they began to drag him towards the Stone Table.

'Stop!' said the Witch. 'Let him first be shaved.'

Another roar of mean laughter went up from her followers as an ogre with a pair of shears came forward and squatted down on Aslan's head. Snip-snip-snip went the shears and masses of curling gold began to fall to the ground. Then the ogre stood back and the children, watching from their hiding-place, could see the face of Aslan looking all small and different without its mane. The enemies also saw the difference.

'Why, he's only a great cat after all' cried one.

'Is that what we were afraid of?' said another.

And they surged round Aslan, jeering at him, saying things like 'Puss, Puss! Poor Pussy,' and 'How many mice have you caught today, Cat?' and 'Would you like a saucer of milk, Pussums?'

'Oh, how can they?' said Lucy, tears streaming down her cheeks. 'The brutes, the brutes!' for now that the first shock was

over the shorn face of Aslan looked to her braver, and more
beautiful, and more patient than ever.

'Muzzle him!' said the Witch. And even now, as they worked
about his face putting on the muzzle, one bite from his jaws
would have cost two or three of them their hands. But he never
moved. And this seemed to enrage all that rabble. Everyone was at
him now. Those who had been afraid to come near him even after
he was bound began to find courage, and for a few minutes the
two girls could not even see him – so thickly was he surrounded
by the whole crowd of creatures kicking him, hitting him, spitting
on him, jeering at him.

At last the rabble had had enough of this. They began to drag
the bound and muzzled Lion to the Stone Table, some pulling and
some pushing. He was so huge that even when they got him there
it took all their efforts to hoist him on to the surface of it. Then
there was more tying and tightening of cords.

At last the Witch drew near. She stood by Aslan's head. Her face
was working and twitching with passion, but his looked up at the
sky, still quiet, neither angry nor afraid, but a little sad.

The children did not see the actual moment of the killing. They
couldn't bear to look and had covered their eyes.

b) As soon as the wood was silent again Susan and Lucy crept out
into the open hill-top. The moon was getting low and thin clouds
were passing across her, but still they could see the shape of the
Lion lying dead in his bonds. And down they both knelt in the
wet grass and kissed his cold face and stroked his beautiful fur –
what was left of it – and cried till they could cry no more. And
then they looked at each other and held each other's hands for
mere loneliness and cried again; and then again were silent. At last
Lucy said 'I can't bear to look at that horrible muzzle. I wonder
could we take it off?' So they tried. And after a lot of working at it
(for their fingers were cold and it was now the darkest part of the
night) they succeeded. And when they saw his face without it they
burst out crying again and kissed it and fondled it and wiped away
the blood and the foam as well as they could. And it was all more
lonely and hopeless and horrid than I know how to describe.

'I wonder could we untie him as well?' said Susan presently.
But the enemies, out of pure spitefulness, had drawn the cords so
tight that the girls could make nothing of the knots.

I hope no one who reads this book has been quite as miserable
as Susan and Lucy were that night; but if you have been – if
you've been up all night and cried till you have no more tears left
in you – you will know that there comes in the end a sort of

quietness. You feel as if nothing was ever going to happen again. At any rate that was how it felt to these two. Hours and hours seemed to go by in this dead calm, and they hardly noticed that they were getting colder and colder. But at last Lucy noticed two other things. One was that the sky on the east side of the hill was a little less dark than it had been an hour ago. The other was some tiny movement going on in the grass at her feet. At first she took no interest in this. What did it matter? Nothing mattered now! But at last she saw that what-ever-it-was had begun to move up the upright stones of the Stone Table. And now whatever-they-were were moving about on Aslan's body. She peered closer. They were little grey things.

'Ugh' said Susan from the other side of the Table. 'How beastly! They are horrid little mice crawling over him. Go away, you little beasts.' And she raised her hand to frighten them away.

'Wait!' said Lucy, who had been looking at them more closely still. 'Can't you see what they're doing?'

Both girls bent down and stared.

'I do believe –' said Susan. 'But how queer! They're nibbling away at the cords!'

'That's what I thought,' said Lucy. 'I think they're friendly mice. Poor little things – they don't realize he's dead. They think it'll do some good untying him.'

c) It was quite definitely lighter now. Each of the girls noticed for the first time the white face of the other. They could see suddenly mice nibbling away at the ropes; dozens and dozens, even hundreds, of little field mice. And at last, one by one, the ropes were all gnawed through.

The girls cleared away the remains of the gnawed ropes. Aslan looked more like himself without them. Every moment his dead face looked nobler, as the light grew and they could see it better.

In the wood behind them a bird gave a chuckling sound. It had been so still for hours and hours that it startled them. Then another bird answered it. Soon there were birds singing all over the place.

It was quite definitely early morning now, not late night.

They walked to the eastern edge of the hill and looked down. Then at last, the red turned to gold along the line where the sea and the sky met and very slowly up came the edge of the sun. At that moment they heard from behind them a loud noise – a great cracking, deafening noise as if a giant had broken a giant's plate.

'What's that?' said Lucy, clutching Susan's arm.

'I – I feel afraid to turn round,' said Susan; 'something awful is happening.'

'They're doing something worse to Him,' said Lucy. 'Come on!' And she turned pulling Susan round with her.

The rising of the sun had made everything look so different – all the colours and shadows were changed – that for a moment they didn't see the important thing. Then they did. The Stone Table was broken into two pieces by a great crack that ran down it from end to end; and there was no Aslan.

'Oh, oh, oh!' cried the two girls, rushing back to the Table.

'Oh, it's too bad,' sobbed Lucy; 'they might have left the body alone.'

'Who's done it?' cried Susan. 'What does it mean? Is it more magic?'

'Yes!' said a great voice behind their backs. There, shining in the sunrise, larger than they had seen him before, shaking his mane (for it had apparently grown again) stood Aslan himself.

'Oh, Aslan!' cried both the children, staring up at him, almost as much frightened as they were glad.

'Aren't you dead then, dear Aslan?' said Lucy.

'Not now,' said Aslan.

'You're not – not a –?' asked Susan in a shaky voice. She couldn't bring herself to say the word ghost. Aslan stooped his golden head and licked her forehead. The warmth of his breath and a rich sort of smell that seemed to hang about his hair came all over her.

'Do I look it?' he said.

'Oh, you're real, you're real! Oh, Aslan!' cried Lucy, and both girls flung themselves upon him and covered him with kisses.

C. S. Lewis

3 LIVING TOGETHER

Assemblies

REMEMBRANCE

a) Father hear the prayer we offer
   Readings **58a**: First World War facts and *Anthem for Doomed Youth*, Wilfred Owen; or **60**: *Disabled*, Wilfred Owen
   Prayer **50**

b) I vow to thee my country, all earthly things above
   Reading **58b**: *Testament of Youth*, Vera Brittain, and *The Dead*, Rupert Brooke
   Prayer **51**

c) Travel on, travel on, there's a river that is flowing
   Reading **58c**: *Testament of Youth*, Vera Brittain, and *This is No Case of Petty Right or Wrong*, Edward Thomas
   Prayer **50**

d) Tomorrow is a highway, broad and fair
   Reading **59**: *The Armistice*, Vera Brittain
   Prayer **53**

See also readings **61**: *Ecclesiasticus XLIV*; with **62**: *Micah IV* .

INTERNATIONAL CO-OPERATION

a) We ask that we live and we labour in peace
   Readings **63**: *Preamble to the Charter of the United Nations, 1945*; and **62**: *Micah IV*
   Prayer **52**

b) O brother Man, fold to thy heart thy brother
   Reading **72**: *Space Between the Bars*, Donald Swann
   Prayer **62**

PEACE

a) If I had a hammer, I'd hammer in the morning
Reading **64**: *The White Flag*, Spike Milligan
Prayer **57**

b) Kum ba yah, my Lord, Kum ba yah!
Reading **65**: *Feed My Little Ones*, C. Day Lewis
Prayer **56**

INTERDEPENDENCE

a) I belong to a family, the biggest on earth
Reading **66**: *Alf*, Colin Morris
Prayer **53**

b) The sheep's in the meadow, the cow's in the corn *or* Now
join we, to praise the creator
Readings **67**: *Statistics*, C. Rajendra; and **68**: *The Arithmetic
of Poverty*, D. Appadurai
Prayers **58** and **66**

c) In Christ there is no East or West
Reading **69**: *1941*, Yevgeny Yevtushenko
Prayers **63** and 52

UNITY

a) I belong to a family, the biggest on earth
Reading **73**: *Unity*, Carolyn Scott
Prayer **61**

b) O Jesus, I have promised
Reading **71**: *The Story of Taizé*, J. L. G. Balado
Prayer **63**

c) Life could be good and rich and whole/The church's one
foundation
Reading **72**: *Space Between the Bars*, Donald Swann
Prayers **55** and **64**

d)   O brother Man, fold to thy heart thy brother
Reading **133**: *Modern Affirmations of Faith and Hope*
Prayers **61** and **63**

See also readings **156–161**: *Mister God, This is Anna*, Fynn

Prayers

REMEMBRANCE

50 O Lord, we remember those who gave their lives that we might live. May we work for the ideal for which they died, that wars may cease, old hatreds be forgotten, and the brotherhood of man replace the feuds of nations: for the sake of Jesus Christ, our Lord.

51 Father of all men and lover of souls,
   as on this day we hold in grateful remembrance
   those who died in time of war,
   we pray that the leaders of the nations
   may seek your righteousness
   so that the whole world may find your peace:
   through Jesus Christ our Lord.

Frank Colquhoun, **N. P. P.**

INTERNATIONAL CO-OPERATION

52 O God, who made of one blood all nations of men to dwell on the face of the earth, and sent your blessed Son to preach peace to them that are far off, and to them that are near: grant that all the peoples of the world may work together for the common good, through Jesus Christ our Lord.

Bishop Cotton (adapted)

53 Break down, O Lord, the barriers of fear, of hostility and of mis-understanding that divide the nations from one another; and prosper all counsels that make for sanity and love, for a just and enduring peace: through Jesus Christ our Lord.

N. P. P. *(adapted)*

PEACE

54 Let us all protect one another.
Let us all enjoy together.
Let us act valiantly together.
May spiritual knowledge ever shine before us.
Let us never hate one another.
And let Peace and Peace and Peace reign everywhere.

The Rig Veda

55 Almighty God, from whom all thoughts of truth and peace
proceed; kindle, we pray thee, in the hearts of all men the true
love of peace; and guide with thy pure and peaceable wisdom
those who take counsel for the nations of the earth; that in
tranquility thy kingdom may go forward, till the earth be filled
with the knowledge of thy love: through Jesus Christ our Lord.

Bishop Francis Paget 1851–1911

INTERDEPENDENCE

56 Let us pray for the life of the world:
that every nation may seek the way that leads to peace;
that human rights and freedoms may everywhere be respected;
and that the world's resources may be ungrudgingly shared;
for Jesus Christ's sake.

C. P. P. W. (*adapted*)

57 Lord of the nations and friend of the poor,
strengthen in the leaders of today's world
a belief in human dignity and in basic human rights;
a belief in the values of justice, freedom and peace;
in love and generosity,
in reason rather than force.
So may the nations grow in mutual respect and understanding,
and recognize that the problem of world poverty
is the concern and responsibility of them all.
Grant it for Christ's sake.

Frank Colquhoun, N. P. P., based on words in the Brandt Report

58 Most merciful God, we commend to your care the men, women
and children of our world who are suffering anxiety and distress
through lack of food.

    Strengthen and support them in their need; and grant that the
nations may grow in their concern for one another and in their
readiness to share all your gifts; that all may live together in the
fellowship, freedom and joy of your kingdom; through Jesus
Christ our Lord.

Morning, Noon and Night

UNITY

59 O God,
    Let us be united,
    Let us speak in harmony,
    Let our minds apprehend alike.
    Common be our prayer;
    Common be the end of our assembly;
    Common be our resolution;
    Common be our deliberations.
    Alike be our feelings;
    Unified be our hearts;
    Common be our intentions;
    Perfect be our unity.

A Hindu prayer from **The Rig Veda**

60 Let us pray for the holy Church of God,
    that Christians in their diversity
    may learn to respect one another,
    to understand one another,
    to love one another and to work together
    as members of the body of Christ, for Jesus' sake.

Unity Book of Prayers (*adapted*)

61 We pray, Lord, for men throughout the world:
    that we may share to the full in the work of your Son,
    revealing you to men and reconciling men to you;
    that we may learn to love one another, as you have loved us;
    and that we may more and more show the unity, love and
    kindness which is your will and your gift; for Jesus Christ's sake.

C. P. P. W. (*adapted*)

62 Jesus, by your death you broke down the barriers between Jew
and Gentile, Greek and barbarian, male and female, slave and
freeman. Heal the tragic divisions of our world, between East and
West, black and white, Arab and Jew, so that each man may
respect his brother as someone for whom you died.

C. P. P. W

63 Give us peace in our time, O Lord:
peace and reconciliation among the nations:
peace and unity within the churches;
peace and harmony in our communities and our homes;
peace and love in all our hearts;
for the sake of Jesus Christ our Saviour.

Frank Colquhoun, N. P. P.

64 God of all grace and lover of all nations, we pray for peace in our
hearts and in our homes, in our nation and in the world; the peace
of your will, the peace of our need; in the name of Christ our
Lord.

Frank Colquhoun, N. P. P.

Readings

REMEMBRANCE

Three Assemblies for Remembrance Day

8a) What are we to remember? At the 11th hour of the 11th day of the 11th month 1918 an armistice was signed to end the war to end wars. In that war 10 million were killed, 21 million were wounded and 7 million were missing. A new feature of the war had been the trench warfare with lines of dugouts.

17 April 1917 Aisne: allied losses 180,000, gain nil;
20 Sept. 1917 Menin Road: British losses 22,000, gain 800 yds;
25 Sept. 1917 Polygon Wood: British loss 17,000, gain 1,000 yards;
12 Oct. 1917 Paschendaele; British loss 13,000 in 3 hours, gain 100 yds.

Wilfred Owen was one of the first war poets. He won the M. C. and was killed by machine gun fire on 4 November 1918. He had been planning a book of poems just before he was killed. The following is from the Preface:

'This book is not about heroes. English poetry is not yet fit to speak of them.

Nor is it about deeds, or lands, nor anything about glory, honour, might, majesty, dominion, or power, except War.

Above all I am not concerned with Poetry.

My subject is War, and the pity of War.

The poetry is in the pity.

Yet these elegies are to this generation in no sense consolatory. They may be to the next. All a poet can do today is warn. That is why the true Poets must be truthful.'

Anthem for Doomed Youth

1 What passing-bells for these who die as cattle?
Only the monstrous anger of the guns.
Only the stuttering rifles' rapid rattle
Can patter out their hasty orisons.

2 No mockeries now for them; no prayers nor bells;
   Nor any voice of mourning save the choirs, –
   The shrill, demented choirs of wailing shells;
   And bugles calling for them from sad shires.

3 What candles may be held to speed them all?
   Not in the hands of boys, but in their eyes
   Shall shine the holy glimmers of goodbyes.
   The pallor of girls' brows shall be their pall;
   Their flowers the tenderness of patient minds,
   And each slow dusk a drawing down of blinds.

Wilfred Owen

58b) The idealism of the early part of the First World War is reflected
      in this passage from Vera Brittain's *Testament of Youth*, her
      account of her life in the war, written in the 1930s. She had gone
      to Somerville College, Oxford, in October 1914, although her
      fiancé, Roland, who would have gone to Oxford as well, joined the
      army instead. He was later killed, as was her brother.

   'One chilly May evening (in 1915) the English
tutor . . . showed us her latest acquisition from Blackwell's – the
newly published first edition of Rupert Brooke's *1914* . . . For the
young to whom Rupert Brooke's poems are now familiar as
classics, it must be impossible to imagine how it felt to hear them
for the first time just after they were written. With my grief and
anxiety then so new, I found the experience so moving that I
should not have sought it had I realised how hard composure
would be to maintain. Silently I struggled for it as I listened to the
English tutor's grave, deliberate voice reading the sonnets,
unhackneyed, courageous, and almost shattering in their
passionate, relevant idealism:

   Glad from a world grown old and cold and weary,
   Leave the sick hearts that honour could not move,
   And half-men, and their dirty songs and dreary –

But not, oh, surely not,
   all the little emptiness of love?

Was that really what Rupert Brooke had felt? Was it what Roland
would come to feel? Almost more bearable was the sonnet on 'The
Dead', with what might become its terribly personal application:

These laid the world away; poured out the red
Sweet wine of youth; gave up the years to be
Of work and joy . . .

How would Rupert Brooke have written, I wonder had he lived
until 1933? . . . Would he still have thought that Holiness and
Nobleness and Honour described the causes for which those
sacrifices of youth and work and immortality were offered?'

Vera Brittain

The Dead

Blow out, you bugles, over the rich Dead!
There's none of these so lonely and poor of old,
But, dying, has made us rarer gifts than gold.
These laid the world away; poured out the red
Sweet wine of youth; gave up the years to be
Of work and joy, and that unhoped serene,
That men call age; and those who would have been,
Their sons, they gave, their immortality.
Blow, bugles, blow! They brought us, for our dearth,
Holiness, lacked so long, and Love, and Pain.
Honour has come back, as a king, to earth,
And paid his subjects with a royal wage;
And nobleness walks in our ways again;
And we have come into our heritage.

Rupert Brooke

58c) Vera Brittain left Oxford to nurse, and was in 1917 sent to France.

'Our train next day did not leave until the afternoon, so I spent
the morning in the English Church at Boulogne commemorating
the Third Anniversary of the War . . . Dreaming in the soft light
that filtered through the high, stained-glass windows, I saw the
congregation as a sombre rainbow, navy-blue and khaki, scarlet
and grey, and by the time that the "Last Post" – with its final
questioning note which now always seemed to me to express the
soul's ceaseless inquiry of the Unseen regarding its ultimate
destiny – had sounded over us as we stood in honour of the dead
who could neither protest nor complain, I was as ready for
sacrifices and hardships as I had ever been in the early idealistic
days. This sense of renewed resolution went with me as I stepped

from the shadowed quiet of the church into the wet, noisy streets
of Boulogne. The dead might lie beneath their crosses on a
hundred wind-swept hillsides, but for us the difficult business of
continuing the War must go on in spite of their departure; the sirens
would still sound as the ships brought their drafts to the harbour,
and the wind would flap the pennons on the tall mast-heads.'

Vera Brittain

Even after the initial idealism and optimism faded there was still a
grim determination that it must be a war to end wars, a disaster
out of which would emerge a better life for people. This can be
seen, for instance, in the poems of Edward Thomas written on
active service between 1915 and 1917 when he was killed at Arras.

This is No Case of Petty Right or Wrong

This is no case of petty right or wrong
That politicians or philosophers
Can judge. I hate not Germans, nor grow hot
With love of Englishmen, to please newspapers.
Beside my hate for one fat patriot
My hatred of the Kaiser is love true: –
A kind of god he is, banging a gong.
But I have not to choose between the two,
Or between justice and injustice. Dinned
With war and argument I read no more
Than in the storm smoking along the wind
Athwart the wood. Two witches' cauldrons roar.
From one the weather shall rise clear and gay;
Out of the other an England beautiful
And like her mother that died yesterday.
Little I know or care if, being dull,
I shall miss some thing that historians
Can rake out of the ashes when perchance
The phoenix broods serene above their ken.
But with the best and meanest Englishman
I am one in crying, God save England, lest
We lose what never slaves and cattle blessed.
The ages made her that made us from dust:
She is all we know and live by, and we trust
She is good and must endure, loving her so:
And as we love ourselves we hate her foe.

Edward Thomas

59 The Armistice

When the sound of victorious guns burst over London at 11 a.m.
on November 11th 1918, the men and women who looked
incredulously into each other's faces did not cry jubilantly: 'We've
won the War!' They only said: 'The War is over' . . . Outside the
Admiralty a crazy group of convalescent Tommies were collecting
specimens of different uniforms and bundling their wearers into
flag-strewn taxis; with a shout they seized two of my companions
and disappeared into the clamorous crowd, waving flags and
shaking rattles. Wherever we went a burst of enthusiastic cheering
greeted our Red Cross uniform, and complete strangers adorned
with wound stripes rushed up and shook me warmly by the hand.
After the long, long blackness, it seemed like a fairy-tale to see the
street lamps shining through the chill November gloom . . .
Already this was a different world from the one that I had known
during four life-long years, a world in which people would be
light-hearted and forgetful, in which themselves and their career
and their amusements would blot out political ideals and great
national issues. And in that brightly lit, alien world I should have
no part. All those with whom I had really been intimate were
gone . . .

The War was over; a new age was beginning; but the dead were
dead and would never return.

The War Generation: Vale. V. B. 1933. Verse two.

For us they live till life itself shall end,
The frailties and the follies of those years,
Their strength which only pride of loss could lend,
Their vanished hopes, their sorrows and their tears;
But slowly towards the verge the dim sky clears,
For nobler men may yet redeem our clay
When we and war together, one wise day,
Have passed away.

Vera Brittain, **The Testament of Youth**

60 Disabled

He sat in a wheeled chair, waiting for dark,
And shivered in his ghastly suit of grey.
Legless, sewn short at elbow. Through the park
Voices of boys rang saddening like a hymn,

Voices of play and pleasures after day,
Till gathering sleep had mothered them from him.

About this time town used to swing so gay
When glow-lamps budded in the light blue trees,
And girls glanced lovelier as the air grew dim, –
In the old times, before he threw away his knees.
Now he will never feel again how slim
Girls' waists are, or how warm their subtle hands;
All of them touch him like some queer disease.

There was an artist silly for his face,
For it was younger than his youth, last year.
Now, he is old; his back will never brace;
He's lost his colour very far from here,
Poured it down shell-holes till the veins ran dry,
And half his lifetime lapsed in the hot race,
And leap of purple spurted from his thigh.

One time he liked a blood-smear down his leg,
After the matches, carried shoulder-high.
It was after football, when he'd drunk a peg,
He thought he'd better join. – He wonders why.
Someone had said he'd look a god in kilts,
That's why; and may be, too, to please his Meg;
Aye, that was it, to please the giddy jilts
He asked to join. He didn't have to beg;
Smiling they wrote his lie; aged nineteen years.

Germans he scarcely thought of; all their guilt
And Austria's, did not move him. And no fears
Of Fear came yet. He thought of jewelled hilts
For daggers in plaid socks; of smart salutes;
And care of arms; and leave; and pay arrears;
Esprit de corps; and hints for young recruits.
And soon he was drafted out with drums and cheers.

Some cheered him home, but not as crowds cheer Goal.
Only a solemn man who brought him fruits
Thanked him, and then inquired about his soul.

Now, he will spend a few sick years in Institutes,
And do what things the rules consider wise,
And take whatever pity they may dole.

Wilfred Owen

INTERNATIONAL CO-OPERATION

61 Ecclesiasticus XLIV

And some there be, which have no memorial; who are perished, as though they had never been; and are become as though they had never been born; and their children after them. But these were merciful men, whose righteousness had not been forgotten . . . Their bodies are buried in peace; but their name liveth for evermore. The people will tell of their wisdom, and the congregation will shew forth their praise.

62 Micah IV

Out of Zion shall go forth the law, and the word of the Lord from Jerusalem.
He shall judge between many peoples, and shall decide for strong nations afar off.
And they shall beat their swords into ploughshares, and their spears into pruning hooks;
Nation shall not lift up sword against nation, neither shall they learn war any more.

63 Preamble to the Charter of the United Nations, 1945

We, the Peoples of the United Nations, determined to save succeeding generations from the scourge of war, which twice in our lifetime has brought untold sorrow to mankind, and to reaffirm faith in fundamental human rights, in the dignity and worth of the human person, in the equal rights of men and women and of nations large and small, and to establish conditions under which justice and respect for the obligations arising from treaties and other sources of international law can be maintained, and to promote social progress and better standards of life in larger freedom, and for these ends to practise tolerance and live together in peace with one another as good neighbours, and to unite our strength to maintain international peace and security, and to ensure, by the acceptance of principles and the institution of methods, that armed force shall not be used, save in the common interest, and to employ international machinery for the promotion of the economic and social advancement of all peoples, have resolved to combine our efforts to accomplish these aims.

PEACE

64 The White Flag

The two great Generals and the two great Armies faced each other across one great battlefield. The two great Generals marched about their two great Armies as they faced each other across one great battlefield. One great General said to himself, 'We can't hold out against this other great Army much longer,' and the other great General said, 'We can't hold out against this other Army much longer,' so the first great General said to one of his great Sergeants, 'Hoist a white flag,' and the second great General said to his great Sergeant 'Hoist a white flag.'

Private Fred Lengths was commanded by one great General to haul up the flag. At the same time, Private Norrington Blitt had also been signalled by his General to hoist their white flag, and so the two great Armies stood surrendering to each other across the battlefield. It was very quiet, and the two white flags were the only movement seen.

Three days passed, and one great General said 'What's happened?', as did the other great General. Both great Generals were informed that each side had surrendered to the other. 'Impossible,' said the first General.

'It can't be true,' said the second General.

'My arms are aching,' said Private Blitt, as did Private Lengths.

'How long have they had their flag up?' said the first great General.

'Three days,' at which time the second great General had asked the same question, and received the same answer.

'Tell them *we* surrendered – *first!*'

The message was shouted across the great battlefield.

'No, no,' was the reply. '*We* surrendered first.' Neither side wanted to lose the initiative. Stalemate.

The two great Generals met in a tent in the middle of a field. 'According to my notes,' said the first, 'our flag went up at one minute to eleven on the 1st April.'

'So did ours,' was the reply.

'But,' said the first General, 'I gave the order to put the white flag up at a quarter to eleven . . . ' and was met with the same reply. Stalemate II.

The first General screwed his eyes up, screwed his knees up, his nose, teeth and ears. 'Tell you what – my peace flag is whiter than yours.'

'Nonsense,' was the furious reply. 'Hold ours up to the light –
not a stain in sight. We use the new Bluinite.'

'Bluinite!' guffawed the facing General. 'My dear fellow, Rinso,
the new white Rinso, is my answer to you. That's why I say my
flag is whiter.'

'The window test!' they said simultaneously.

In due course, a window was brought, against which the two
flags were held. Alas, both were of the same degree of white
intensity. Stalemate III.

Meantime, the makers of Bluinite and Rinso had heard of the
conflict.

'You aren't going to let that lot get away with it,' said the
Managing Director of Bluinite to the first General, at which time,
as you can guess, Sir Jim Rinso was inciting the second General.

'I will prove who surrendered first,' he said, as the first great
atomic blast exterminated them.

Spike Milligan, from **A Dustbin of Milligan**

65 Feed My Little Ones

How many children starving, did you say?
A million? Five million? It is sad,
Tragic really.
But after all, they are
Thousands of miles away,
Remote as the Black Death
Or the dying stars. Oh, I do sympathise:
But I could never count much beyond ten –
Tragedy multiplied by millions fades
Into a faceless limbo of statistics
And leaves imagination cold on the outside.
Charity, I say, must begin at home.

Let charity begin at home.
Think of one child,
Your own or the next-door neighbour's.
Tetter the pretty skin with sores,
Let the bones show through it
Like ribs of a stranded wreck.
This is your child –
This derelict with the animal breath of famine
Whimpering through his frame.

He understands nothing,
Nothing he knows but a mother long sucked dry
Of milk and tears, a father drained of hope.
You are that father, you are that mother,
Your child. Imagine. Is it so hard to imagine?

Thousands of miles away,
Yet still they are next-door neighbours
Within the giant stride,
The magical ring of compassion.
Let one child plead for all,
As the Christ-child spoke for all
Innocents bundled away into a bloodless limbo.

This need not be so.
Our target is mankind's conscience:
Not by the wringing of hands
Shall our concern be measured
But in shelter, seed and ploughshares,
That hope may be reborn.
Put one stranger's child
To the breast of your warm compassion.
Find its father a share in earth,
His only birthright.

Sow a few handfuls of seeds and give that child its future.

C. Day Lewis, Poet Laureate, a poem written for Oxfam

INTERDEPENDENCE

66 Alf

Let's be fanciful for a moment and demonstrate our global
inter-dependence by considering the antics of one such mythical
Englishman. His day begins as he steps out of his pyjamas – a
garment which originated in the East Indies, and he washed with
soap invented by the ancient Gauls. He shaves, a masochistic rite
first developed by the ancient priests of Sumer and made a little
less unpleasant by the use of a razor made of steel, an iron-carbon
alloy discovered in Turkestan. Then, down to breakfast. The table
cloth is probably made of cotton from Uganda and the cutlery of

South African or Rhodesian chrome, nickel from Canada and vanadium from Peru. A cup of Indian tea or Kenyan coffee, a slice of Danish bacon, an egg from poultry whose foodstuffs have been imported from any of thirty countries, ranging from Iceland and Chile to Japan, and he's ready to go.

Alf then dons a close-fitting suit, a form of dress native to the Asiatic steppes; he adjusts his tie, which is, of course, the vestigial remnant of the shoulder shawl of a 7th-century Croat. Then complete with hat which originated in Eastern Asia, and umbrella, invented by the Chinese, he will dash for the train (which, thank God, we British *did* invent). He pauses to buy a newspaper using coins which first made their appearance in ancient Lydia. Then he settles back to scan the day's news – which will be set out in Arabic characters on a Chinese innovation, paper, by means of a German process. He'll snort with disgust at the antics of those dreadful foreigners, and thank a Hebrew God in an Indo-European language that he is 100 per cent – a decimal system invented by the Greeks – English, a word of course derived from Angle, a district in Holstein.

But as Alf would say, we really ought to have been minding our own business all those centuries. He could then have cut a dashing figure in a wolf-skin with a face decorated in woad.

There is no escaping the fact that we are hopelessly indebted to all Mankind for the very sinews of our life. A thousand tiny filaments join us to men of every race under the sun.

Colin Morris, from **Hammer of the Lord**

67 Statistics

Statistically
it was a rich island
income per capita
one million
per annum

Naturally
it was a shock to hear
half the population
had been carried off
by starvation
Statistically
it was a rich island

A U.N. Delegation
(hurriedly despatched)
discovered however
a smallish island
with a total population
of – 2
Both inhabitants
regrettably
not each a millionaire
as we'd presumed
But one the island owner
Income per annum:
Two million
The other
his cook/chauffeur
shoeshine boy/butler
gardener/retainer
handyman/labourer
field nigger etc. etc.
The very same
recently remaindered
by malnutrition

Statistically
it was a rich island
Income per capita
per annum
one million

C. Rajendra, Malaysia

68 The Arithmetic of Poverty

Decide, mother,
who goes without.
Is it Rama, the strongest?
who may not need it
that day.
Or Bala, the weakest?
who may not need it
much longer.
Or perhaps, Sita?
who may be expendable.

Decide, mother,
kill a part
of yourself
as you resolve
the dilemma.

Decide, mother,
decide . . .

D. Appadurai, India

UNITY

69 1941

In 1941, Mama took me to Moscow. There I saw our enemy for
the first time. If my memory is right, nearly 20,000 German war
prisoners were to be marched in a single column through the
streets of Moscow.

The pavements swarmed with onlookers, cordoned off by
soldiers and police. The crowd were mostly women – Russian
women with hands roughened by hard work, lips untouched by
lipstick and thin hunched shoulders which had borne half the
burden of the war. Every one of them must have had a father or a
husband, a brother or a son killed by the Germans.

They gazed with hatred in the direction from which the column
was to appear. At last we saw it.

The generals marched at the head, massive chins stuck out, lips
folded disdainfully, their whole demeanor meant to show
superiority over their plebeian victors . . .

The women were clenching their fists. The soldiers and
policemen had all they could do to hold them back.

All at once something happened to them.

They saw German soldiers, thin, unshaven, wearing dirty,
blood-stained bandages, hobbling on crutches or leaning on the
shoulders of their comrades; the soldiers walked with their heads
down.

The streets became dead silent – the only sound was the
shuffling of boots and the thumping of crutches.

Then I saw an elderly woman in broken-down boots push
herself forward and touch a policeman's shoulder, saying: 'Let me
through.' There must have been something about her that made
him step aside.

She went up to the column, took from inside her coat something wrapped in a coloured handkerchief and unfolded it. It was a crust of black bread. She pushed it awkwardly into the pocket of a soldier, so exhausted that he was tottering on his feet. And now, suddenly from every side women were running towards the soldiers, pushing into their hands bread, cigarettes, whatever they had.

The soldiers were no longer enemies. They were people.

Yevgeny Yevtushenko

70 Fishers of Men

'Let there be light',
God said, 'Unite'
The bigots cried, 'Not so
We will be separate below
How you rule Heaven is Your own affair;
We can but hope your many mansions there
Are not another Biblical mistake.
Elect must be the souls we take.
Pie in the sky in separate dishes,
And God help all the little fishes.'

Joan Brockelsby

71 The Story of Taizé

The community founded in France at Taizé by Brother Roger in 1949 has become the centre of a stimulating Christian experience for young and old, Protestant and Catholic. People flock to Taizé to discuss, to think, to be silent, above all to pray and worship. And from it many go out to share their experience and beliefs with others in their home lands and beyond, in Africa, in Asia and in South America.

It was clear from the start that Taizé would be a 'parable of unity' and as such called to play an active role by its example in the reconciliation of separated Christians. How could such a community not become a leaven of brotherhood – at least do everything in its power to be such? The Rule was to call each brother to have the 'unity of the Body of Christ' as his passionate concern. There could be no question of making Taizé into a

'Protestant concern' to be set up in parallel with similar Catholic institutions.

Reformed and Lutheran brothers were mingled in the community from quite early days. By the 1960s there were brothers of the Anglican Communion. There is no break with his Church when a person becomes a brother of Taizé – just as the Rule encourages each brother to be full of affection for his parents, whether father and mother understand his vocation or not. The community is no new church. Then in 1969 a young Belgian doctor was to become the first Catholic to enter the community. Cardinal Marty, the archbishop of Paris, was in full agreement with that step. Since then, other Catholics have become brothers, including a small number of priests . . . Taizé can only be described as 'a fully ecumenical community'. We cannot make it belong to any one isolated tradition of the Church . . .

Young people made journeys, without any publicity, to all parts of the world . . . Not tourism, and not an attempt to 'get people involved in the Council of Youth'. People were sent from one to another as 'living letters', a means of creating a link between groups whose search may be closely related but who had not met. By those visits a network slowly came into being, a network of reciprocity between continents. The following lines are from Zaire in Africa: 'How can we make good the errors of the past, except by refusing to repeat them? When young Europeans come to Africa today that means not coming as colonisers or evangelising missionaries. They are not to come as bringers of "civilisation" but should come to meet a people . . . No communion is possible until we realise that we are all in the same house, and that the flames threatening one wall (be they the situation in the Far East, consumer society in Europe, or underdevelopment in the Third World) will not spare the people living on the other side of the building. Europe cannot wash its hands of Africa. The problems which arise here, in spite of all the dykes you may build, are bound to have a repercussion in Europe, sooner or later. Each one may not yet feel it personally, but we shall only make good the wrongs of the past all together.'

Extracts from the Rule of Taizé
Christ's path is a way of light: I am, but also you are, the light of the world . . . If the light of Christ is to penetrate you, it is not enough to contemplate it as though you were purely spirit; you have to set out resolutely, body and soul, along that path . . .
If your praying is to be genuine, you need to be at grips with the demands of real work. If your attitude remains careless and

half-hearted you will also be incapable of true intercession. Your prayer becomes total when it is one with your work . . .

True joy begins within. Perfect joy lies in the utter simplicity of peaceful love. Such joy requires no less than your whole being in order to shine out . . .

Simplicity is a way of openness towards our neighbour. Simplicity lies in the free joy of a brother who has given up any obsession with his own progress or backsliding, to keep his eyes fixed on the light of Christ. As peace with Christ involves peace with your neighbour, seek reconciliation, make amends where you can.

J. L. G. Balado

72 Space Between the Bars

My father . . . met my Mother, a [Russian] Moslem, on the Roumanian front in the First World War when he was working as a Red Cross doctor in Russia . . . My mother's parents thought she was giving up her faith which would have been disaster for a Moslem. In fact they were married by a tolerant and rather nervous Lutheran. He wasn't too sure what the rules were. My mother never gave up her faith, and as her son and my father's son I have a tendency to enjoy mixed marriages, mixed faiths, mixed peoples and mixed occurrences. In fact I welcome them. It's part of the dance. My aim now is to suggest that we are only on the brink of enjoying the variety and excitement that a true appreciation of world religions can give, nor have we savoured the differences between peoples to the full, mostly because we fear instead of welcome the divergences . . .

It was Michael Flanders who showed me that there were humourous ways of expressing oneself on serious subjects. To a group of very cheerful sixth formers at Holland Park School I once gave a talk called 'Pacifism with Songs'. I adumbrated all these fearful matters of wars and killing, and when I had reminded the young audience of what people did to each other in the name of righteousness, I suddenly broke into the *Ostrich Song* at the piano and then played *The Reluctant Cannibal*. Neither of these are specifically pacifist songs. The first points to the dangers of burying one's head in the sand in a minefield; the second suggests in the paradoxical form of all Michael's sketches, that if a cannibal wished to refuse to eat humans he would have had a tricky time with his father; and that this tricky time may be

similar to the tricky time people have who now say you should not
fight people . . .

[It is helpful if these two songs can be played.]

Donald Swann

73 Unity

'Ye are all one in Jesus Christ' (St Paul)

'A gulf bridged makes a cross
A split defeated is a cross'

(L. Van Der Post)

It is our failures that are obvious: men fight, they starve, and they
pray in separate buildings to different gods. Men are divided
within themselves.

But there is in all men something that is the same, and there are
signs of this as well:

A In the Meditation Room at the United Nations Building in New
York, a shaft of light cuts across the altar of iron ore. The shaft
streams from an unknown source. It represents a unity between
men.

B In Coventry Cathedral, on the high altar, stands a cross of nails.
Another stands before an altar in Dresden. In the Cathedral
bookshop on a cross of nails postcard are the words:

'The Cross of Nails is a relic that grew out of the destruction of
the cathedral in 1940. As the roof burnt, 14th century hand-forged
nails which had fastened together its beams, littered the sanctuary.
The following morning, the inspiration came to shape three of the
nails into the form of a cross. The cross has become the symbol of
Coventry Cathedral's ministry of international reconciliation.'

C At London Airport a chapel of St George serves twelve million
people who pass through the airport every day, and the thirty-five
thousand who work there. It is a single chapel for the use of
Roman Catholics, Anglicans and Free Churchmen.

D In Johannesburg at Easter time, Africans borrow a painting from
the Cathedral to hang in the churches in the African reserves. The
painting is called Simon of Cyrene. It shows a black man carrying
a cross. It was painted by a white European: the English artist,
Delmar Banner. He painted it to show the sharing of the Negro in
the burden of the cross, and the sharing of Christ in the burden of
the Negro.

Unity does not belong to nationality or race or faith alone. Unity
belongs to all mankind.

*Freely adapted from **Unity** by Carolyn Scott, taken from **One***

4 MANKIND IN THE WORLD

Assemblies

SOME MORAL TALES

1 When to Speak and when to be Silent

To everything, turn, turn, turn
Ecclesiastes 3, 1–9 (10–15)
Readings **74a**: *Watch Your Tongue*, and **74b**: *The Royal
    Chatterbox*
Prayer **81**

2 You Can't Please Everyone

When a knight won his spurs in the stories of old/Be thou my
    guardian and my guide
Reading **75**: *Taking the Donkey to Market* (based on Aesop)
Prayers **73** and **74**

3 Three Sufi Stories

a) God moves in a mysterious way
    Reading **76**: *The Smuggler*
    Prayers **82** and **91**

b) Eternal ruler of the ceaseless round
    Reading **81**: *What's in a Name?*
    Prayers **71**, **52** and **53**

c) Love is something if you give it away
    Reading **77**: *Treasure in the Basket*
    Prayers **82**, **75** and **76**

4 Work

Father hear the prayer we offer
Reading **78**: *A Pig Named Percy*
Prayers **81** and **82**

5 *Working Together*

Life would be good and rich and whole/Help us to
   help each other Lord
Reading **79**: *The Quail*
Prayer **71**

6 *Gifts – Talents*

Awake my soul and with the sun
Reading **80**: *The Magic Mirror*
Prayer **71**

See also readings **82**: *Spoilt Broth*; **129**: *Blind Men and the
   Elephant*; and **121** *Washing Dishes*

COMMUNITY

1 *Love Your Neighbour*

a)   Heavenly Father, may thy blessing
     Reading: Romans 12, 9–21
     Prayer **77**

b)   When I needed a neighbour, were you there, were you
        there?
     Reading **86**: *Chopsticks*, John R. Hogan
     Prayer **68**

c)   Help us to help each other, Lord
     Reading **82**: *Spoilt Broth*, H. L. Gee
     Prayer **71**

d)   If I had a hammer, I'd hammer in the morning
     Reading **79**: *The Quail*
     Prayer **78**

e)   He who would valiant be
     Reading **169**: *Mrs Bedonebyasyoudid*, Charles Kingsley
     Prayer **81**

f)   Dear Lord and Father of Mankind
     Reading **170**: *Mrs Doasyouwouldbedoneby*, Charles Kingsley
     Prayer **82**

See also readings **77**: *Treasure in the Basket*; and **83**: *The Rock*,
   T. S. Eliot (a series of extracts)

2 The Foundations

a) The church's one foundation/City of God, how broad and
    far
    Readings **85**: *The Brick*, Michel Quoist; and Matthew 7,
    21–7
    Prayer **70**

b) And did those feet in ancient times/Lead us, heavenly
    Father, lead us/Father hear the prayer we offer
    Reading **83**: *The Rock*, T. S. Eliot (a series of extracts)
    Prayer **65**

c) God is love; his the care
    Reading **84**: *Over the Great City*, Edward Carpenter
    Prayers **74** and **69**

FAMILY

a) Dear Lord and Father of Mankind
    Reading **87**: *Good Fruit Salad*
    Prayer **75**

b) Lead us, heavenly Father, lead us
    Reading **89**: *The Need to be Nasty*, P. Okeden
    Prayers **84** and **86**

c) Now thank we all our God/Give me joy in my heart, keep
    me praising/The bell of creation is swinging for ever
    Reading **88**: *Adolescence*, Doris Odlum
    Prayers **82** and **83**

d) Was I really once a child?/Lord of all hopefulness, Lord of
    all joy
    Reading **91**: *Coping with Grandpa*, Joy Davidman
    Prayer **77**

e) Travel on, travel on, there's a river that is
    flowing/or as for (d)
    Reading **92**: *Old Age*, Anon.
    Prayers **65** and **68**

See also reading **124**: *Yugoslav Father to Son*; and **90**:
Maternity, Bernadine Bishop

LOVE

a) Gracious Spirit, Holy Ghost
   Readings: 1 Corinthians 13, 1–13, Colossians 3, 12–15
   Prayer **77**

b) God is love; His the care
   Readings **94**: *The Velveteen Rabbit*, M. Williams Bianco;
      and **95**: *Love*, Ken Walsh
   Prayer **80**

c) Love divine, all loves excelling
   Reading **93**: *Love*, Michel Quoist
   Prayer included

See also readings **84**: *Over the Great City*, Edward Carpenter;
   99: *November Third*, Miyazawa Kenji; and **96**: *These I have Loved*, Rupert Brooke

PREJUDICE AND TOLERANCE

1 *What is it?*

Love is something if you give it away
Readings **98**: *Which Half?* Ken Walsh; and Ephesians 4,
   25–32
Prayer **77**

2 *Race*

a) If I had a hammer, I'd hammer in the morning
   Reading **101**: *Common Assault*, Joan Brockelsby
   Prayers **82** and **52**

b) I belong to a family, the biggest on earth/In Christ there is
      no East or West
   Reading **102**: *The Refrigeration of Silas Hunt*, C. Astle
   Prayers **83** and **53**

3 *The Age Gap*

Possible hymns – Sing we of the modern city/Father hear the
   prayer we offer/All who love and serve your city/He who
   would valiant be/Lord of all hopefulness, Lord of all joy.
Readings **100a–c**: *Purple Papers*, John Ward

COURAGE

1 In faith

a)   Soldiers of Christ arise
Reading: Ephesians 6, 10–17
Prayer **85**

b)   Fight the good fight with all thy might
Reading **104b**: *Androcles and the Lion*
Prayer **79**

c)   He who would valiant be/When a knight won his spurs, in
the stories of old
Reading **103**: *St George's Day*, W. H. Elliott
Prayer **78**

d)   Once to every man and nation
Reading **69**: *1941*, Yevgeny Yevtushenko
Prayers **86** and **92**
See also readings **97**: *Ahimsa or the Way of Non-violence*,
Mahatma Gandhi; and **127**: *Good and Evil*,
Kahlil Gibran

2 Bravery

a)   Readings **166–168**: *Emma and I*, Sheila Hocken (see
Section b). There are always accounts of physical bravery
which can be used. These include local incidents
reported in the press and accounts of famous feats such
as the ascent of Everest or the Transglobe expedition.
Suitable biographies include those of Mother Theresa;
Dietrich Bonhoeffer etc.

b)   Soldiers of Christ arise
Reading **104a**: *Mary Verghese*
Prayer **78**

FREEDOM

a)   Wealthy man, you are imprisoned
Reading **105**: *Mr. Mandragon*, G. K. Chesterton
Prayer **83**

b) When in His own image
   Reading **107**: *Freedom and My Neighbour*, Jim Bates
   Prayer **80**

c) The bell of creation is swinging for ever
   Reading **108**: *Freedom*, Kahlil Gibran
   Prayer **68**

d) If I had a hammer, I'd hammer in the morning
   Reading **106**: *Four Freedoms*, Franklin D. Roosevelt
   Prayer **67**

HAPPINESS

1 *Individual*

a) Give me joy in my heart, keep me praising
   Reading **115**: *The Saratoga*, F. W. Boreham
   Prayer **80**

b) Glad that I live am I
   Reading **113**: *Solitary Delights*, Tachibana Akemi
   Prayers **78** and **86**

c) Morning has broken
   Reading **112**: *On a Bicycle*, Yevgeny Yevtushenko
   Prayers **11** and **68**

2 *With Others*

a) For the beauty of the earth
   Reading **111**: *Canoe Story*, Geoffrey Summerfield
   Prayers **75** and **76**

b) Love is something if you give it away
   Reading **114**: *Boasting Song*, Margaret Rose
   Prayer **68**

c) Give me joy in my heart, keep me praising
   Reading **109**: *How to be Happy*, Thomas Merton
   Prayer **78**

d) For the beauty of the earth
   Reading **110**: *Happiness and Vision*, William Blake
   Prayers **13** and **86**

USE OF TIME

1 *Use of Time*

a)   To everything turn, turn, turn
Reading: Ecclesiastes 3, 1–8, 10–15
Prayer **81**

b)   Dear Lord and Father of Mankind
Reading **116**: *Use of Time*, Michel Quoist
Prayer included

c)   New every morning is the love
Readings **139**: *Just for Today*; and Ephesians 4, 25–32; 5,
15–17
Prayers **83** and **82**

d)   Father hear the prayer we offer
Readings **125**: *Go Placidly*, Anon.; and **126**: *Life*, Ken
Walsh
Prayer **86**

e)   Be thou my guardian and my guide
Reading **43**: *The Three Apprentices*, Mary Tayler
Prayers **81** and **83**
Other suitable readings may be found in Sirach (Ecclesiastichs)
5 and 6.

2 *Born anew*

a)   The bell of creation is swinging for ever
Reading **117**: *Headington Hill*, C. S. Lewis
Prayer **80**

b)   Give me joy in my heart, keep me praising
Reading **118**: *Born for this Moment*, Monica Furlong
Prayer **71**

USE OF TALENTS

a)   Fill thou my life, O Lord my God
Readings **119**: *Work is Love*, Kahlil Gibran; and 122: *We
are Transmitters*, D. H. Lawrence
Prayer **71**

b)   Awake my soul and with the sun
Readings **121**: *Washing Dishes*, Martin Buber; and **122**: *We
are Transmitters*, D. H. Lawrence.
Prayers **82** and **83**

c)   Lord of all hopefulness, Lord of all joy
Reading **120**: *Digging*, Seamus Heaney
Prayer **78**

d)   Give me joy in my heart, keep me praising
Reading **123**: *The Minstrel*, Joan Hasler
Prayer **80**

e)   Father hear the prayer we offer
Reading **78**: *A Pig Named Percy*
Prayer **76**

f)   Glad that I live am I
Reading **80**: *The Magic Mirror*
Prayers **78** and **82**

VALUES

1 *Statements of Values*

a)   Dear Lord and Father of Mankind
Reading **125**: *Go Placidly*, Anon.
Prayer **86**

b)   Father hear the prayer we offer
Reading **124**: *Yugoslav Father to Son*
Prayer **78**

c)   O brother Man, fold to thy heart thy brother
Reading **133**: *Modern Affirmations of Faith and Hope*
Prayer **83**

d)   Lord of all hopefulness, Lord of all joy
Reading **132**: *Just for Today*
Prayer **81**

Other suitable hymns: Praise my soul the king of heaven/Give
me joy in my heart, keep me praising

2 *Points of view*

a)   We ask that we live and we labour in peace
     Reading **129**: *Blind Men and the Elephant*
     Prayer **75**

b)   God's spirit is in my heart/I belong to a family, the biggest
        on earth
     Reading **81**: *What's in a Name?*
     Prayer **76**

c)   Sing we of the modern city
     Reading **131**: *People Matter*, Stephen Hopkinson; or **83**:
        The Rock, T. S. Eliot (a series of extracts)
     Prayers **76** and **71**

d)   For the beauty of the earth/Glad that I live am I
     Reading **130**: *The Madman's Will*, Music-hall monologue
     Prayers **83** and **86**

e)   Once to every man and nation
     Readings **127**: *Good and Evil*, Kahlil Gibran; and **83I**: *The
        Rock*, T. S. Eliot
     Prayers **85**, **69** and **70**

See also reading **75**: *Taking the Donkey to Market*, based on
Aesop

Prayers

65 Father, into whose world we come and from whose world finally we must go; we thank you for all those people, great and humble, who have maintained the fabric of the world's life in the past and left us a great inheritance. May we take up and encourage what is good, and hand it on to those who come after, believing that our work in your name will not be wasted. This we ask through Jesus Christ our Lord.

C. P. P. W.

66 Heavenly Father we cannot believe that poverty, famine or sickness are the conditions under which you intend men to live. And yet famine is still normal for most people. Sickness still takes its toll. We believe that these are evils to be fought and yet that mankind is not equipped to fight them by itself. Grant us your love with which to fight them and meanwhile give strength to those who suffer and to those who try to help them; through Jesus Christ our Lord.

C. P. P. W. (*much adapted*)

67 Lord God we pray for the life of the world; that human rights and freedom may everywhere be respected; and that the world's resources may be ungrudgingly shared, through Jesus Christ our Lord.

C. P. P. W. (*adapted*)

68 Let us all protect one another.
Let us all enjoy together.
Let us act valiantly together.
May spiritual knowledge ever shine before us.
Let us never hate one another.
And let Peace and Peace and Peace reign everywhere.

The Rig Veda

69 May the strength of God pilot us.
May the power of God preserve us.
May the wisdom of God instruct us.

May the hand of God protect us.
May the way of God direct us.

St Patrick 389–461

70 May the shield of God defend us.
   May the host of God guard us against the snares of evil and the
      temptations of the world.
   May Christ be with us, Christ before us, Christ in us, Christ over us.
   May thy salvation, O Lord, be always ours this day and for
      evermore.

St Patrick 389–461

71 O Lord God open our ears to hear what you are saying to us in the
      things that happen to us and in the people we meet;
   Open our eyes to see the needs of the people around us;
   Open our hands to do our work well, to help when help is
      needed;
   Open our hearts to love you and our fellow men;
   for Jesus Christ's sake.

C. P. P. W. (*adapted*)

72 May it be your will, O Lord, that no man fosters hatred against us
   in his heart, and that we foster no hatred in our hearts against any
   man; that no man fosters envy of us in his heart, and that we
   foster no envy in our hearts of any man.

The Talmud

73 O Lord God, in the darkness of uncertainty when we don't know
   what to do, when decisions are hard to take; Lord give us light to
   guide us.

C. P. P. W. (*adapted*)

74 Grant us, O Lord, in all our duties your help, in all our
   perplexities your guidance, in all our dangers your protection, and
   in all our sorrows your peace; through Jesus Christ our Lord.

St Augustine 354–430

75 Lord, make us instruments of your peace.
   Where there is hatred, let us sow love;
   Where there is injury, pardon;
   Where there is discord, union;

Where there is doubt, faith;
Where there is despair, hope;
Where there is darkness, light;
Where there is sadness, joy;

St Francis of Assisi 1181–1226

76 Grant that we may not so much seek to be consoled as to console;
to be understood as to understand; to be loved as to love; through
the love of your Son, Jesus Christ our Lord.

St Francis of Assisi 1181–1226

77 O God of love who has given us a commandment that we should
love one another, even as you loved us, we pray you to give us a
mind forgetful of past ill-will and a heart to love our fellow men,
for the sake of Jesus Christ our Lord.

Coptic liturgy of St Cyril (*adapted*)

78 Take from us, O God,
All pride and vanity,
All boasting and forwardness,
And give us the true courage that shows itself by gentleness,
The true wisdom that shows itself by simplicity,
And the true power that shows itself by modesty;
through Jesus Christ our Lord.

Charles Kingsley 1819–1875

79 Let us not pray to be sheltered from dangers, but to be fearless in
facing them.
Let us not beg for the stilling of pain, but for the heart to conquer
it.
Let us not look for allies in life's battlefield, but to our own
strength.
Let us not crave in anxious fear to be saved, but hope for the
patience to win freedom.
Grant that we may not be cowards, O Lord, feeling your mercy in
our success alone;
but let us find the grasp of your hand in our failures.

Rabindranath Tagore 1861–1941, **Fruit Gathering** (*adapted*)

80 O Lord our God, grant us grace to desire you with our whole
heart; that so desiring we may seek and find you; and so finding

you may love you, and loving you may hate those sins from which
you have redeemed us.

St Anselm 1033–1109

81 O Lord forgive us that we have allowed the days and hours to pass
away without any endeavour to accomplish your will. Help us to
remember that every day is your gift and ought to be used
according to your command, through Jesus Christ.

Samuel Johnson 1708–1784 (adapted)

82 Give us your Spirit, Lord, to make us people who build your
Kingdom not people who pull it down. Help us to want things
your way, not our way, for Jesus Christ's sake.

C. P. P. W. *(adapted)*

83 Grant us, O Lord, to know that which is worth knowing, to love
that which is worth loving, to praise that which can bear with
praise, to hate what in your sight is unworthy, to prize what to
you is precious, and to do what is pleasing to you, through Jesus
Christ our Lord.

Thomas à Kempis 1380–1471 (adapted)

84 Heavenly Father,
Help us to trust you enough to obey you; to follow though this
will be to fail you; to persist, that after failure we may hear you
come again to us. Through Jesus Christ our Lord.

C. P. P. W. *(adapted)*

85 Teach us good Lord to serve thee as thou deservest; to give and
not to count the cost, to fight and not to heed the wounds, to toil
and not to seek for rest, to labour and not to ask for any reward
save that of knowing that we do thy will, through Jesus Christ our
Lord.

Ignatius Loyola 1491–1556

86 Show us good Lord,
    the peace we should seek,
    the peace we must give,
    the peace we can keep,

the peace we must forego,
and the peace you have given in Jesus Christ our Lord.

C.P.P.W.

87 The things, good Lord, that we pray for, give us your grace to
labour for.

Sir Thomas More 1478–1535

88 Lord, you know how busy we must be this day. If we forget you,
do not forget us.

Sir Jacob Astley before the Battle of Edgehill 1642

89 O God, help us not to despise or oppose what we do not
understand; through Jesus Christ our Lord.

William Penn 1644–1718

90 May the blessing of the Lord rest and remain upon all his people
in every land, of every tongue.

A Book of Prayers for Schools, S. C. M. 1936

91 May the Lord forgive what we have been; sanctify what we are
and order what we shall be; for His Name's sake.

A Book of Prayers for Schools, S. C. M. 1936

92 May God give us light to guide us, courage to support us, and love
to unite us, this day and for evermore.

A Book of Prayers for Schools, S. C. M. 1936

93 The Lord make us to increase and abound in love, one towards
another and towards all men, now and ever.

A Book of Prayers for Schools, S. C. M. 1936

I Readings

SOME MORAL TALES

74a Watch Your Tongue

Once upon a time a powerful and hasty tempered king ruled a far off country. This king had a favourite horse which he loved more than anything else. One day the horse fell ill. The king summoned all the vets, all the doctors. He tried every remedy, but the horse became worse. The king was distraught. He told the doctors and courtiers that anyone who spoke to him of the horse's death would be hanged.

One night the horse died. Who was to tell the king? No one was willing, until finally one young man agreed to do it. He went to the king and in answer to his enquiry after the horse he said: 'He is lying in his stall. He does not eat, doesn't drink, doesn't sleep and doesn't breathe.' The king stood up. 'You're telling me he's dead.' he exclaimed. 'It is you, your Majesty, who has said it, and you are right,' the young man answered!

The king soon calmed down and congratulated the young man on the way he had broken the news. He explained that he had been brought up to know what damage his tongue could do and to learn to control it. He had learned to say nothing to hurt others or himself.

A Buddhist story

74b The Royal Chatterbox

Once upon a time there was a brave and handsome king. He had only one fault – he never stopped talking. His Chief Minister knew he ought to warn the king that he was making himself look foolish by his everlasting chatter, but he was afraid of the king's anger.

Soon, however, the Minister's chance came. Near the palace lived a talkative turtle who entertained two wild geese who were wintering there. When it was time to go the geese offered to take the turtle with them. Each goose would take one end of a stick in his mouth and the turtle would hold the middle of the stick in his mouth. 'But,' they said, 'you will have to keep your mouth shut.'

The turtle was delighted and agreed at once. Everything went well until they were over the palace. Then a boy standing on top of a hill called out to the turtle. It was too much for the talkative turtle – he opened his mouth to reply and fell to the ground, smashing himself to death on the palace courtyard.

The king and his Minister looked at the shattered body. 'What a lesson to all those who cannot keep their mouths shut,' said the Minister. The king looked at him suspiciously, but he hurried on. 'You, I know Sire, realise that those who are always talking often fail to listen to others and to hear new ideas; and how this often lands them in a mess.'

The king looked thoughtful and for once did not reply. From that moment he ceased to be a chatterbox.

A Buddhist story

75 Taking the Donkey to Market

There was once a farmer who went to market with his son to sell his donkey. The three of them were walking along when a woman called out 'Why are you both walking when one of you could ride on the donkey?' The farmer immediately put his son on the donkey and they moved on. At a crossroads some old men were chatting. 'Fancy the boy riding while his father walks' one said loudly. 'I don't know what the young are coming to these days.' The farmer at once lifted the boy down and got up himself, and on they went. 'Look at that man riding while that poor child has to walk' said one woman to another. 'What a shame.' The farmer told his son to get up behind him. When they were in sight of the market they passed a group of youths. They began to call out after them 'Poor old donkey – he'll be ruined carrying those two. Wouldn't buy him! Why don't you carry him?' Once more the farmer stopped. This time he made the donkey lie down, tied its legs together and slung it from a pole. Then with great difficulty he and his son took each end of the pole and slowly they staggered on, carrying the donkey. To enter the market they had to cross a bridge. Unbalanced by their load, the farmer slipped and let go of the donkey which fell into the water and was drowned.

As they walked home the farmer said bitterly to his son 'It serves me right. Next time I will make up my own mind what is right and do it – trying to please everyone ends up by pleasing nobody and accomplishing nothing.'

Based on Aesop

76 The Smuggler

Nasrudin once became a smuggler. Every day at dawn he came on a donkey to the customs post. His donkey was searched, he was searched – nothing. Every evening he came back to the village, striding cheerfully past the customs, nothing to be found. Yet he became richer and richer and the whole village knew and spoke of his smuggling. One customs officer in particular took it as a challenge. He kept Nasrudin for hours, checking and searching, day after day. Nothing.

A year or so later the official retired. He went to see Nasrudin and begged him to satisfy his curiosity and tell him what he had smuggled. The answer, of course, was – donkeys.

The Mullah told this story to teach the villagers that all the great truths are under our noses – that complicated theories and way-out ideas often distract us from the simple truth.

A Sufi story

77 Treasure in the Basket

One day Mullah Nasrudin had a visit from one of the villagers, Abdul Ali. Abdul told him a sad story. The wind had blown all his figs off the tree and they were too bruised to sell. His family would starve without the flour, rice and olive oil he had hoped to buy with the proceeds. Could Nasrudin possibly lend him some money? Just until the grape harvest?

Nasrudin pointed to a basket on a high shelf. 'Help yourself, Abdul, take what you need. But return it as soon as you can so that it can be used to help others.'

'Of course' said Abdul, emptying every last coin from the basket. 'You can depend on me. Allah be with you', and he departed.

The time of the grape harvest came and went – no Abdul. Four years passed before Nasrudin had another visit from him. About to thank him for returning the money, Nasrudin looked at him as he entered uneasily, eyes looking shiftily round the room, and so he waited. They talked of this and that and Abdul began to relax. Eventually he sighed, 'Fate is against me. My goat has died and we have no milk, no yoghourt. Unless I can buy a new goat my youngest child will die.' 'See that basket on the high shelf? That is where I keep the money to help those in trouble.' Abdul was up in a flash – but the basket was empty.

'Someone must have borrowed the money and not returned it,' said Nasrudin sadly. Abdul fled – but could not go fast enough to escape the Mullah's warning. 'Life is like that basket. A man cannot always be taking and never giving. Neither baskets nor lives fill themselves with treasure.'

A Sufi story

78 A Pig Named Percy

A pig once lived in a little cottage with a fine large garden. Year in, year out the pig tended his garden, growing vegetables and fine plants. He worked from dawn to sunset, and his produce became famous for its excellent quality. He won prizes at vegetable shows and sold his surplus far and wide. But as the years passed he become more and more discontented, feeling that there must be easier ways of earning a living.

Finally, one spring day, he could bear it no longer. He packed a bag, shut up his cottage and set out. Soon he heard some tuneful violin music and met Thomas the Cat merrily playing away. He thought it looked an easy way to earn a living and asked Thomas to teach him. He agreed at once, but when Percy pulled the bow across the strings there was a discordant screech. 'Never mind' said Thomas, 'Just practise five hours a day and you'll master it in a few years.' Percy hurriedly said good-bye and went on his way.

Next he saw a dog sitting by his front door pushing a pole up and down in some milk to make cheese. Percy asked to try, but soon found his arms were tired out and the milk had not even begun to thicken. So he decided that was not the job for him and continued on his journey.

As he was enjoying his walk through the clover meadows he met a man pottering round his beehives. 'What a pleasant life', he thought, 'nothing to do but take the honey combs.' The man willingly agreed to show him what to do and Percy put on the gloves and veil and went to the honey comb. At once the bees were everywhere, stinging him viciously. He yelped with pain and set off for home as fast as his legs could carry him.

Once home, he sank into a chair, surveyed all his prize plants and vegetables and decided that in future he would stick to doing what he enjoyed and could do so well.

A fable

79 The Quail

In the old days men used to catch flocks of quail by stealing up and throwing a large net over them. As they struggled they become entangled in the nets and could be caught very easily.

The chief quail thought hard and long and calling all the surviving birds to him he suggested a way out. Next time the net was thrown over a group of them each bird took hold of the net and they all flew up with the net. They draped it on a tree and flew down. Time and again they did this, till the fowlers were in despair.

The birds were delighted at their success, but they began to boast about it, to claim the credit for the idea and even to complain that they had the heaviest part of the net to carry. Quarrels broke out and friends became enemies. One day they were so busy quarrelling that they did not hear a fowler approach and when he threw the net they were so angry with each other that they did not carry the net off. Each bird struggled for his own freedom, all became entangled in the net and most were caught.

The chief quail, who was one of the surviving birds, said to the rest 'Now I hope you have learned your lesson. We must work together and think of each other.' The quail nodded. They knew – now.

A fable

80 The Magic Mirror

Do you need a magic mirror? Have you ever looked at yourself and decided that you don't like what you see?

There was once a prince who was in just that situation. In his youth he had been tall, dark and handsome, but now when he looked at himself he saw dark rings round rather bloodshot eyes, pale wrinkled skin, the beginnings of a double chin and far too much stomach. Alarmed, he sent for the doctors, who prescribed vitamins and iron tablets and a variety of diets. Nothing made much difference and the prince became more and more miserable. Then a wise man who came to the court heard of his problem and guaranteed a cure. He told him that he must find a magic mirror in the hills. It would only be visible in the early hours after sunrise and until he found it he was not to look in another mirror. Well, the prince got up early day after day and searched for the magic mirror. He had to go to bed early to be ready, and he always came back with a good appetite.

One morning the court was roused by the prince striding into the palace, triumphant, holding up a mirror. 'I've found it – and it works!' He was delighted. 'Bring me the old man.' When the wise man came to him the prince told him how he had recovered his good looks. Gone were the wrinkles, the yellow complexion, the sagging skin. He asked the secret of the magic mirror, but the wise man confessed that it was an ordinary mirror which he had put in the hills the previous day. The 'secret' was simple – it was the long walks, early nights and sensible food which had brought about the change.

The prince laughed at the trick, but he did not forget the lesson that fitness, like any other gift, has to be worked at.

Folk story

81 What's in a Name?

Once upon a time a Turk, a Persian, an Arab and a Greek were travelling together. None of them understood the others' languages but a Sufi wise man who was with them understood them all and translated for them, so they got on well together.

One day, however, the Sufi left them for a few hours in a market. When he came back they were quarrelling violently about how to spend their last coin. The Turk wanted Uzum, the Persian Angur, the Arab Inab and the Greek Staphylia. The Sufi took one look, demanded the coin and went off. He came back with four bunches of grapes which he distributed among his companions. Each was delighted, for each got what he wanted; only the words were different.

The Sufi turned to them and said 'Now perhaps you can see how foolish you were to argue when you were really agreed.'

A Sufi story

COMMUNITY

82 Spoilt Broth

A very old tale from India says there were once four foolish beggars, clothed in rags, who by chance met in a beggars' hut near a small village. All day they had been holding out bowls in the market-place, begging charity of those who moved to and fro. As the sun was setting and the shadows were lengthening, they limped to the hut. There they sat round a very small fire of sticks, all of them discontented and suspicious.

Now it happened that the first beggar had nothing in his wooden bowl except a little meat. The second had his bowl half filled with vegetables. A few spices lay at the bottom of the third beggar's bowl; and all that the fourth beggar had collected were four or five handfuls of rice.

So there in the hut, as twilight deepened, the four foolish beggars talked and grumbled until one suggested that if they put water in the pot hanging over the fire and if each threw into it the contents of his own bowl, there would be broth enough for everyone.

The idea of enjoying a savoury supper was loudly acclaimed, and the pot having been filled, the beggars sat round eagerly.

But the first beggar, who thought himself a cunning fellow, realised that if the other three threw in spices, vegetables and rice, why, there would be no need for *him* to share his little store of meat. So, in the half-light he pretended to drop his meat in the pot, afterwards chuckling to think that he would enjoy a tasty supper, and still have his meat all for himself.

As it happened, the second beggar did the same with his vegetables; the third with his spices; and the fourth with his rice, each pretending to throw everything he had into the common pot, all hiding their food under their rags.

They say there was no end of quarrelling in the beggars' hut that night when the pot was lifted off the fire, and *nothing* was found in it except hot water.

H. L. Gee, 500 Tales to Tell Again

83 The Rock

I 60–74

The world turns and the world changes,
But one thing does not change.
In all of my years, one thing does not change.
However you disguise it, this thing does not change:
The perpetual struggle of Good and Evil.
Forgetful, you neglect your shrines and churches;
The men you are in these times deride
What has been done of good, you find explanations
To satisfy the rational and enlightened mind.

Second, you neglect and belittle the desert.
The desert is not remote in southern tropics,
The desert is not only around the corner,
The desert is squeezed in the tube-train next to you,
The desert is in the heart of your brother.
The good man is the builder, if he build what is good.

II 38–55
What life have you if you have not life together?
There is no life that is not in community,
And no community not lived in praise of GOD.
Even the anchorite who meditates alone,
For whom the days and nights repeat the praise of GOD,
Prays for the Church, the Body of Christ incarnate.
And now you live dispersed on ribbon roads,
And no man knows or cares who is his neighbour
Unless his neighbour makes too much disturbance,
But all dash to and fro in motor cars,
Familiar with the roads and settled nowhere.
Nor does the family even move about together,
But every son would have his motor cycle,
And daughters ride away on casual pillions.

Much to cast down, much to build, much to restore;
Let the work not delay, time and the arm not waste;
Let the clay be dug from the pit, let the saw cut the stone,
Let the fire not be quenched in the forge.

III 1–19

The Word of the LORD came unto me, saying:
O miserable cities of designing men,
O wretched generation of enlightened men,
Betrayed in the mazes of your ingenuities,
Sold by the proceeds of your proper inventions:
I have given you hands which you turn from worship,
I have given you speech, for endless palaver,
I have given you my Law, and you set up commissions,
I have given you lips, to express friendly sentiments,
I have given you hearts, for reciprocal distrust.
I have given you power of choice, and you only alternate
Between futile speculation and unconsidered action.
Many are engaged in writing books and printing them,
Many desire to see their names in print,

Many read nothing but the race reports.
Much is your reading, but not the Word of GOD,
Much is your building, but not the House of GOD.
Will you build me a house of plaster, with corrugated roofing,
To be filled with a litter of Sunday newspapers?

III 37–76

We build in vain unless the LORD build with us.
Can you keep the City that the LORD keeps not with you?
A thousand policemen directing the traffic
Cannot tell you why you come or where you go.
A colony of cavies or a horde of active marmots
Build better than they that build without the LORD.
Shall we lift up our feet among perpetual ruins?
I have loved the beauty of Thy House, the peace of Thy sanctuary.
I have swept the floors and garnished the altars.
Where there is no temple there shall be no homes,
Though you have shelters and institutions,
Precarious lodgings while the rent is paid,
Subsiding basements where the rat breeds
On sanitary dwellings with numbered doors
Or a house a little better than your neighbour's;

When the Stranger says: 'What is the meaning of this city?
Do you huddle close together because you love each other?'
What will you answer? 'We all dwell together
To make money from each other'? or 'This is a community'?
And the Stranger will depart and return to the desert.
O my soul, be prepared for the coming of the Stranger,
Be prepared for him who knows how to ask questions.

O weariness of men who turn from GOD
To the grandeur of your mind and the glory of your action,
To arts and inventions and daring enterprises,
To schemes of human greatness thoroughly discredited,
Binding the earth and the water to your service,
Exploiting the seas and developing the mountains,
Dividing the stars into common and preferred,
Engaged in devising the perfect refrigerator,
Engaged in working out a rational morality,
Engaged in printing as many books as possible,
Plotting of happiness and flinging empty bottles,
Turning from your vacancy to fevered enthusiasm

For nation or race or what you call humanity;
Though you forget the way to the Temple,
There is one who remembers the way to your door:
Life you may evade, but Death you shall not.
You shall not deny the Stranger.

T. S. Eliot

84 Over the Great City

Over the great city,
Where the wind rustles through the parks and gardens,
In the air, the high clouds brooding,
In the lines of street perspective, the lamps, the traffic,
The pavements and the innumerable feet upon them.
I Am: make no mistake – do not be deluded.

Think not because I do not appear at the first glance – because the
    centuries have gone by and there is no assured tidings of me –
    that therefore I am not there.
Think not because all goes its own way that therefore I do not go
    my own way through all.
The fixed bent of hurrying faces in the street – each turned
    towards its own light, seeing no other – yet I am the Light
    towards which they all look.
The toil of so many hands to such multifarious ends, yet my
    hand knows the touch and twining of them all.

All come to me at last.
There is no love like mine;
For all other love takes one and not another;
And other love is pain, but this is joy eternal.

Edward Carpenter, **Oxford Book of Mystical Verse**

85 The Brick

The bricklayer laid a brick on the bed of cement.
Then, with a precise stroke of his trowel spread another layer
And without a by-your-leave, laid on another brick.
The foundations grew visibly,
The building rose, tall and strong, to shelter men.

I thought, Lord, of that brick buried in the darkness at the base of
the big building.
No one sees it, but it accomplishes its task, and the other bricks
need it.
Lord, what difference whether I am on the roof-top or in the
foundations of your building, as long as I stand faithfully at the
right place?

Michel Quoist

86 Chopsticks

In Korea there is a legend about a native warrior who died and
went to heaven. 'Before I enter,' he said to the gatekeeper, 'I
would like you to take me on a tour of hell.' The gatekeeper found
a guide to take the warrior to hell. When he got there he was
astonished to see a great table piled high with the choicest foods.
But the people in hell were starving. The warrior turned to his
guide and raised his eyebrows.

'It's this way,' the guide explained. 'Everybody who comes here
is given a pair of chopsticks five feet long, and is required to hold
them at the end to eat. But you just can't eat with chopsticks five
feet long if you hold them at the end. Look at them. They miss
their mouths every time, see?'

The visitor agreed that this was hell indeed and asked to be
taken back to heaven post-haste. In heaven, to his surprise, he saw
a similar room, with a similar table laden with very choice foods.
But the people were happy: they looked radiantly happy.

The visitor turned to the guide: 'No chopsticks I suppose?' he
said. 'Oh yes,' said the guide, 'they have the same chopsticks, the
same length, and they must be held at the end, just as in hell. But
you see these people have learned that if a man feeds his
neighbour, his neighbour will feed him also.'

John R. Hogan

FAMILY

87 Good Fruit Salad

A Japanese husband stood with his wife and their son and
daughter on the platform at a meeting. In his staccato
Japanese-style English he said, 'I am father. I am like coconut.
You know coconut? Hard outside – soft inside. This is mother.

She is like peach. You know peach? Soft and lovely outside – hard inside. This is son. He is like banana. You know banana? Soft outside, soft inside, not straight and very slippery! This is daughter. She is like chestnut. Prickly outside and she explodes when heated. But now we are all changed. We make good fruit salad.

Himmat, Bombay

88 Adolescence

One girl of 15 told me that she had made a list of all the criticisms that she had received during the past month. These emanated from her parents, her brothers and sisters, her teachers, her school mates and other girl friends, and also from the boys she knew. The list was formidable and many of the criticisms were self-contradictory. They included the following items from her family: inconsistency, unpredictability, arguing, being unreasonable, rude and aggressive manner, bad temper, irritability, moodiness, quarrelsomeness, grumbling and dissatisfaction with everything in the home, dislike of clothes after buying them and refusing to wear them, untidiness, lack of interest in appearance, too much time spent on appearance, always looking in mirror, wanting to use make-up (this during the previous six months), upsetting brothers or sisters by being bossy and interfering, being slow and late for everything, rushing and being slapdash, always wanting to be out with friends, no interest in the home or family, not wanting to help with housework, apparent hostility to parents. Teachers said she was not really trying and complained of her lack of concentration, carelessness in work, not doing homework, always seeming tired, being apathetic, excitable, disturbing in class, noisy in corridors, forgetting books, and generally irresponsible. Friends accused her of moodiness, unpredictability, bossiness, possessiveness, and jealousy, or of wanting other friends; and made criticisms of her appearance and every detail of her behaviour. Boy friends were critical of her appearance, moodiness, unpredictability, going with other boys, jealousy and possessiveness.

Doris Odlum, **Journey through Adolescence**

89 The Need to be Nasty

Do you know that time, towards the end of Christmas Day, when the goodwill sometimes runs out? Exhausted parents flop in their chairs among the debris; children, bloated but cheerful, play with their new possessions on the rug; and then, all of a sudden, all hell breaks loose. Children start to fight, there are tears and tantrums, someone's new toy gets broken and it will be surprising if parents don't lose their tempers too – with each other and the children.

The goodwill has run out. It has been a strain being kind and grateful and feeling that everything must be enjoyed. We can't keep up being nice any more; it's time to be nasty, to be ungrateful, unkind. Adult or child we probably feel we hate our rotten family, and if not on Christmas Day, then certainly we feel it sometimes.

I think one of the best thing about families is you can be nasty, really nasty, and they will still be around tomorrow when you love them.

For instance, you can come home from school after a difficult day and refuse your tea, or fly off the handle and slam doors. You can come home from work full of depression or suppressed fury and be a bear with a sore head. You can have a rotten day at home and be thoroughly nasty to the family: and they may fight back, or tell you what they think or just take it – but with any luck they will take it and be around to be nice to later.

I know plenty of people who will accept me when I'm being nice, when I'm trying hard, when I'm on my best behaviour. But I have a sneaking feeling that if they knew the worst side of my nature the smile of welcome would pretty soon freeze. I don't feel at all sure if I am really acceptable – because I also need to be nasty, to be bad-tempered, to be difficult, to express the frustration and the unhappiness and the anger which are part of every person's experience.

And that's where a family comes in. A family will not only allow me to show my better self – it will allow me to be my worst self. At home my feelings are almost sure to emerge – at home I can sometimes be bad-tempered, ungrateful, sulky, miserable – I can be nasty – and still be put up with. And that seems to me one of the best things a person or a group of people can do for another – allow someone to be at their worst and still care about them and not walk out. And in the family we can all do this for each other.

A family can be like a trampoline. It can absorb the shocks of our worst moments, our ghastly failures, our antisocial behaviour and keep sending us back to meet life. We need it when we're small and have to find someone to take our frustration and rage – we need it in adolescence when we're mixed up and moody and rebellious and so often need to be difficult. We need it all through life, and people on their own desperately need others who will accept them in this kind of way.

I think my family is marvellous, and not least because when I
am moody and difficult, when I find fault with everyone, then
they tell me how impossible I am, but they still stick around, they
make me feel I matter in spite of it, and they should know,
because they've seen me at my worst. In fact they love me enough
to allow me to be nasty – and who will do that for me, except the
infuriating family that I love so much.

P. Okeden

90 Maternity

Consider this advertisement: 'Wanted. Young person to act as
nursery nurse, playleader, psychologist, cook, weightlifter,
medical expert, nightwatcher, accident prevention officer and
general organiser. Permanent position of the utmost
responsibility. No supervision. 168-hour week. No experience or
qualifications required.'

Of course we never see such an advertisement, and if we did we
should be puzzled and worried. But this is what is involved when
a young girl answers the responsibilities of motherhood. There is
no other task so vast and open-ended which anyone takes on with
so little preparation as maternity.

Bernadine Bishop

91 Coping with Grandpa

Once upon a time there was a little old man. His eyes blinked and
his hands trembled; when he ate he clattered the silverware
distressingly, missed his mouth with the spoon as often as not,
and dribbled a bit of his food on the table-cloth. Now he lived
with his married son, having nowhere else to live, and his son's
wife was a modern young woman who knew that in-laws should
not be tolerated in a woman's home.

'I can't have this,' she said. 'It interferes with a woman's right
to happiness.'

So she and her husband took the little old man gently but firmly
by the arm and led him to the corner of the kitchen. There they
set him on a stool and gave him his food, what there was of it, in
an earthenware bowl. From then on he always ate in the corner,
blinking at the table with wistful eyes.

One day his hands trembled rather more than usual, and the
earthenware bowl fell and broke.

'If you are a pig,' said the daughter-in-law, 'you must eat out of a trough.' So they made him a little wooden trough, and he got his meals in that.

This comple These people had a four-year-old son of whom they were very fond. One suppertime the young man noticed his boy playing intently with some bits of wood and asked what he was doing.

'I'm making a trough,' he said, smiling up for approval, 'to feed you and Mamma out of when I get big.'

The man and his wife looked at each other for a while and didn't say anything. They cried a little. Then they went to the corner and took the little old man by the arm and led him back to the table. They sat him in a comfortable chair and gave him his food on a plate, and from then on nobody ever scolded when he clattered or spilled or broke things.

One of Grimm's fairy tales, this anecdote has the crudity of the old simple days: the modern serpent's tooth method would be to lead Grandpa gently but firmly to the local asylum, there to tuck him out of sight as a case of senile dementia. But perhaps crudity is what we need to illustrate the naked and crude point of the Fifth Commandment: honour your parents lest your children dishonour you. Or, in other words, a society that destroys the family destroys itself.

Joy Davidman, **Smoke on the Mountain**

92 Old Age

What do you see, tell me, what do you see?
Who are you seeing when looking at me?
A crabbit old woman, not very wise,
Uncertain of habit, with far away eyes,
Who seems not to notice the things that you do,
And forever is losing a stocking or shoe?
Is that what you're thinking, is that what you see?
Then open your eyes, for you're not seeing me.

I'll say who I am as I sit here so still,
As I rise at your bidding and eat at your will.
I'm a small child of 10 with a father and mother,
Sisters and brothers who love one another;
A young girl of 16 with wings on her feet,
Dreaming that soon her true sweetheart she'll meet;
A bride at just 20, my heart gives a leap,
Remembering the vows I promised to keep.

At 25 now I have bairns of my own,
Who need me to build a secure happy home.
A woman of 30, my children grow fast,
Bound to each other with ties that should last.
At 40, my grown-up sons soon will be gone,
But my man stays beside me to see I don't mourn.
At 50 once more babies play round my knee,
Again we know children my loved one and me.

Dark days are upon me, my husband is dead;
I look at the future, I shudder with dread.
My children are busy with bairns of their own;
I think of the years and the love I have known.
I'm an old woman now, grace and vigour depart,
But thousands of memories live in my heart.
Inside it you see, a girl still dwells,
And now and again my tired heart swells.

Anon.

LOVE

93 Love

There are two loves only, Lord,
Love of myself and love of you and of others,
And each time that I love myself, it's a little less love for you and
    for others,
It's a draining away of love,
It's a loss of love,
For love is made to leave self and fly towards others.
Each time it's diverted to myself, it withers, rots and dies.
Love of self, Lord, is a poison that I absorb each day;
Love of self offers me a cigarette and gives none to my neighbour;
Love of self chooses the best part and keeps the best place;
Love of self indulges my senses and supplies them from the table
    of others;
Love of self speaks about myself and makes me deaf to the words
    of others;
Love of self chooses, and forces that choice on a friend;
Love of self puts on a false front, it wants me to shine,
    over-shadowing others;

Love of self is self-pitying and overlooks the suffering of others;
Love of self advertises my ideas and despises those of others;
Love of self thinks me virtuous, it calls me a good man;
Love of self induces me to earn money, to spend it for my
    pleasure, to save it for my future;
Love of self advises me to give to the poor in order to ease my
    conscience and live in peace;
Love of self puts my slippers on and ensconces me in an easy
    chair;
Love of self is satisfied with myself, it gently rocks me to sleep.

What is more serious, Lord, is that love of self is a stolen love.
It was destined for others, they needed it to live, to thrive, and I
    have diverted it.
So the love of self creates human suffering.
So the love of men for themselves creates human misery,
All the miseries of men,
All the sufferings of men:

The suffering of the boy whose mother has slapped him without
    cause, and that of the man whose boss has reprimanded him
    in front of the other workers;
The suffering of the ugly girl neglected at a dance, and that of the
    woman whose husband doesn't kiss her any more;
The suffering of the child left at home because he's a nuisance,
    and that of the grandfather made fun of because he's too old;
The suffering of the worried man who hasn't been able to confide
    in anyone, and that of the troubled adolescent whose worries
    have been ridiculed;
The suffering of the desperate man who jumps into the canal, and
    that of the criminal who is going to be executed;
The suffering of the unemployed man who wants to work, and
    that of the worker who ruins his health for a ridiculous wage;
The suffering of the father who has to pile his family into a single
    room next to an empty house, and that of the mother whose
    children are hungry while the remains of someone's party are
    thrown into the dustbin;
The suffering of one who dies alone, while his family, in the
    adjoining room, wait for his death, drinking coffee.
All sufferings,
All injustices, bitternesses, humiliations, griefs, hates, despairs,
All sufferings are an unappeased hunger,
A hunger for love.

So men have built, slowly, selfishness by selfishness, a disfigured
    world that crushes them;
So men on earth spend their time feeding their self-love,
While around them others with outstretched arms die of hunger.
They have squandered love.
I have squandered your Love, Lord.
Tonight I ask you to help me to love.

Grant us, Lord, to spread true love in the world.
Grant that by me and by your children it may penetrate a little into
    all circles, all societies, all economic and political systems, all
    laws, all contracts, all rulings;
Grant that it may penetrate into offices, factories, apartment
    buildings, cinemas, dance-halls;
Grant that it may penetrate the hearts of men and that I may
    never forget that the battle for a better world is a battle of
    love, in the service of love.

Help me to love, Lord,
    not to waste my powers of love,
    to love myself less and less in order to love others more and
    more,
That around me, no one should suffer or be hurt because I have
    stolen the love they needed to live.

Son, you will never succeed in putting enough love into the heart
    of man and into the world,
For man and the world are hungry for an infinite love,
And God alone can love with a boundless love.
But if you want, son, I give you my life,
Draw it within you.
I give you my heart, I give it to my sons.
Love with my heart, son,
And all together you will feed the world, and you will save it.

Michel Quoist, **Prayers of Life**

94 The Velveteen Rabbit

'What is REAL?' asked the rabbit one day, when they were lying
side by side near the nursery fender, before Nana came to tidy the

room. 'Does it mean having things that buzz inside you and a stick-out handle?'

'Real isn't how you are made,' said the skin horse. 'It's a thing that happens to you. When a child loves you for a long, long time, not just to play with, but REALLY loves you, then you become Real.'

'Does it happen all at once, like being wound up,' he asked, 'or bit by bit?'

'It doesn't happen all at once,' said the skin horse. 'You become. It takes a long time. That's why it doesn't often happen to people who break easily, or have sharp edges, or who have to be carefully kept. Generally, by the time you are Real, most of your hair has been loved off, and your eyes drop out and you get loose in the joints and very shabby.'

M. Williams Bianco

95 Love

Love is glad when you are glad
Is sad when you are sad
Is hurt when you are.
Love is never so wrapped in himself
He can't listen to you,
And hear you.
Love accepts you exactly as you are –
Is happy for your strengths
Is sorry for you in your weakness,
(However unacceptable it may appear)
Stands beside you in your struggle.
Love knows no time
And is always available.
Love may criticize what you do
But never you,
And looks with you
For the right path, for you
Love makes no judgements
And has a deep respect for you;
Love shares his all with you
His time, his possessions, his talents.
Love grows by sharing himself;

Love drives out fear;
Love is eternal and never dies:
Love cares.

Ken Walsh

96 These I have Loved

These I have loved:
White plates and cups, clean-gleaming,
Ringed with blue lines; and feathery, faery dust;
Wet roofs, beneath the lamp-light; the strong crusts
Of friendly bread; and many-tasting food;
Rainbows; and the blue bitter smoke of wood;
And radiant raindrops couching in cool flowers;
And flowers themselves, that sway through sunny hours,
Dreaming of moths that drink them under the moon;
Then, the cool kindliness of sheets, that soon
Smooth away trouble; and the rough male kiss
Of blankets; grainy wood; live hair that is
Shining and free; blue-massing clouds; the keen
Unpassioned beauty of a great machine;
The benison of hot water; furs to touch;
The good smell of old clothes; and others such –
The comfortable smell of friendly fingers,
Hair's fragrance, and the musty reek that lingers
About dead leaves and last year's ferns . . .

Rupert Brooke

PREJUDICE AND TOLERANCE

97 Ahimsa or the Way of Non-violence

Non-violence is 'not a resignation from all real fighting against wickedness'. On the contrary, the non-violence of my conception is a more active and real fight against wickedness than retaliation whose very nature is to increase wickedness. I seek entirely to blunt the edge of the tyrant's sword, not by putting up against it a sharper-edged weapon, but by disappointing his expectation that I would be offering physical resistance. The resistance of the soul that I should offer would elude him. It would at first dazzle him and at last compel recognition from him, which recognition would not humiliate but would uplift him.

Non-violence to be a potent force must begin with the mind. Non-violence of the mere body without the co-operation of the mind is non-violence of the weak or the cowardly, and has therefore no potency. If we bear malice and hatred in our bosoms and pretend not to retaliate, it must recoil upon us and lead to our destruction.

Readings from Mahatma Gandhi

98 Which Half?

I must concentrate
On the half of my argument
That is right,
And the half of his argument
That is wrong,
And so we can argue
For ever –

But if I could add
The half of his argument
That is right,
To the half of my argument
That is right,
We could move
Towards
A solution.

Ken Walsh

99 November Third

Bending neither to the rain
Nor to the wind
Nor to snow nor to summer heat,
Firm in body, yet
Without greed, without anger,
Always smiling serenely.
Eating his four cups of rough rice a day
With bean paste and a few vegetables,
Never taking himself into account
But seeing and hearing everything,
Understanding
And never forgetting.

If there is a sick child in the east
He goes and tends him.
If there is a tired mother in the west
He goes and shoulders her rice-sheaves.
Everyone calls him a fool.
Neither praised
Nor taken to heart.

That man
Is what I wish to be.

Miyazawa Kenji

100 Purple Papers

a) Mr Brawny,

For several weeks I have been meaning to write and tell you what I think of your so-called Youth Club, but have refrained from so doing in the hope that some improvement might take place in the behaviour of the teenagers who seem to belong to it. However, last night was the last straw and I can hold it in no longer.

Because I am unfortunate enough to have a bus shelter outside my front door I have to endure rowdyism till past midnight every Friday. My little front garden is treated as a dustbin – especially for fish and chip papers, bottles and beer cans – and as I lie in bed I am treated to a whole dictionary of abuse in order to amuse their sluttish girl friends. But even the worm turns, so last night I got out of bed, opened the window and shouted at them. 'Call yourselves a Church Youth Club,' I said. 'I've never seen so much as one of you in St Beamend's. Get off home! Decent folk are in bed by this time.'

This produced raucous laughter and to my astonishment one lewd-looking youth in a black jacket full of brass studs sauntered up to my front door, stuck a firework in the keyhole and lit it from his cigarette. The explosion was enough to wake the neighbourhood. I shook my fist at them and threatened to get the police, but they jeered, made cheeky and disgusting gestures with their fingers and moved slowly away down the street.

How much longer, Mr Brawny, are we to put up with all this? The Rector shall know of it and if he refuses to close your club down I shall have it out with him. Most of the Church Council think it's a disgrace anyway. There was a time when St Beamend's had a flourishing branch of the Girls' Friendly Society and we held lovely dances, but this, it's outrageous! The world has gone mad. It will not be tolerated.

I remain resolute,
Mrs Starch

From Ted Brawny, Club Leader, to the Rector

Dear Mr Evergreen,
No doubt, Mrs Starch has given you an earful. I am sorry, I really am. They're not all like that, you know. It's just an element but I admit things has got badly out of hand lately. It's help I need, like. How can I know what's going on all the time? You know how often I've caught them snogging in the boiler house and dragged them out! Now there's this business of unscrewing the tap from the Mothers' Union tea urn. Goodness knows where it's gone.

Rector, what I'm saying is I've got to resign. It's only right, like. I can't do it single-handed. Fred Weaknees was supposed to be coming as my assistant but he never turned up. I put two windows back in last week but there's no end to it. I've been thinking. I've done the Friday night club for nearly six years now but I've hardly been what you might call a success, like. I've let the Church down and I've let you down.

Sorry,
Ted Brawny

From the Secretary of the local Spastics Society to the Revd Herbert Evergreen

Dear Rector,
Will you please convey the heartfelt thanks of the members of the Spastics Committee to all those young people who did so magnificently with their sponsored walk. To raise £125 is a tremendous achievement and we have great pleasure in offering them our sincere congratulations. Well done, St Beamend's.

Yours sincerely,
Mary Newpenny,
Honorary Secretary

b) From the Rector to Ted Brawny

Oh! My Dear Ted,
You think you've let me down! Upon my soul, dear boy, you are
one of the very few real workers we've got here. Let me put it to
you frankly – what on earth would we do without you? If you
resign I shall be at my wits' end to find another youth leader.
Look at the enclosed letter from the Secretary of the Spastics
Society. You casually mentioned that the youngsters were doing a
sponsored walk and I had no idea the result would be £125! Wait
till I see Mrs Starch. I'll apologise to her, of course, because I feel
ashamed of the way she's been treated, but I'll try to get her to see
that it's only too easy for a minority to give the majority a bad
name.

Let's have a talk. I know you can see how important it is to give
young people something better to do than hang around pubs and
coffee bars. How about coming back to breakfast in the Rectory
after Holy Communion on Sunday morning.

I never thanked you for putting that weed killer all over the
church paths. The wardens should see to it but you know what
they are like!!

> Your sincere friend,
> Herbert Evergreen,
> Rector

From the Treasurer of the Silver Threads Club
to the Revd Herbert Evergreen

Dear Rector,
I enclose the profit from last Saturday's American Tea. It is only
£3.43p but the Silver Threads Club Committee would like to point
out that we don't think we have done badly considering the
complete lack of co-operation from the church. You yourself, so I
am told, forgot to announce it at morning service. How can you
expect people to work hard for your new lighting fund if you take
so little interest? But what's a thousand times worse is that that Mr
Brawny had got nothing ready for us whatsoever in the Hall. The
tables were not put out and he had not bothered to put the heat
on. It was freezing! Our Committee will most certainly not be
holding future efforts in aid of your lighting fund.

Finally, I see from your parish magazine that you lavish praise on the Friday Night Youth Club for raising £125 in a Sponsored Walk. Well, in my opinion, they have done far more than £125 worth of damage to the school hall so it's a great pity they don't have the decency to offer it to the Church with their apologies for being such nuisances. You should hear what Mrs Starch has to say.

Yours faithfully,
Mrs Cool,
Hon. Treasurer,
Silver Threads Club

The Rector's reply

Dear Mrs Cool,
Thank you for the sum of £3.43p. We are most grateful and I enclose a receipt. Please don't think that your efforts were not appreciated – they are – but I feel it is my duty to point out that the Silver Threads Club Committee is labouring under a misunderstanding. Mr Edward Brawny is NOT a caretaker. We used to have a verger and caretaker but he left suddenly three weeks after my induction to this parish. His reason for leaving was that I am too High Church, a statement I found more than a little puzzling as he used to go and sit in the bar of 'The Green Dragon' whilst services were in progress. We advertised for a new verger and caretaker without success and would have been in dire straits if Mr Brawny had not taken on these duties out of sheer goodness of heart rather than see the church suffer.

I'm sorry that I failed to announce the American Tea. A notice about it (on a scruffy piece of paper) was handed to me AFTER the morning service. I announced it in the evening. These things will happen. Let there be no ill feeling. We all do our best for the good of the church, don't we?

Your sincere friend,
Herbert Evergreen,
Rector

c) Ted Brawny to the Rector

Dear Rector,

I've been thinking. I'll keep on with the club after all. As you know there was none last night and I was that tired I turned in pretty early. But when I'd dropped off I was woke again with singing. It was the mob in the street outside my window. I went down and let them in. We brewed up and had a good talk, like, about everything. They promised to pull together with me and to jump on the yobbish element. Then Gladys said would I be Jeff's best man. 'Blimey!' I says, 'I didn't even know you was going out together.' But they insisted that they'd been to see you and you'd said they mustn't get married just to make things look straight and above board and they agree, like, but said they love each other and would have got married later in any case. I don't mind being a General Factotum as long as they would help a bit, like. I tried to knock that into their thick heads and I think I got it home to a few. It's a great life if you don't weaken! I'll be their Best Man.

See you Sunday,
Ted

John Ward

101 Common Assault

A South African farmer was charged with beating an African convict labourer to death, and found guilty of common assault by the jury, sentence, eighteen months imprisonment.

I killed a man,
And in my dreams
The anger that suffused my brain
Returns to scatter all my peace;
And drunkard shivering madness
Once again claims me.
There at my feet he lies
Shattered battered shell,
His empty hands clawing no more
In mute futility,
But curled in trust with death.
I turn the sudden emptiness that lies there
With my foot.

And lo, his face is black,
And in relief, I laugh with joy.

So did the judge and jury at my trial,
Common assault they called my murder
Counting my guilt in months, not years.
Fed me glib sympathy and gentle lies,
That I should suffer so, for a bad black.
All the long days I dream my innocence away,
But in the night comes agony again:
I dream I face another Judgement court,
From whose decision there is no appeal
Whose sentence is eternity.
Silent the Judge turns, facing me openly,
I scream with horror for His face is black.

Joan Brockelsby

102 The Refrigeration of Silas Hunt

In this story by Mordecai Johnson, President of Howard
University (as told to Donald Robinson), we are shown how the
brotherhood of man depends on our ability to see ourselves as
others see us.

I saw him the moment I entered the dining car that September
day in 1948, a handsome, dark-skinned young man, sitting
alone. He looked miserable.

'May I sit with you?' I said.

'Help yourself,' he muttered. He didn't glance up. I studied the
menu while he stared dejectedly at the table.

'What's wrong, son?' I asked.

Slowly he turned towards me. His eyes widened. 'Why, you're
Dr. Johnson,' he said. 'You don't know me, but I know you. My
name is Silas Hunt, a friend of Lawyer Scipio Jones, of Little
Rock, Arkansas.'

'Well, I'll be blessed,' I exclaimed. 'I'm well acquainted with
the distinguished Mr. Jones, and I'm happy to meet his friend.
Now, tell me, what's the trouble?'

'I'm on my way to the University of Arkansas,' he said. 'I'm the
first Negro ever to be admitted to the law school.'

That didn't seem anything to be despondent about. And I said
so.

'You don't understand. I don't want to go. I don't want to go at
all.'

'Why not?'

'It will be awful. The students are going to cut me dead. They won't talk to me, won't have anything to do with me. They're going to treat me like dirt.'

'Yes' – I had to say it – 'that could well be what will happen to you.'

The boy went glumly on. 'I was all set for a law school in Illinois. Then Mr. Jones got the University of Arkansas to admit a Negro student to the law school for the first time. He wrote me that I had an obligation to my race to go. I suppose he's right.'

He paused and drank a little water. 'Those students are going to plain refrigerate me.'

What could I say to the boy? I knew how right he might be. With every turn of the wheels he became more miserable. And apprehensive. Unfortunately, I couldn't stay with him to the end. I had to change trains. Weeks later a friend told me what happened.

When the train pulled into Fayetteville, where the university is, young Hunt saw a crowd of thirty-odd white students standing on the platform. As he stepped down, they pressed towards him.

Hunt's heart sank. His worst fears rose.

A lanky youth pushed forward right at him. 'Is your name Hunt?' he said.

'Yes, that's my name,' Hunt answered, his forehead wet with perspiration.

The white youth stuck out his hand. 'Welcome to the University of Arkansas,' he said. 'And step over here. I want to introduce you to some of your friends.'

It seems that, the night before, a number of law students had been having a get together. Suddenly one of them blurted out: 'Say, how would you feel if you were the first Negro to enter the University of Arkansas law school? How would you like it?'

They talked it over. They knew that the Negro would expect to be 'refrigerated'. (They actually used the same word that young Hunt had used.) They made up their minds, then and there, to see that Hunt led as normal a life at the University as he would at any law school in the U.S.A. As a first move they decided to meet his train.

'These fellows here are not all of your friends,' the lanky white youth said to Hunt as he made the introductions. 'There are more – many more.'

There were.

C. Astle

COURAGE

103 St. George's Day

This is St. George's Day. And if that has meant anything to you at
all you must have had in your minds for just a moment or so that
old figure of romance, the legendary St. George of England, clad
perhaps in shining armour, galloping forth in the keen morning
air with his gay pennon fluttering in the breeze and a dare-devil
gallantry in his eyes, to challenge any dragon in his path and to
offer battle to any evil thing that he might discover at its vile work
of terrorizing, corrupting, and enslaving human life.

We shall never get the best out of ourselves unless there lingers
still within us something of the spirit of St. George, prompting us
to take risks sometimes, if risks there be, to venture boldly
without counting too closely the cost when truth is at stake, to
have faith enough to do and to dare for the sake of what is right
amidst all the tangles of argument and motive and interest that
confront us in this modern world.

So I have to ask myself whether I can say in sober fact that this
spirit of old romance still lives in the hearts of our English folk.
Let me try at any rate to be fair about it. It would be foolish, for
example, to suppose that chivalry is gone because it does not dress
as St. George used to dress. For all I know there may be a very
gentle and perfect knight living in your own street, but I am
certain that you have never seen him mount his restless charger
just after breakfast and canter gracefully past your door on his way
to the wars. It is much more likely that he is a little man in
spectacles carrying an attaché case and hurrying to catch a train on
the Underground. Times change and fashions with them, but
chivalry still may be the burning motive of a life which to casual
eyes may seem quite dull and commonplace. Nevertheless, if you
knew more of such a life, with its desperate ideals and its almost
incredible foolishness in following them in such an age as this, in
the stubborn fight that it is putting up against enormous odds, in
its patient struggle day by day for the good of others, you might
take off your hat and get the unaccustomed thrill of knowing that
a St. George and nobody less was passing by.

In like manner the dragons of modern life have discarded for
the most part their slimy scales and no longer roar with fiery
breath at any who approach them. On the contrary the evils of
today have a friendly look. Sometimes they fawn upon us like
little lost dogs, and plead with us to be kind to them since they are

quite harmless and very much misjudged. But when we look around us at the chaos that they have made, at the degradation and despair that they have brought to home after home, we recognise them for what they are and see clearly that by voice and pen, by will and resolve, they must be faced and fought to the end.

Fight then if you can, for the sake of others as well as for your own, with something of the high-hearted gallantry, something of the gay abandon, something of the grim tenacity of St. George.

W. H. Elliott

104a Mary Verghese

A very special kind of courage is needed to face illness and suffering but those who have it are an inspiration to sick and healthy alike. One of the bravest was Mary Verghese. Mary was an Indian, a young doctor generally believed to have a very promising career in front of her. Then, one day, suddenly, her car crashed into a milestone and was catapulted down a bank, to lie, a mangled heap of metal, at the bottom. When Mary was rescued her injuries included a fractured back and she was paralysed from the neck down with no hope of walking or moving again. However, Mary's arms were not affected, and neither was her head.

Mary was determined to live as full a life as possible. Her first step was to have three operations to fuse the vertebrae in her spine and make it rigid. This meant that she could sit up and use a wheelchair. Mary was a Christian and believed that God would bring her into full medical work again. She knew, too, that if she could continue she could bring hope and courage as well as skill and medical help to those who were ill.

Mary thought God was leading her to work with leprosy patients. She practised handling instruments in the operating theatre from her wheelchair and eventually she was able to continue her surgical work.

Mary has been in charge of the leprosy ward in Vellore Christian Medical College. She has helped hundreds of patients by her surgery, reconstructing damaged limbs and improving their confidence and their appearance by plastic surgery. Even more important in some ways, however, is the inspiration she has given by having herself overcome such a devastating tragedy and showing such courage and perseverance in the face of her own incurable paralysis.

104b Androcles and the Lion

Androcles was a Greek tailor, living in the days of the Roman empire. He was a Christian, and lived in fear of arrest by the Roman soldiers, for the Emperor was persecuting the Christians. The latest sport, he had heard, was to put them in one of the great arenas and let out captured lions to feed on them. Androcles was a very ordinary, rather timid man, and feared that he would never have the courage to stand up for Jesus or to suffer such a terrible death.

One day, as he travelled about his business in the foothills, he heard a great roar of pain. There, in a clearing in the trees, he saw a great lion trying to pull a huge thorn out of its foot where it was obviously deeply embedded. Androcles' pity for the animal overcame his fear, for he loved all animals, and he walked slowly up to the lion, holding out his hand. When he touched the lion's leg it quickly pulled it away but made no attempt to attack. Encouraged, Androcles grabbed the leg firmly with one hand and with the other reached right down between the pads in its foot and with a sharp tug removed the thorn. The lion roared, stared at Androcles and then stalked off between the trees.

Not long after this incident Androcles was arrested as a Christian. He had the opportunity to give up his religion but refused, in spite of being told that he would be fed to the lions the next day if he remained a Christian. He was taken to the jail near the arena and his guard told him that they had caught some new beasts a few days earlier who had been starved so that they would be suitably hungry for the show next day.

The next afternoon Androcles was taken to the stadium. He knelt on the sand in the centre of the arena, and with the excited murmur of the crowds in his ears he tried to pray. The excitement mounted as the lion was let out. It came rushing at him, snarling. But then, just as Androcles felt his last moment had come, the lion stopped in its tracks. There was a pause as he felt its rough tongue licking him. The crowd was silent with amazement. Androcles opened his eyes and there was this fully grown lion sitting beside him. As he stared the lion raised its paw and at last Androcles understood. It was the lion which he had helped a few days earlier. Androcles put his arms round its neck and wept with relief and gratitude.

The Emperor and the crowd were dumbfounded, but the Emperor was touched when he heard the story. He pardoned Androcles and some stories will tell you he released the lion as well. It was generally agreed that the tailor's courage in helping

the lion in the first place as well as his courage in standing up for
his religion both deserved the reward he received.

An old story made famous by the play by George Bernard Shaw

FREEDOM

105 Mr. Mandragon

Mr. Mandragon, the Millionaire, he wouldn't have wine or wife,
He couldn't endure complexity; he lived the simple life.
He ordered his lunch by megaphone in manly, simple tones,
And used all his motors for canvassing voters, and twenty
    telephones;
Besides a dandy little machine,
Cunning and neat as ever was seen
With a hundred pulleys and cranks between,
Made of metal and kept quite clean,
To hoist him out of his healthful bed on every day of his life,
And wash him and brush him, and shave him and dress him to
    live the Simple Life.

Mr. Mandragon was most refined and quietly, neatly dressed,
Say all the American newspapers that know refinement best;
Neat and quiet the hair and hat, and the coat quiet and neat.
A trouser worn upon either leg, while boots adorn the feet;
And not, as any one might expect,
A Tiger Skin, all striped and flecked,
And a Peacock Hat with the tail erect,
A scarlet tunic with sunflowers decked,
That might have had a more marked effect,
And pleased the pride of a weaker man that yearned for wine or
    wife;
But fame and the flagon, for Mr. Mandragon obscured the Simple
    Life.

Mr. Mandragon, the Millionaire, I am happy to say, is dead;
He enjoyed a quiet funeral in a crematorium shed,
And he lies there fluffy and soft and grey, and certainly quite
    refined,
When he might have rotted to flowers and fruit with Adam and all
    mankind,

Or been eaten by wolves athirst for blood,
Or burnt on a big tall pyre of wood,
In a towering flame, as a heathen should,
Or even sat with us here at food,
Merrily taking twopenny ale and cheese with a pocket-knife;
But these were luxuries not for him who went for the Simple Life.

G. K. Chesterton

106 Four Freedoms

We know that enduring peace cannot be bought at the cost of other people's freedom.

We will not be intimidated by the threats of dictators that they will regard as a breach of international law and as an act of war our aid to the democracies which dare to resist their aggression.

There is nothing mysterious about the foundations of a healthy and strong democracy. The basic things expected by our people of their political and economic systems are simple. They are: equality of opportunity for youth and for others; jobs for those who can work; security for those who need it; the ending of special privilege for the few; the preservation of civil liberties for all; the enjoyment of the fruits of scientific progress in a wider and constantly rising standard of living.

These are the simple and basic things that must never be lost sight of in the turmoil and unbelievable complexity of our modern world. The inner and abiding strength of our economic and political systems is dependent upon the degree to which they fulfil these expectations.

In the future days, which we seek to make secure, we look forward to a world founded upon four essential human freedoms.

The first is freedom of speech and expression – everywhere in the world.

The second is freedom of every person to worship God in his own way – everywhere in the world.

The third is freedom from want – which, translated into world terms, means economic understanding which will secure to every nation a healthy peace time life for its inhabitants – everywhere in the world.

The fourth is freedom from fear – which, translated into world terms, means a world-wide reduction of armaments to such a point and in such a thorough fashion that no nation will be in a position to commit an act of physical aggression against any neighbour – anywhere in the world.

This is no vision of a distant millennium. It is a definite basis for a kind of world attainable in our time and generation.

Franklin D. Roosevelt, 'Four Freedoms' Speech, 1941

107 Freedom and My Neighbour

There is a freedom that man fears
The freedom of his fellow man
In the eye of the tyrant
In the eye of the oppressed
In the eye of the neighbour
Who makes his fence too high – or low;
In the eye of the traveller in the tube
Who, like him, eyes the seat he makes for,
There is a freedom that threatens
That disturbs the freedom he has carved out for himself.
So we live
Shut in by fences, regulations, gates.
Apartheid in a thousand forms
Secures us from the freedom of the world
To invade and to destroy
Our liberty of isolation.

For freedom we build our walls,
For freedom we make our bombs,
For freedom we pass our laws,
For freedom we imprison and restrict,
For freedom we create the Ghetto.
And we shall meet no one,
And speak to no one,
And listen to no one
Who does not look as we do,
Think as we do,
Act as we do,
Except at a safe and deferential distance.

Christ came to make men free
Free from their isolation and their fear.
He came –
Homeless – and so at home among all;
In poverty – and so the guest of all;
In weakness – and so at the mercy of all;

Common – and so approachable by all;
A man with time for all,
A man for others.
Jesus, Son of Man.
He was in the world
And nothing came between him and the world,
So that men might be one with him
And one with each other.

Jim Bates

108 Freedom

Pleasure is a freedom-song,
But it is not freedom.
It is the blossoming of your desires,
But it is not their fruit.
It is a depth calling unto a height,
But it is not the deep nor the high.
It is the caged taking wing,
But it is not space encompassed.
Ay, in very truth, pleasure is a freedom-song.
And I fain would have you sing it with fullness of heart; yet I
    would not have you lose your hearts in the singing.

Some of your youth seek pleasure as if it were all, and they are
    judged and rebuked.
I would not judge nor rebuke them. I would have them seek.
For they shall find pleasure, but not her alone;
Seven are her sisters, and the least of them is more beautiful than
    pleasure.
Have you not heard of the man who was digging in the earth for
    roots and found a treasure?

Kahlil Gibran, **The Prophet**

HAPPINESS

109 How to be Happy

There are various ways of being happy, and every man has the
capacity to make his life what it needs to be for him to have a
reasonable amount of peace in it. Why then do we persecute

ourselves with illusory demands, never content until we feel we have conformed to some standard of happiness that is not good for us only, but for *everyone*? Why can we not be content with the secret gifts of the happiness that God offers us, without consulting the rest of the world? Why do we insist, rather, on a happiness that is approved by the magazines and TV? Perhaps because we do not believe in a happiness that is given to us for nothing. We do not think we can be happy with a happiness that has no price tag on it.

If we are fools enough to remain at the mercy of the people who want to sell us happiness, it will be impossible for us ever to be content with anything. How would they profit if we became content? We would no longer need their new product.

The last thing the salesman wants is for the buyer to become content. You are of no use in our affluent society unless you are always just about to grasp what you never have.

Thomas Merton, **Conjectures of a Guilty Bystander**

110 Happiness and Vision

William Blake, who wrote this, was an artist, a mystic and a poet.

I feel that a man may be happy in this world and I know that this world is a world of imagination and vision. I see everything I paint in this world but everybody does not see alike. To the eye of a miser a guinea is far more beautiful than the sun and a bag worn with the use of money has more beautiful proportions than a vine filled with grapes. The tree which moves some to tears of joy is in the eyes of others only a green thing which stands in the way. As a man is, so he sees.

When the sun rises, do you not see a round disk of fire something like a gold piece? O no, no, I see an innumerable company of the Heavenly host crying 'Holy, Holy, Holy, is the Lord God Almighty.' I do not question my bodily eye any more than I would question a window concerning sight. I look through it and not with it.

William Blake

111 Canoe Story

We went in a long canoe, two of us.
He sat in the front, one of us.

I sat in the back, one of us.
We went in a long canoe, two of us.

Water whispered, 'I'm cool, ever so.'
Sun sang, 'I'm hot, hot.'
Breeze sighed, 'I'm not.'
Paddle said, 'Heave ho, ever so.'

He sat, his back to me, and paddled.
I sat, looked at his back, and dandled
My paddle on my knees, and dabbled
My hands, while he talked and babbled
And pushed and paddled and paddled, and paddled.

And paddled. And sweated. And puffed.
I was cool as the water.
He was hot as the sun.
He puffed, heave ho. I sighed, just so.

Sweating and puffing, he turned
And saw my paddle, at rest, on the floor, all alone,
My paddle, dry as a bone.
And he burst. He might have cursed.

He might have cursed, but I grabbed my paddle,
And I paddled and pushed, and poked and thrust,
And we skimmed, bubble-brimmed, across the lake,
While he sat and relaxed and cooled in the breeze.

And I gasped, 'It's hot.'
He smiled, 'I'm not.'
And I said, 'You look cool, ever so.'
And he turned and smiled, 'Heave ho, just so.'

Geoffrey Summerfield

112 On a Bicycle

Under the dawn I wake my two-wheel friend.
Shouting in bed my mother says to me,
'Mind you don't clatter it going downstairs!'
I walk him down he springing step to step;
those tyres he has, if you pat him flat-handed
he'll bounce your hand. I mount with an air

and as light a pair of legs as you'll encounter,
slow into Sunday ride out of the gates,
roll along asphalt, press down on the pedals,
speeding,   fearless,
   ring,
     ring,
       ring . . . .
Flinging along my happiness my fever,
incapable of breaking out of it,
overtaking the lorries on the road
taking each of them in a single swoop
flying behind them through cut open space
hanging on them uphill. Yes I know.
It's dangerous. I enjoy it. They hoot
and lean out and yell out,
'We'll give you a hand on the hills;
give you some speed; after that
you tear along on your own.'
Careering full tilt, pelting along
in a flurry of jokes. Turn a blind eye
to my crazy career; it's the fashion.
You can't tell me how terribly I ride.
One day I'll learn how to ride.
And I spring down at a deserted
ancient lodge by the roadside;
in dim forest light I break lilac,
twine it with ivy on to the handle-bars.
Flying on, flying,
sticking my face down into dark blossom,
get into the city not quite worn out.
I put my bunch of lilac into water,
set the alarm to go at eight o'clock,
sit at the table
   write
     these lines.

Yevgeny Yevtushenko

113 Solitary Delights

What a delight it is
When on the bamboo matting
In my grass-thatched hut,

All on my own,
I make myself at ease.

What a delight it is
When, borrowing
Rare writings from a friend,
I open out
The first sheet.

What a delight it is
When, spreading paper,
I take my brush
And find my hand
Better than I thought.

What a delight it is
When, after a hundred days
Of racking my brains,
That verse that wouldn't come
Suddenly turns out well.

What a delight it is
When, of a morning,
I get up and go out
To find in full bloom a flower
That yesterday was not there.

What a delight it is
When, skimming through the pages
Of a book, I discover
A man written of there
Who is just like me.

What a delight it is
When everyone admits
It's a very difficult book,
And I understand it
With no trouble at all.

What a delight it is
When I blow away the ash,
To watch the crimson
Of the glowing fire
And hear the water boil.

What a delight it is
When a guest you cannot stand
Arrives, then says to you
'I'm afraid I can't stay long,'
And soon goes home.

What a delight it is
When I find a good brush,
Steep it hard in water,
Lick it on my tongue
And give it its first try.

Tachibana Akemi, nineteenth-century Japanese poet

114 Boasting Song

Peter	I can swim like a trout!
Paul	I can climb up the tallest tree!
Peter	When I really strike out,
	Even fish envy me!
Paul	Now I'll tell the truth of it,
	If you'll tell with me.
Peter	I swim with water wings.
Paul	Heights make me dizzy.
Peter	I can play the guitar!
Paul	I'm a champion at wrestling!
Peter	Let's fight then, let's spar.
Paul	No, you play and sing.
Peter	Now why don't you tell the truth?
Paul	If you do, I might.
Peter	I've bought a book of chords.
Paul	I've seen one fight.
Peter	All the girls fall for me,
	For my charm and my carefree smile!
Paul	And they're not slow to see
	That I dress with style!
Peter	Perhaps we should look for two?
Paul	No need to rush.
	I'm scared to speak to them.
Peter	I always blush.

Paul   So we'll lie on the beach,
            Let the sand trickle through our toes,
Peter   And each one tell to each
            What no one else knows:
Paul   Our fears and our fantasies,
Peter   All ten feet tall.
Together   Take them with salt, or don't
            Take them at all!

Margaret Rose

115 The Saratoga

The problem was an acute one. It all happened at Parattah
Junction in Tasmania. I was travelling on the south-bound
express. Having enjoyed a good dinner in the refreshment rooms,
I discovered that I still had five minutes before the train resumed
its journey.

At that very moment, the north-bound express arrived. How
better could I spend my spare five minutes than by strolling along
the platform on the chance of meeting somebody I knew? And,
surely enough, beside one of the central carriages, I caught sight
of a young lady, a minister's daughter, at whose home I had often
been a guest.

I saw at a glance that she was in dire distress.

'Why, Effie!' I exclaimed. 'What's wrong?'

'Oh, I'm in serious trouble,' she replied. 'I've lost my Saratoga!'

'That's dreadful,' I assented sympathetically. 'But look, *you*
take the front part of the train, and *I'll* take the back, and we'll
meet again here in a minute or two!'

I hurried along the carriages that I had assigned to myself,
looking high and low for the elusive Saratoga. I sincerely hoped
that Effie would find it in that portion of the train that I had
allotted to her, for I had to confess to myself that I felt seriously
handicapped in my own search by the lamentable circumstance
that I had no shadow of an idea as to what a Saratoga was!

It sounded as if it might be a special breed of dog, and I poked
with my stick among the bags and boxes, hoping that, with a
frightened yelp, the little beast would dash out at me. But then
again, it might be an article of jewellery, and, for that reason, I
scrutinized the asphalt of the platform and the floors of the
carriages in the frantic hope that I might detect a sudden glitter.

But then, I reminded myself, a Saratoga might conceivably be
some mysterious part of a lady's wearing apparel, and it was

because of this possibility that, fearing to embarrass her, I had refrained from asking Effie for exact particulars of the missing treasure.

At any rate, I searched my half of the train as closely as my limited time would allow, and, on returning to our appointed rendezvous, was delighted to find Effie with her face beaming and the precious Saratoga at her feet. How was I to know that a Saratoga was a species of suitcase? I congratulated her, waved her a hurried goodbye, and caught my own train by the skin of my teeth.

But, to my dying day, I shall never forget the sensation of searching eagerly for a thing without possessing the faintest clue as to what that thing could be.

My experience that day resembles the universal search for happiness. If asked what they were seeking, nine people out of ten – perhaps ninety-nine out of a hundred – would reply that they were seeking happiness. Do they know what they are looking for? Would they recognize it if they saw it? Or is their passionate quest like my own wild pursuit of the Saratoga? . . . .

F. W. Boreham

USE OF TIME

116 Use of Time

All men complain that they haven't enough time. It's because they look at their lives from too human a point of view. There's always time to do what God wants us to do, but we must put ourselves completely into each moment that he offers us.

Be most careful then how you conduct yourselves: like sensible men, not like simpletons. Use the present opportunity to the full, for these are evil days. So do not be fools, but try to understand what the will of the Lord is (Eph. 5, 15–17).

I went out, Lord.
Men were coming out.
They were coming and going,
Walking and running.
Everything was rushing, cars, lorries, the street, the whole town.
Men were rushing not to waste time.

They were rushing after time,
To catch up with time,
To gain time.

Goodbye, sir, excuse me, I haven't time.
I'll come back, I can't wait, I haven't time.
I must end this letter – I haven't time.
I'd love to help you, but I haven't time.
I can't accept, having no time.
I can't think, I can't read, I'm swamped, I haven't time.
I'd like to pray, but I haven't time.

You understand, Lord, they simply haven't the time.
The child is playing, he hasn't time right now . . . Later on . . .
The schoolboy has his homework to do, he hasn't time . . . Later
    on . . .
The student has his courses, and so much work, he hasn't
    time . . . Later on . . .
The young man is at his sports, he hasn't time . . . Later on . . .
The young married man has his new house, he has to fix it up, he
    hasn't time . . . Later on . . .
The grandparents have their grandchildren, they haven't
    time . . . Later on . . .
They are ill, they have their treatments, they haven't
    time . . . Later on . . .
They are dying, they have no . . .
Too late! . . . They have no more time!

And so all men run after time, Lord.
They pass through life running – hurried, jostled, overburdened,
    frantic, and they never get there. They haven't time.
In spite of all their efforts they're still short of time, of a great deal
    of time.
Lord, you must have made a mistake in your calculations.
There is a big mistake somewhere.
The hours are too short,
The days are too short,
Our lives are too short.

You who are beyond time, Lord, you smile to see us fighting it.
And you know what you are doing.
You make no mistakes in your distribution of time to men.
You give each one time to do what you want him to do.

But we must not lose time
>> waste time,
>> kill time,
For time is a gift that you give us,
But a perishable gift,
A gift that does not keep.

Lord, we have time,
We have plenty of time,
All the time that you give us,
The years of our lives,
The days of our years,
The hours of our days,
They are all ours.
Ours to fill quietly, calmly,
But to fill completely, up to the brim . . .

Michel Quoist: **Prayers of Life**

117 Headington Hill

I was going up Headington Hill on the top of a bus. Without
words and (I think) almost without images, a fact about myself was
somehow presented to me. I became aware that I was holding
something at bay, or shutting something out. Or, if you like, that
I was wearing some stiff clothing, like corsets, or even a suit of
armour, as if I were a lobster. I felt myself being, there and then,
given a free choice. I could open the door or keep it shut; I could
unbuckle the armour or keep it on. Neither choice was presented
as a duty; no threat or promise was attached to either, though I
knew that to open the door or to take off the corslet meant the
incalculable. The choice appeared to be momentous but it was also
strangely unemotional. I was moved by no desire or fears. In a
sense I was not moved by anything. I chose to open. Then came
the repercussion on the imaginative level. I felt as if I were a man
of snow at long last beginning to melt.

C. S. Lewis, from **Surprised by Joy**

118 Born for this Moment

During the two years just before and after I was twenty I had two
experiences which led to religious conversion. The first occurred

when I was waiting at a bus stop on a wet afternoon. It was opposite the Odeon cinema, outside the station, and I was surrounded by people, shops, cars. A friend was with me. All of a sudden, for no apparent reason, everything looked different. Everything I could see shone, vibrated, throbbed with joy and with meaning. I knew that it had done this all along, and would go on doing it, but that usually I couldn't see it. It was all over in a minute or two. I climbed on the bus, saying nothing to my friend – it seemed impossible to explain – and sat stunned with astonishment and happiness.

The second experience occurred some months later. I left my office at lunch-time, stopped at a small Greek café in Fleet Street to buy some rolls and fruit, and walked up Chancery Lane. It was an August day, quite warm but cloudy, with the sun glaringly, painfully bright, behind the clouds. I had a strong sense that something was about to happen. I sat on a seat in the garden of Lincoln's Inn waiting for whatever it was to occur. The sun behind the clouds grew brighter and brighter, the clouds assumed a shape which fascinated me, and between one moment and the next, although no word had been uttered, I felt myself spoken to. I was aware of being regarded by love, of being wholly accepted, accused, forgiven, all at once. The joy of it was the greatest I had ever known in my life. I felt I had been born for this moment and had marked time till it occurred.

Monica Furlong, **Travelling In**

USE OF TALENTS

119 Work is Love

Work is love made visible.
And if you cannot work with love but only with distaste, it is better that you should leave your work and sit at the gate of the temple and take alms of those who work with joy.

For if you bake bread with indifference, you bake a bitter bread that feeds but half man's hunger.

And if you grudge the crushing of the grapes, your grudge distils a poison in the wine.

And if you sing though as angels, and love not the singing, you muffle man's ears to the voices of the night.

Kahlil Gibran, **The Prophet**

120 Digging

Between my finger and my thumb
The squat pen rests; snug as a gun.
Under my window, a clean rasping sound
When the spade sinks into gravelly ground:
My father, digging. I look down

Till his straining rump among the flowerbeds
Bends low, comes up twenty years away
Stooping in rhythm through potato drills
Where he was digging.

The coarse boot nestled on the lug, the shaft
Against the inside knee was levered firmly.
He rooted out tall tops, buried the bright edge deep
To scatter new potatoes that we picked
Loving their cool hardness in our hands.

By God, the old man could handle a spade.
Just like his old man.

My grandfather cut more turf in a day
Than any other man on Toner's bog.
Once I carried him milk in a bottle
Corked sloppily with paper. He straightened up
To drink it, then fell to right away
Nicking and slicing neatly, heaving sods
Over his shoulder, going down and down
For the good turf. Digging.

The cold smell of potato mould, the squelch and slap
Of soggy peat, the curt cuts of an edge
Through living roots awaken in my head.
But I've no spade to follow men like them.

Between my finger and my thumb
The squat pen rests.
I'll dig with it.

Seamus Heaney

121 Washing Dishes

A disciple of Rabbi Schmelke's begged his master to teach him how to prepare his soul for the service of God. The master told him to go to Rabbi Abraham, who at that time was still an innkeeper. The disciple did as he was bidden and lived in the inn for several weeks without observing any vestige of holiness in the innkeeper who from morning prayer till night devoted himself to his business. Finally he asked him what he did all day. 'My most important occupation,' said Rabbi Abraham, 'is to clean the dishes properly, so that not the slightest trace of food is left, and to clean and dry the pots and pans, so that they do not rust.' When the disciple returned home and reported to Rabbi Schmelke what he had seen and heard, the rabbi said to him: 'Now you know the answer to what you asked me.'

Martin Buber (trans.), **Tales of the Hasidim**

122 We are Transmitters

As we live, we are transmitters of life.
And when we fail to transmit life, life fails to flow through us.

And if, as we work, we can transmit life into our work life, still
    more life, rushes into us to compensate, to be ready
    and we ripple with life through the days.

Even if it is a woman making an apple dumpling, or a man a stool,
if life goes into the pudding, good is the pudding, good is the
    stool,
content is the woman, with fresh life rippling into her, content is
    the man.

Give, and it shall be given unto you
is still the truth about life.
But giving life is not so easy.
It doesn't mean handing it out to some mean fool, or letting the
    living-dead eat you up.
It means kindling the life-quality where it was not,
even if it's only in the whiteness of a washed pocket handkerchief.

D. H. Lawrence

123 The Minstrel

There was once a minstrel who entertained the lords and ladies with his music and with his dancing and tumbling. He became rich and successful but nowhere could he find true happiness and peace of mind. He gave up all his wealth and became a monk, but he could not read or write or even concentrate on prayer in the same way as other monks. He felt a failure, and became more and more miserable.

Then one day in the crypt of the great church as he gazed at the statue of Mary over the altar he seemed to find some comfort, and standing up he offered his skill as his tribute to God. Faster and faster he leapt and tumbled, somersaulting and twisting backwards and forwards. He felt his old skill returning and danced on till he fell to the floor, exhausted but at peace.

After this the tumbler used to go each day to the crypt, and soon the other monks became curious. One followed him and looked on as he tumbled and danced. He reported what he saw to the abbot who himself went to the crypt the next day and unobserved watched the tumbler. He began by bowing to the altar and asking God to accept his service as the only contribution he could make. He danced until he was exhausted and then the abbot and the monk saw a miracle. The crypt glowed with light and Our Lady appeared to fan and soothe the tumbler, leaving him with the Sign of the Cross.

Several times more the abbot saw the minstrel in the crypt and then he summoned him to him. The minstrel suspected that his secret had been discovered and was in despair, afraid that he would be asked to leave the monastery. The abbot made him explain how he served God and the minstrel reluctantly told the story, although he knew nothing of the miracle. He did know, however, that after his performance he felt peace of mind and contentment.

When he had finished, the abbot raised him from his knees and embraced him, telling him that his service was clearly pleasing to God. After this the tumbler continued his daily service, no longer secretly but openly and with joy. He lived there for many years venerated and respected and legend has it that when he died Our Lady appeared to take his soul to heaven,

And, through the ages, men have quoted this legend to show that every talent can be used to the Glory of God.

Joan Hasler

VALUES

124 Yugoslav Father to Son

During the tragic years of war, a Yugoslav father wrote this letter to his unborn child.

My child, sleeping now in the dark and gathering strength for the struggle of birth, I wish you well. At present you have no proper shape, and you do not breathe, and you are blind. Yet, when your time comes, your time and the time of your mother, whom I deeply love, there will be something in you that will give you power to fight for air and light. Such is your heritage, such is your destiny as a child born of woman – to fight for light and hold on without knowing why.

May the flame that tempers the bright steel of your youth never die, but burn always; so that when your work is done and your long day ended, you may still be like a watchman's fire at the end of a lonely road, loved and cherished for your gracious glow by all good wayfarers who need light in their darkness and warmth for their comfort.

The spirit of wonder and adventure, the token of immortality, will be given to you as a child. May you keep it for ever, with that in your heart which always seeks the gold beyond the rainbow, the pastures beyond the desert, the dawn beyond the sea, the light beyond the dark.

May you seek always and strive always in good faith and high courage, in this world where men grow so tired.

Keep your capacity for faith and belief – but let your judgement watch what you believe.

Keep your power to receive everything – only learn to select what your instinct tells you is right.

Keep your love of life, but throw away your fear of death. Life must be loved or it is lost, but it should never be loved too well.

Keep your delight in friendship – only learn to know your friends.

Keep your intolerance – only save it for what your heart tells you is bad.

Keep your wonder at great and noble things like sunlight and thunder, the rain and the stars, the wind and the sea, the growth of trees and the return of harvests, and the greatness of heroes.

Keep your heart hungry for new knowledge; keep your hatred of a lie; and keep your power of indignation.

Now I know I must die, and you must be born to stand upon the rubbish heap of my errors. Forgive me for this. I am ashamed to leave you an untidy, uncomfortable world. But so it must be. In thought, as a last benediction, I kiss your forehead. Good-night to you – and good morning and a clear dawn.

Passed to Rita Snowden by Sir Carl Berendsen, quoted in
Worship and Wonder

125 Go Placidly

Go placidly amid the noise and haste, and remember what peace there may be in silence. As far as possible without surrender be on good terms with all persons. Speak your truth quietly and clearly; and listen to others, even the dull and ignorant, they too have their story.

Avoid loud and aggressive persons, they are vexations to the spirit. If you compare yourself with others you may become vain and bitter, for always there will be greater and lesser persons than yourself. Enjoy your achievements as well as your plans. Keep interested in your own career, however humble; it is a real possession in the changing fortunes of time. Exercise caution in your business affairs, for the world is full of trickery. But let this not blind you to what virtue there is; many persons strive for high ideals and everwhere life is full of heroism.

Be yourself. Especially, do not feign affection. Neither be cynical about love for, in the face of all aridity and disenchantment, it is perennial as the grass. Take kindly the counsel of the years, gracefully surrendering the things of youth. Nurture strength of spirit to shield you in sudden misfortune. But do not distress yourself with imaginings. Many fears are born of fatigue and loneliness. Beyond a wholesome discipline, be gentle with yourself.

You are a child of the universe, no less than the trees and the stars; you have a right to be here. And whether or not it is clear to you, no doubt the universe is unfolding as it should. Therefore be at peace with God, whatever you conceive Him to be, and whatever your labours and aspirations, in the noisy confusion of life keep peace with your soul. With all its sham, drudgery and broken dreams, it is still a beautiful world. Be careful. Strive to be happy.

Anon. (found in old Saint Paul's Church, Baltimore: dated 1692)

126 Life

Life is now
This moment,
What I can see, hear, feel,
Now
Here.

In me and around me
With what I have,
With things just as they are –
Now.

Ken Walsh

127 Good and Evil

And one of the elders of the city said, Speak to us of Good and
    Evil.
And he answered:
Of the good in you I can speak, but not of the evil.
For what is evil but good tortured by its own hunger and thirst?
Verily when good is hungry it seeks food even in dark caves,
    and when it thirsts it drinks even of dead waters.

You are good when you are one with yourself.
Yet when you are not one with yourself you are not evil.
For a divided house is not a den of thieves; it is only a divided
    house.
And a ship without a rudder may wander aimlessly among
    perilous isles yet sink not to the bottom.
You are good when you strive to give of yourself.
Yet you are not evil when you seek gain for yourself.

For when you strive for gain you are but a root that clings to the
    earth and sucks at her breast.
Surely the fruit cannot say to the root, 'Be like me, ripe and full
    and ever giving of your abundance.'
For to the fruit giving is a need, as receiving is a need to the root.

You are good when you are fully awake in your speech.
Yet you are not evil when you sleep while your tongue staggers
    without purpose.
And even stumbling speech may strengthen a weak tongue.

You are good when you walk to your goal firmly and with bold
   steps.
Yet you are not evil when you go thither limping.
Even those who limp go not backward.
But you who are strong and swift, see that you do not limp before
   the lame, deeming it kindness.

You are good in countless ways, and you are not evil when you are
   not good,
You are only loitering and sluggard.
Pity that the stags cannot teach swiftness to the turtles.

In your longing for your giant self lies your goodness: and that
   longing is in all of you.
But in some of you that longing is a torrent rushing with might to
   the sea, carrying the secrets of the hillsides and the songs of the
   forest.
And in others it is a flat stream that loses itself in angles and bends
   and lingers before it reaches the shore.
But let not him who longs much say to him who longs little,
'Wherefore are you slow and halting?'
For the truly good ask not the naked, 'Where is your garment?'
   nor the houseless, 'What has befallen your house?'

Kahlil Gibran

128 Green Blackboards

The school is up-to-date.
Proudly, the principal tells of all the improvements.
The finest discovery, Lord, is the green blackboard.
The scientists have studied long, they have made experiments;
We know now that green is the ideal colour, that it doesn't tire the
   eyes, that it is quieting and relaxing.
It has occurred to me, Lord, that you didn't wait so long to paint
   the trees and the meadows green.
Your research laboratories were efficient, and in order not to tire
   us, you perfected a number of shades of green for your modern
   meadows.
And so the 'finds' of men consist in discovering what you have
   known from time immemorial.
Thank you, Lord, for being the good Father who gives his
   children the joy of discovering by themselves the treasures of his
   intelligence and love,

But keep us from believing that – by ourselves – we have invented
   anything at all.

Michel Quoist

129 Blind Men and the Elephant

Once upon a time the prince of an Indian city asked the wise men
to tell him about the gods and the purpose of life. One man told
him one thing, another something else. They quarrelled among
themselves and attacked each other in front of the prince who was
thoroughly confused and angered.

Finally the prince called on all the blind men in the city to come
to the market place. Then he had an elephant brought from a
distant city. Such an animal had never been seen before. The
prince told each blind man to feel the animal and report what he
found, to himself and to the wise men. Each man in turn went to
the elephant and came back to describe it.

The first felt its head and thought it like a pot; the second, who
had taken its ear, contradicted him, saying it was like a fan. The
one who felt the tusk thought it a plough handle, the trunk was
compared to a snake, its feet to pillars, its back to a barn, its tail to
a rope and the tuft on the end of its tail to a feather duster. As
each man heard the others' reports they began to contradict each
other and to squabble. Each thought he was right and the others
wrong. Tempers rose and soon fighting broke out.

The wise men were amused by all this, but the next day the
prince called them together. He told them that they had done just
the same as the blind men when he asked them about the gods.
Each had taken a narrow view and not tried to understand anyone
else's view. Ideas, he said, had to be looked at all over and from
every angle if they were to be understood.

A Buddhist story

130 The Madman's Will

In a work-house ward that was cold and bare,
   The doctor sat on a creaking chair,
By the side of a dying madman's bed.
   'He can't last much longer,' the doctor said.
But nobody cares if a pauper lives,
   And nobody cares when a pauper's dead.

The old man sighed, the doctor rose,
   And bent his head o'er the ricketty bed,
To catch the weak words one by one –
   To smile – as the dying madman said:
'Beneath my pillow when I am gone –
   Search – hidden there you will find it still!'
'Find what, old madman?' the doctor asked,
   And the old man said, as he died, 'My WILL.'
How they all laughed at the splendid jest –
   A pauper madman to leave a will.
And they straightened him out for his final rest,
   In the lonely graveyard over the hill,
And the doctor searched for the paper and found
   The red-taped parchment – untied it with zest,
While the others laughingly gathered round
   To hear the cream of the madman's jest.
Then the doctor with mocking solemnity said,
   'Silence, my friends,' and the will he read.
'I leave to the children the green fields,
   The fresh country lanes for their play,
The stories of fairies and dragons,
   The sweet smell of heather and hay.
I leave to young maidens romantic
   The dreaming which all maidens do,
And the wish that some day in the future
   Their happiest dreams will come true.
To youth I leave all youth's ambition,
   Desire, love, impetuous hate.
And to youth with years I leave wisdom,
   And the hope that it comes not too late.
I leave to old people sweet memories,
   And smiles that endure to the last,
With never a fear for the future,
   And not a regret for the past.
I die without earthly possessions,
   Without the last word of a friend,
To you all I leave good cheer and friendship
   That lasts through all time to the end.
I leave to the wide world my blessing
   In the hope that the long years will find
That my wishes shall grow like a flower
   And bring God's good peace to mankind.'
The ward doctor laid down the parchment,
   His smile had gone, turned into pain.

The faces around laughed no longer,
  But grew grave with regret that was vain.
'No wonder that he looks so happy,
  While we who derided are sad,
For the things he has left are the best things in life –
  I wonder if he *was* mad?'

Music-hall monologue of 1925

131 People Matter

We must concern ourselves with getting not the most out of
people, but the best. We must rethink our plans for industry and
housing with an eye to the kind of life and atmosphere people
would find in them rather than to planning efficiency. We must
care about people being happy in their job rather than adjusted or
conditioned to it; we must think of machines as just extensions of
men, rather than their owners. Now there's plenty of evidence that
this is what man as a whole is demanding. He may do it noisily, in
marches or protest, or quietly, by turning his back on it, as the
Flower People do. He can run away into the private world of drugs,
or he can live at secondhand through mass communications . . .

We have reached an extraordinary degree of mastery over things
at the very moment when we are least able to get on terms with
human beings – 'You can control,' said an Indian, 'half a million
horsepower, but you can't keep your temper.'

What we must do is to recognise that people and our
relationships with them matter more than our ability to handle
things. It is really more important, for instance to be on terms of
understanding with one's children than to maintain one's car at
the peak of condition; it is more important to respect people's
right to be themselves than it is to manipulate them into being
something different.

Stephen Hopkinson, 'More from 10 to 8' on Radio 4

132 Just for Today

Just for today, I will try to live through this day only and not
tackle my whole life problem at once. I can do something for
twelve hours which would appal me if I felt that I had to keep it
up for a lifetime.

Just for today I will be happy. Most folks are as happy as they
make up their minds to be.

Just for today, I will adjust myself to what is, and not try to adjust everything to my own desires. I will take my luck as it comes and fit myself to it.

Just for today, I will try to strengthen my mind. I will study, I will learn something useful, I will not be a mental loafer, I will read something that requires effort, thought and concentration.

Just for today, I will exercise my soul in three ways: I will do somebody a good turn and not get found out; if anybody knows of it, it will not count. I will do at least two things I don't want to do, just for exercise. I will not show anyone that my feelings are hurt. They may be hurt, but today I will not show it.

Just for today, I will be agreeable, I will look as well as I can, dress becomingly, talk low, act courteously, criticize not one bit, not find fault with anything and not try to improve or regulate anybody except myself.

Just for today I will have a programme. I may not follow it exactly but I will have it. I will save myself from two pests: hurry and indecision.

Just for today I will have a quiet half hour all by myself and relax. During this half hour, sometime, I will try to get a better perspective of my life.

Just for today I will be unafraid. Especially I will not be afraid to enjoy what is beautiful and to believe that as I give to the world so the world will give to me.

From the L. P. **Just for today**, *VE–R297264–8, Pye records for Victor Maddern Enterprises Ltd*

133 Modern Affirmations of Faith and Hope

(a) We believe in one *World* – full of riches meant for everyone to enjoy, and one race, the family of mankind, learning to live together by way of common enterprise, mutual esteem, and sacrificial care.

We believe in one *Life* – exciting and positive, which enjoys all beauty, integrity, and science, uses the discipline of work to enrich society, harmonises with the life of Jesus, and perfects body, mind, and spirit.

We believe in one *Morality* – love, which means sharing, sharing the joys and sorrows of others, bringing people together as true friends, working to overcome the causes of poverty, injustice, ignorance, fear, and loneliness – love, which is partially seen in the care of our friends and families, generously portrayed in the lives of the saints, and supremely revealed in our Lord.

We believe in one *God* – witnessed to in the Bible and experienced in many cultures, revealed simply and unforgettably in the life and victorious death of Jesus, and present with us still as the spirit of forgiveness, compassion, renewal, and hope.

We believe in one *Consummation* – the final defeat of sin and disease through a constructive revolution in society, individuals, and nations, and the uniting of all things in Christ.

Based on a form used at St Paul's Cathedral, Calcutta, 1970

(b) We believe that there is hunger,
war,
oppression,
tyranny,
hatred.
We believe that there can be plenty,
peace,
equality,
freedom,
love.
We believe that there is doubt, despair, hatred.
We believe that there can be faith, hope, love – if we do
   something.
We resolve to do something, to try
TO MAKE LOVE
TO MAKE HOPE
TO MAKE BELIEVE

Adapted from a form used at an ecumenical student conference of the
University of California, Berkeley

5 PEOPLE AND GOD

Assemblies

RELIGION

a) Thy kingdom come! On bended knee
   Reading **134**: *The Meaning of Religion*, Mahatma Gandhi
   Prayers **54, 63, 82** and **94**

b) Fill thou my life, O Lord my God
   Reading **135**: *Religion*, Kahlil Gibran
   Prayers **71** and **95**

c) Father hear the prayer we offer
   Reading **142**: *The Story of My Heart*, Richard Jefferies
   Prayers **83** and **95**

WORSHIP

a) We ask that we live and we labour in peace
   Reading **136**: *Worship*, Joan Hasler
   Prayers **68, 94** and **101**

b) Immortal, invisible, God only wise
   Reading **137**: *God as Light*, Joan Hasler
   Prayers **97, 98** and **99**

c) Immortal, invisible, God only wise
   Readings **138**: *The Invisible Spirit*, Chandogya
      Upanishad; and **140**: *Spirit in All Things*,
      Mundaka Upanishad
   Prayers **68, 99** and **100**

d) Come down, O love divine
   Reading **139**: *The Search for the Spirit*, Chandogya
      Upanishad
   Prayers **68, 75, 83** and **94**

e) Morning has broken
   Reading **142**: *The Story of My Heart*, Richard Jefferies; see

also **24**: *Autumn*, Forrest Reid; and **25**: *God's Grandeur*,
Gerard Manley Hopkins
Prayers **9**, **11**, **100** and **101**

f) Give me joy in my heart, keep me praising, *or* O praise ye
the Lord
Readings **143**: *The Winthrop Woman*, Anya Seton; and **144**:
The Ganges at Night, Svetlana Alliluyeva
Prayers **4**, **11**, **12** and **101**

g) Fill thou my life, O Lord my God
Reading **141**: *Vision of God*, Baba Kuhi of Shiraz
Prayers **71**, **86**, **96** and **100**

PARABLES OF JESUS

a) O Jesus I have promised
Mark 4, 3–9: reading **145**: *The Seed*, Rex Chapman

b) Lord thy word abideth
Luke 14, 16–24: reading **146**: *One Big Party*, Rex
Chapman

c) Fight the good fight with all your might
Luke 18, 1–8: reading **147**: *The Unjust Judge and the Ideal
Man*, Rex Chapman

d) I danced in the morning
Matthew 11, 16–19: reading **148**: *The Lord of the Dance*,
Rex Chapman

MIRACLES OF JESUS

a) When in His own image
Mark 2, 3–12: reading **149**: *Which Way to Go?*, Rex
Chapman

b) Fill thou my life, O Lord my God
Mark 5, 1–3 and 9–20: reading **150**: *Legion and Those
Pigs*, Rex Chapman

c) God's spirit is in my heart
Mark 7, 31–37: reading **151**: *Inner Loneliness*, Rex
Chapman

THE COMMANDMENTS

a)   Lord of all hopefulness, Lord of all joy
     Readings: Exodus 20, 20–21; Mark 12, 30–31 and **152**:
        Thou Shalt Nots of Missionaries, Joy Davidman
     Prayers **61**, **67** and **95**

b)   Praise my soul the King of heaven/Lead us heavenly
        father, lead us/At the name of Jesus
     Reading **153**: *What Shape is an Idol?*, Joy Davidman
     Prayers **66**, **69**, **75** and **96**

c)   Morning has broken
     Reading **154**: *The Martian Student*, Joy Davidman
     Prayers **71**, **81** and **85**

d)   Sing we of the modern city
     Reading **91**: *Coping with Grandpa*, Joy Davidman
     Prayers **65**, **71** and **76**

e)   Blest are the pure in heart
     Reading **155**: *The Genies of Today*, Joy Davidman
     Prayers **4**, **65** and **83**

Prayers

94 We worship and adore the framer and former of the universe; governor, disposer, keeper; Him on whom all things depend; mind and spirit of the world; from whom all things spring; by whose spirit we live; the divine spirit diffused through all; God all-powerful; God always present; God above all other gods; Thee we worship and adore.

Seneca 4 BC–65 AD, Roman Stoic

95 O Holy Spirit, giver of light and life, impart to us thoughts higher than our own thoughts, and prayers better than our own prayers and powers beyond our own powers, that we may spend and be spent in the ways of love and goodness, after the perfect image of our Lord Jesus Christ.

E. Underhill

96 O Lord Jesus Christ, who art the Way, the Truth and the Life, we pray Thee suffer us not to stray from Thee who art the way: nor to distrust Thee who art the Truth nor to rest in any other thing than Thee, who art the Life. Teach us by the Holy Spirit what to believe, what to do, and where to take our rest. We ask it for Thy own name's sake.

Desiderius Erasmus 1466–1536

97 Lord God, Light of the minds that know thee, Life of the souls that love thee, and Strength of the thoughts that seek thee; help us so to know thee that we may truly love thee, and so to love thee that we may fully serve thee, whose service is perfect freedom; through Jesus Christ our Lord.

Gelasian Sacramentary

98 Almighty and everlasting God, with whom nothing is obscure, nothing dark, send forth thy light into our hearts that we may perceive the brightness of thy Law, and walking in thy holy way may fall into no sin, through thy beloved Son and our beloved example, Jesus Christ.

St Gregory 550–604

99 Eternal Light, shine into our hearts,
Eternal Goodness, deliver our thoughts from evil,
Eternal Power, support our prayer,
Eternal Wisdom, enlighten the darkness of our ignorance,
Eternal Pity, have mercy upon us, that with all our heart and
mind and soul and strength we may seek thy face, and be
brought by thy infinite mercy to thy holy presence; through
Jesus Christ our Lord.

Alcuin 735–804

100 God is in the water, God is in the dry land, God is in the heart.
God is in the forest, God is in the mountain, God is in the cave.
God is in the earth, God is in heaven. . . .
Thou art in the tree, thou art in its leaves,
Thou art in the earth, thou art in the firmament.

Govind Singh, Sikh

101 Hast thou not seen how all in the Heavens and in the Earth
uttereth the praise of God? – the very birds as they spread their
wings? Every creature knoweth its prayer and its praise! and God
knoweth what they do.

The Koran

Readings

RELIGION

134 The Meaning of Religion

By religion, I do not mean formal religion, or customary religion, but that religion which underlies all religions, which brings us face to face with our Maker.

I have not seen Him, neither have I known Him. I have made the world's faith in God my own.

To me God is Truth and Love; God is ethics and morality; God is fearlessness. God is the source of Light and Life, and yet He is above and beyond all these. God is conscience. He is even the atheism of the atheist . . . He is a personal God to those who need His personal presence. He is embodied to those who need His touch. He is all things to all men . . . With Him ignorance is no excuse. And withal He is ever forgiving for He always gives us the chance to repent. He is the greatest democrat the world knows, for He leaves us 'unfettered' to make our own choice between evil and good. He is the greatest tyrant ever known, for He often dashes the cup from our lips and, under the cover of free will, leaves us a margin so wholly inadequate as to provide only mirth for Himself . . .

To see the universal and all-pervading Spirit of Truth face to face one must be able to love the meanest of creation as oneself. And a man who aspires after that cannot afford to keep out of any field of life. That is why my devotion to truth has drawn me into the field of politics.

I am endeavouring to see God through service of humanity, for I know that God is neither in heaven, nor down below, but in every one.

Indeed religion should pervade every one of our actions.

Here religion does not mean sectarianism. It means a belief in ordered moral government of the universe. It is not less real because it is unseen. This religion transcends Hinduism, Islam, Christianity, etc. It does not supersede them. It harmonises them and gives them reality.

After long study and experience, I have come to the conclusion that (1) all religions are true; (2) all religions have some error in them; (3) all religions are almost as dear to me as my own Hinduism, in as much as all human beings should be as dear to one as one's own close relatives. My own veneration for other faiths is the same as that for my own faith; therefore no thought of conversion is possible.

I do not believe in the exclusive divinity of the Vedas. I believe the Bible, the Koran and the Zend Avesta to be as much divinely inspired as the Vedas. My belief in the Hindu scriptures does not require me to accept every word and every verse as divinely inspired. . . . I decline to be bound by any interpretation, however learned it may be, if it is repugnant to reason or moral sense.

Mahatma Gandhi

135 Religion

And an old priest said, Speak to us of Religion.
And he said:
Have I spoken this day of aught else?
Is not religion all deeds and all reflection,
And that which is neither deed nor reflection, but a wonder and a
    surprise ever springing in the soul, even while the hands hew
    the stone or tend the loom?
Who can separate his faith from his actions, or his belief from his
    occupations?
Who can spread his hours before him, saying, 'This for God and
    this for myself;
This for my soul and this other for my body'?
All your hours are wings that beat through space from self to self.
He who wears his morality but as his best garment were better
    naked.
The wind and the sun will tear no holes in his skin.
And he who defines his conduct by ethics imprisons his song-bird
    in a cage.
The freest song comes not through bars and wires.
And he to whom worshipping is a window, to open but also to
    shut, has not yet visited the house of his soul whose windows
    are from dawn to dawn.

Your daily life is your temple and your religion.
Whenever you enter into it take with you your all.
Take the plough and the forge and the mallet and the lute,
The things you have fashioned in necessity or for delight.

For in reverie you cannot rise above your achievements nor fall
  lower than your failures.
And take with you all men:
For in adoration you cannot fly higher than their hopes nor
  humble yourself lower than their despair.

And if you would know God, be not therefore a solver of riddles.
Rather look about you and you shall see Him playing with your
  children.
And look into space; you shall see Him walking in the cloud,
  outstretching His arms in the lightning and descending in rain.
You shall see Him smiling in flowers, then rising and waving
  His hands in trees.

Kahlil Gibran, **The Prophet**

WORSHIP

136 Worship

We ask that we live and we labour in peace.

God, the Supreme Being, the Creator, is worshipped by men of
many religions, under many names. Jews and Christians see him
in the Psalms –

  Make a joyful noise unto God, all ye lands;
  Sing forth the honour of his name: make his praise glorious.
  Say unto God, How terrible art thou in thy works! through the
    greatness of thy power shall thine enemies submit themselves
    unto thee.
  All the earth shall worship thee, and shall sing unto thee; they
    shall sing to thy name. Se-lah.

Muslims, too, worship God in the name of Allah. In the Koran,
their holy book, we read – Say: 'We believe in Allah and that
which is revealed to us; we believe in what was revealed to
Abraham, Ishmael, Isaac, Jacob, and the tribes; to Moses and
Jesus and the other prophets. We make no distinction between
any of them, and to Allah we have surrendered ourselves.'
Thoughout the Koran is insistence on the Oneness of God – the
opening, repeated several times in all five daily prayers, is –

Praise be to Allah, Lord of the Creation,
The Compassionate, the Merciful,
King of Judgement-day!
You alone we worship, and to You alone we pray for help.
Guide us to the straight path,
The path of those whom You have favoured,
Not of those who have incurred Your wrath,
Nor of those who have gone astray.

Hindus have many gods, but they are generally considered different aspects of the One Supreme Being. 'As different streams, having different sources, all find their way to the sea, so, O Lord, the different paths which men take all lead to thee.'

Joan Hasler

137 God as Light

Immortal, invisible, God only wise.

In many religions light is used as the symbol of God, goodness and love overcoming the evil of darkness or guiding the pilgrim through life by shedding light on the true way. Similarly candles or lamps are often lit in the course of worship or at special festivals like the Hindu Diwali or the Jewish Hanukkah.

For Christians the most famous passage about light is in St John's Gospel.

All that came to be had life in him
and that life was the light of men,
a light that shines in the dark,
a light that darkness could not overpower.
He came as a witness
as a witness to speak for the light,
so that everyone might believe through him.
He was not the light,
only a witness to speak for the light.
The Word was the true light
that enlightens all men;
and he was coming into the world.

There is an equally important passage in the Muslim Koran –

God is the light of heaven and earth. His light may be compared
to a niche which contains a lamp, the lamp within glass, and the
glass as it were a star of pearl. It is lit from a blessed olive tree
neither eastern nor western. Its oil would almost shine forth if
no fire touched it. Light upon Light; God guideth to His Light
whom He will.

In Hindu literature, too, the light of Truth is the End of the
journey. 'The light of lights He is, in the heart of the Dark shining
eternally' (Bhagavad–Gita 13).

Joan Hasler

138 The Invisible Spirit

'Bring me a fruit from this banyan tree.'
'Here it is, father.'
'Break it.'
'It is broken, Sir.'
'What do you see in it?'
'Very small seeds, Sir.'
'Break one of them, my son.'
'It is broken, Sir.'
'What to you see in it?'
'Nothing at all, Sir.'
Then his father spoke to him: 'My son, from the very essence in
the seed which you cannot see comes in truth this vast banyan tree.
    Believe me, my son, an invisible and subtle essence is the Spirit
of the whole universe. That is Reality. That is Atman. THOU ART
THAT.'
    'Explain more to me, father,' said Svetaketu.
    'So be it, my son.
    Place this salt in water and come to me tomorrow morning.'
Svetaketu did as he was commanded, and in the morning his
father said to him:
    'Bring me the salt you put into the water last night.'
    Svetaketu looked into the water, but could not find it, for it had
dissolved.
    His father then said: 'Taste the water from this side.
How is it?'
    'It is salt.'
    'Taste it from the middle. How is it?'
    'It is salt.'
    'Taste it from that side. How is it?'

'It is salt.'

'Look for the salt again and come again to me.'

The son did so, saying: 'I cannot see the salt. I only see water.'

His father then said: 'In the same way, O my son, you cannot see the Spirit. But in truth he is here.

An invisible and subtle essence is the Spirit of the whole universe. That is Reality. That is Truth. THOU ART THAT.'

Chandogya Upanishad

139 The Search for the Spirit

Even as a man, O my son, who has been led blindfold from his land of the Gandharas and then left in a desert place, might wander to the East and North and South, because he has been taken blindfolded and left in an unknown place, but if a good man took off his bandage and told him 'In that direction is the land of the Gandharas go in that direction,' then, if he were a wise man, he would go asking from village to village until he would have reached his land of the Gandharas; so it happens in this world to a man who has a Master to direct him to the land of the Spirit. Such a man can say: 'I shall wander in this world until I attain liberation; but then I shall go and reach my Home.'

This invisible and subtle essence is the Spirit of the whole universe. That is Reality. That is Truth.

Chandogya Upanishad

140 Spirit in All Things

My son! There is nothing in this world, that is not God. He is action, purity; everlasting Spirit. Find Him in the Cavern; gnaw the knot of ignorance.

Shining, yet hidden, Spirit lives in the cavern. Everything that sways, breathes, opens, closes, lives in spirit; beyond learning, beyond everything, better than anything; living, unliving.

It is the undying blazing Spirit, that seed of all seeds, wherein lay hidden the world and all its creatures. It is life, speech, mind, reality, immortality . . .

He who has found Spirit, is Spirit.

Mundaka Upanishad

141 Vision of God

In the market, in the cloister – only God I saw.
In the valley and on the mountain – only God I saw.
Him I have seen beside me oft in tribulation;
In favour and in fortune – only God I saw.
In prayer and fasting, in praise and contemplation,
In the religion of the Prophet – only God I saw.
Neither soul nor body, accident nor substance,
Qualities nor causes – only God I saw.
I open mine eyes and by the light of His face around me
In all the eye discovered – only God I saw.
Like a candle I was melting in His fire:
Amidst the flames outflanking – only God I saw.
Myself with mine own eyes I saw most clearly,
But when I looked with God's eyes – only God I saw.
I passed away into nothingness, I vanished,
And lo, I was the All-living – only God I saw.

Baba Kuhi of Shiraz

142 The Story of My Heart

The story of my heart commences seventeen years ago. In the
glow of youth there were times every now and then when I felt the
necessity of a strong inspiration of soul-thought. My heart was
dusty, parched for want of the rain of deep feeling: my mind arid
and dry, for there is a dust which settles on the heart as well as
that which falls on a ledge. It is injurious to the mind as well as to
the body to be always in one place and always surrounded by the
same circumstances. A species of thick clothing slowly grows
about the mind, the pores are choked, little habits become a part
of existence and by degrees the mind is inclosed in a husk. When
this began to form I felt eager to escape from it, to throw it off like
heavy clothing, to drink deeply once more at the fresh fountains of
life. An inspiration – a long deep breath of the pure air of thought
– could alone give health to the heart.

   There was a hill to which I used to resort at such periods. The
labour of walking three miles to it, all the while gradually
ascending, seemed to clear my blood of the heaviness accumulated
at home. On a warm summer day the slow continued rise required
continual effort, which carried away the sense of oppression. The
familiar everyday scene was soon out of sight; I came to other

trees, meadows, and fields; I began to breathe a new air and to have a fresher aspiration . . .

Moving up the sweet short turf, at every step my heart seemed to obtain a wider horizon of feelings; with every inhalation of rich pure air, a deeper desire. The very light of the sun was whiter and more brilliant here. By the time I had reached the summit I had entirely forgotten the petty circumstances and the annoyances of existence. I felt myself, myself. There was an intrenchment on the summit, and going down into the fosse I walked round it slowly to recover breath. On the south-western side there was a spot where the outer bank had partially slipped, leaving a gap. There the view was over a broad plain, beautiful with wheat, and enclosed by a perfect amphitheatre of green hills. Through these hills there was one narrow groove, or pass, southwards, where the white clouds seemed to close in the horizon. Woods hid the scattered hamlets and farmhouses, so that I was quite alone.

I was utterly alone with the sun and the earth. Lying down on the grass, I spoke in my soul to the earth, the sun, the air, and the distant sea far beyond sight . . .

With all the intensity of feeling which exalted me, all the intense communion I held with the earth, the sun and sky, the stars hidden by the light, with the ocean – in no manner can the thrilling depth of these feelings be written – with these I prayed, as if they were the keys of an instrument, of an organ, with which I swelled forth the notes of my soul, redoubling my own voice by their power . . .

Finally I rose, walked half a mile or so along the summit of the hill eastwards, to soothe myself and come to the common ways of life again. Had any shepherd accidentally seen me lying on the turf, he would only have thought that I was resting a few minutes; I made no outward show. Who could have imagined the whirlwind of passion that was going on within me as I reclined there! I was greatly exhausted when I reached home. Occasionally I went upon the hill deliberately, deeming it good to do so; then, again, this craving carried me away up there of itself. Though the principal feeling was the same, there were variations in the mode in which it affected me.

Through every grass blade in the thousand, thousand grasses; through the million leaves, veined and edge-cut, on bush and tree; through the song-notes and the marked feathers of the birds; through the insects' hum and the colour of the butterflies; through the soft warm air, the flecks of clouds dissolving – I used them all for prayer.

Richard Jefferies

143 The Winthrop Woman

A ray of sunlight started down between the tree trunks. It touched
the pool with liquid gold. The pool became transparent to its
green depths and her self was plunged in those depths and yet
upraised with joy upon the rushing wind. The light grew
stronger and turned white. In this crystal whiteness there was
ecstasy. Against the light she saw a wren fly by; the wren was
made of rhythm, it flew with meaning, with a radiant meaning.
There was the same meaning in the caterpillar as it inched along
the rock, and the moss, and the little nuts which had rolled across
the leaves.

And still the apperception grew, and the significance. The
significance was bliss, it made a created whole of everything she
watched and touched and heard – and the essence of this created
whole was love. She felt love pouring from the light, it bathed her
with music and with perfume; the love was far off at the source of
the light, and yet it drenched her through. And the source and she
were one.

The minutes passed. The light moved softly down, and faded
from the pool. The ecstasy diminished, it quietened, but in its
stead came a serenity and sureness she had never known.

Anya Seton, from **The Winthrop Woman**

144 The Ganges at Night

There were no famous temples in Kalakankar, no historical
monuments, no rare sights in this lonely land, with its scorched
earth and dirty village. The colours were not bright, the peasants
wore nothing but plain white, the dusty foliage of the trees was
dull. There was nothing exotic about the place, none of the
fairy-tale quality that tourists sought in India. But instead, present
in everything, permeating everything, there was an impossible
deep sound, like that of an organ. If you remained very quiet, if
you sat still gazing at the river, you too would hear it. You would
sense it coming as a slow, reverberating gong, as the quietly
breathing heart of a mighty, eternal life, in which everything – the
earth, the river, the sky, the birds, and man – found itself
blended. Even he who knows not God, who does not believe in
Him, would, without knowing it, thank Him for the peace that
filled his soul, and involuntarily, as though against his will, the
words would escape him: 'Lord what bliss!'

Svetlana Alliluyeva, from **Only One Year**

PARABLES OF JESUS

145 The Seed

Mark 4, 3–9

I watched the small child, Lord, as he ran to his parents. He was
  bubbling with enthusiasm, with joy, with some – for him –
  tremendous piece of news.
His mother was smiling, seeking to share his excitement.
His father looked worried, preoccupied.
He probably only heard the garbled and incoherent remarks.
The one who has ears to hear did hear and shared something of
  what the child was eager to communicate.
The other heard, but did not understand.
Seed falls where it is directed, but not all of it grows.
It is strange, Lord, how different people react in different ways to
  the same situation.
It is strange how I react differently to life at different timès.
Sometimes I share the excitement of the child.
I see clearly ahead.
I understand the issues.
I know the way to go.
My eyes are sharply focused.
The seed grows and bears fruit.
Why can't it be like this always, Lord?
Sometimes I find myself wrestling with an issue, and yet cannot
  see the wood for the trees.
Nothing goes right.
There seems to be nothing I can do.
It is as if the thistles were choking life out of the seed.
Sometimes my interest is aroused.
I begin to get to grips with a job.
Then suddenly the mood changes. Lethargy takes control, and
  enthusiasm becomes a thing of the past.
Interest withers for lack of moisture.
Sometimes I wander wondering what to do.
Life becomes time to be passed.
Nothing stirs any interest.
All seeds have become meals for the birds.
Develop my insight, Lord, into the many different situations in
  which I find myself.
Let the seed grow within me and bear fruit.

Let me hear your gospel in the particular moments of my life, and
understand.

Rex Chapman

146 One Big Party

Luke 14, 16–24

Your Kingdom, Lord, is here and now.
It is in this place, at this moment in time, with these people.
You are calling men together, to your feast.
You stand waiting, a focus among men, the centre around whom
   we are to converge.
You are at the core of community.
You are at the heart of shalom.
You are at the meeting-point of reconciliation.
Your feast is laid ready – the universal Eucharist.
Mankind is invited.
We are the guests.
I urgently want mankind to be united, the world to be one.
The invitation to drop in for the party is easily accepted for there
   and then, in another place, at some other time, with unspecified
   people.
I can demonstrate and shout for a future Utopia with the best of
   them.
But it is here and now, in this place, at this time, in this situation,
   with these people that your Kingdom is to be found.
Ground my faith in this fact, Lord.
It is with the friendly, the amusing, the hostile, the
   compassionate, the anxious, the joyful, the angry, the
   grief-ridden, the insincere, the tearful, the unlovable, the
   honest men, women and children with whom I meet today that
   your Kingdom is to be found.
Press home your invitation, Lord.
Widen my horizons.
Enable me to see your presence speaking through the people I
   meet.
Before it is too late.
Before tomorrow comes.

Rex Chapman

147 The Unjust Judge and the Ideal Man

Luke 18, 1–8

If even an unjust judge gives way to persistence in a cause that is
  right, how much more readily will you listen, Lord, to a man's
  just desire.
Built into every man in an ideal man.
He may not know it, he may not think much about it, but it is
  there as the standard against which the real is measured.
It is seen in a man's ambitions, in his actions, in his dreams.
The ideal man is the sort of person the flesh and blood man wants
  to be, or even feels he is.
He is the guide who motivates action, the image who drives
  ambition, the myth who moulds behaviour.
The ideal man is the shadow image with whom we try to merge.
That adolescent boy, Lord, has a vision of competence, greatness
  in sport, and works hard at imitation.
That young man is eager to reach the top of the business world.
This woman strives to fulfil her motherhood.
This man is a thinker. His ideal man, spurring him on from the
  depths of his soul, is the free and independent and profound
  commentator on life.

Lord, all these people persist in their pursuit of the ideal man
  within, and seek to turn him into reality.
The ideal man within me has been created by the influences of
  many people, many events.
Fashion him in your image, the image of the new man, the real
  Adam.
Grant me strength to persist in reflection, meditation, prayer on
  the nature of who man is, who I am, what he ought to be like,
  what I ought to be like.
Let me persist in faith in you.
Be with me, be within me fashioning my being into conformity
  with you.

Rex Chapman

148 The Lord of the Dance

Matthew 11, 16–19

I feel pressurized, Lord,
Squeezed by the demands that are made of me,

Caught in the crossfire of opinions of what I ought to do, of who I
    ought to be.
One man activates deep feelings, emotions, buried guilt within
    me.
Another has definite views that hide a latent judgement.
Yet another wants to mould me into his own image.
I feel pressurized into dancing to a multitude of tunes.
It is emotional blackmail, and it is remarkably effective.
My mind is in turmoil.
So many tunes are being piped at once.
For comfort I feel as if I must satisfy them all.
Yet this is impossible.
They are contradictory tunes.
I lack the resources to pay off the blackmail.

John the Baptist lived an ascetic life.
And he, so they said, was as mad as a hatter.
You played it the other way, Lord.
You enjoyed a good meal with your friends – a pity they were so
    unacceptable.
And you, so they said, were a layabout.
It is impossible to win this game, Lord,
    to satisfy all demands, all expectations.
The rules are fixed so that the piper always wins.

'And yet God's wisdom is proved right by its results.'
You are the wisdom of God.
You are the 'Lord of the Dance'.
You withstood the pressures of life to reach the goal of full
    manhood.
Strengthen me, Lord, when under pressure.
Lead me in the dance.

Rex Chapman

MIRACLES OF JESUS

149 Which Way to Go?

Mark 2, 1–12

'Your sins are forgiven. Arise and walk. Take up your bed and go.'
But where to, Lord?
No destination is mentioned.

' "Cheshire Puss", Alice began, "would you tell me please which
   way I ought to go from here?"
"That depends a good deal on where you want to get to", said the
   Cat.
"I do not much care where", said Alice.
"Then it does not matter which way you go", said the Cat.'

What happened to the man once sick of the palsy when he finally
   reached home with his bed on his back?
You forgave him, Lord.
You removed the invisible bonds that bound him to his bed.
You enabled him to carry away that which had held him captive.
What happened to him next?
Which way would he go?
You made him responsible for himself, Lord.
He was no longer to be carried, no longer someone else's
   responsibility.
Which way would he go?
At the moment of his release there is joy, confidence, exhilaration
   at the new life he could now lead.
He was free!
Yet freedom has to be grasped, seized, taken to heart and
   continually renewed.

Overcome my hesitations, my drawing back in anxiety.
Lead me in this way.
Let me take up my bed and follow.

Rex Chapman

150 Legion and those Pigs

Mark 5, 1–20

'They begged Jesus to leave the district.'
Their economy would be ruined, if you made pigs behave like
   lemmings.
It is unusual.
It is peculiar.
It does not allow for convincing explanation.
It asks awkward questions.
We cannot get it taped, organized.
You threaten security.
We are quite happy looking after our pigs.

It is true that Legion is often to be heard shouting among the
   tombs.
But we keep away from there, especially after dark, and he does
   not trouble us.
Please go.
I am a little afraid of this power of yours.
It is too powerful.
You are master of one whom 'no one was strong enough to
   master'.
To commit myself totally to you, Lord, is a demanding thing to
   ask.
To be honest, there is part of my life I want to keep to myself.
There I can do as I please.
There I can be sole authority.
There I can be master.
There I can be lord.
To commit myself totally to you, Lord, would be to open to you
   the doors of this very private apartment.
I do not want you in, and yet I do.
It looks like being a life-long struggle, Lord, between that part of
   me that wants to control myself and the part that trusts to you.
Struggle with me, Lord.
And win.

Rex Chapman

151 Inner Loneliness

Mark 7, 31–7

How great was his isolation, Lord.
Thank God he could see and smell and touch.
But he could not hear.
He could not speak.
He could not speak a word of sorrow but had to keep it bottled up
   within.
He could not communicate and share so many of the feelings and
   emotions and thoughts that welled up inside him.
He could not hear the joy of children.
He could not hear the word of comfort, consolation,
   encouragement that one man can pass to another.
He could not listen to the wisdom of others nor to the infectious
   laughter that raises the spirits.

Around his world was a barrier of silence.
Lord, you can break through all barriers.
Stay, Lord, and banish all isolation, inner loneliness.
Stay, Lord, and use me to banish the loneliness of others.

Rex Chapman

THE COMMANDMENTS

152 Thou Shalt Nots of Missionaries

There is a tale of a missionary in a dark corner of Africa where the men had a habit of filing their teeth to sharp points. He was hard at work trying to convert a native chief. Now the chief was very old, and the missionary was very Old Testament – his version of Christianity leaned heavily on thou-shalt-nots. The savage listened patiently.

'I do not understand,' he said at last. 'You tell me that I must not take my neighbour's wife.'

'That's right,' said the missionary.

'Or his ivory, or his oxen.'

'Quite right.'

'And I must not dance the war dance and then ambush him on the trail and kill him.'

'Absolutely right!'

'But I cannot do any of these things!' said the savage regretfully. 'I am too old. To be old and to be a Christian, they are the same thing!'

Not a very funny story, perhaps; there is too bitter a point in the laugh. For, if all the truth were told, how many of us, in our hearts, share the cannibal's confusion? How many thousands picture Christianity as something old, sapless, joyless, mumbling in the chimney corner and casting sour looks at the young people's fun? How many think of religion as the enemy of life and the flesh and the pleasures of the flesh; a foe to all love and all delight? How many unconsciously conceive of God as rather like the famous lady who said 'Find out what the baby is doing and make him stop'?

That is, how many of us both inside the Church and out have reduced the good news out of Nazareth to a list of thou-shalt-nots?

Joy Davidman

153 What Shape is an Idol?

I worship Ganesa, brother, god of wordly wisdom, patron of
shopkeepers. He is in the shape of a little fat man with an
elephant's head; he is made of soapstone and has two small rubies
for eyes. What shape do you worship?

I worship a Rolls-Royce sports model, brother. All my days I
give it offerings of oil and polish. Hours of my time are devoted to
its ritual; and it brings me luck in all my undertakings; and it
establishes me among my fellows as a success in life. What model
is your car, brother?

I worship my house beautiful, sister. Long and loving
meditation have I spent on it; the chairs contrast with the rug, the
curtains harmonize with woodwork, all of it is perfect and holy.
The ash trays are in exactly the right place, and should some
blasphemer drop ashes on the floor, I nearly die of shock. I live
only for the service of my house, and it rewards me with the envy
of my sisters, who must rise up and call me blessed. Lest my
children profane the holiness of my house with dirt and noise, I
drive them out of doors. What shape is your idol, sister? Is it your
house, or your clothes, or perhaps even your worth-while and
cultural club?

I worship the pictures I paint, brother . . . I worship my job;
I'm the best darn publicity expert this side of Hollywood . . . I
worship my golf game, my bridge game . . . I worship my
comfort; after all, isn't enjoyment the goal of life? . . . I worship
my church; I want to tell you, the work we've done in missions
beats all other denominations in this city, and next year we can
afford that new organ, and you won't find a better choir
anywhere . . . I worship myself . . . What shape is your idol?

Joy Davidman

154 The Martian Student

The Martian student swooping dangerously low over the United
States in his flying saucer scribbled with his writing tentacle. He
had chosen an ideal morning for taking notes – a fine summer
Sunday, with all the natives coming out of their houses and
obligingly spreading themselves around for his observation. But
he was in a desperate hurry. Only one more week till his thesis
was due, and without it he hadn't an earth-man's chance of
passing his comparative anthropology course.

As it turned out, though, he needn't have worried. The report he wrote was brilliant, comparing favourably for accuracy and insight with the best work of our earthly anthropologists. In several Martian colleges professors have read it aloud as a shining example of what modern scientific methods can do.

'Like so many primitive life forms [thus went the Martian's report] the creatures of the third planet are sun worshippers. One day in every seven is set apart for the adoration of their deity, weather permitting. Their rituals vary, and each apparently involves a special form of dress; but all are conducted in the open air, and most seem to require the collection of enormous crowds. Some creatures gather in vast arenas, to watch strangely garbed priests perform elaborate ceremonies involving a ball and variously shaped instruments of wood. [The significance of the ball as a solar symbol, of course, is known to every Martian schoolboy.] Others, no doubt the mystics and solitaries of their religion, prefer to address the ball themselves with long clubs, singly, or in groups of two or four, wandering in green fields. Some, stripping themselves almost naked in their ecstasy, go down to the seashore in great throngs and there perform their rites, often hurling themselves into the waves with frenzied cries. [This practice is unmistakably based on the dogma, found also among the semi-intelligent crustaceans of Venus, that the sun is a sea-god born anew each morning from the ocean; the use of large brightly coloured balls in these seaside rituals is confirmatory evidence.] After the ceremonial immersion, devotees have been observed to anoint themselves with holy oils and stretch themselves out full length with eyes closed, in order to surrender themselves entirely to silent communion with the deity.

'Human sacrifice, sad to say, is also practised, the instrument of death being a four-wheeled metal car which may be employed in various ways. Often a chosen victim is run down and crushed. Even more frequently the sacrifice is voluntary; devotees enter the cars, and either work themselves into a frenzy by travelling at high speeds until they dash themselves to bits against other cars or stationary objects – or else congregate in vast throngs, too closely packed to move, and allow the sun's rays beating upon the hot metal to cook them slowly to death.

'There exists, however, a small sect of recalcitrants or heretics that does not practise sun worship. These may be identified by their habit of clothing themselves more soberly and completely than the sun worshippers. They too gather in groups, but only to hide from the sun in certain buildings of doubtful use, usually with windows of glass coloured to keep out the light. It is not clear whether these creatures are simply unbelievers or whether they are excommunicated from sun worship for some offence – we have not been able to discover what goes on within their buildings, which may perhaps be places of punishment. But it is noteworthy that their faces and gestures show none of the almost orgiastic religious frenzy with which the sun worshippers pursue their devotions. In fact, they usually appear relaxed and even placid, thus indicating minds blank of thought or emotion; in this connection, see Dr. Duerf's monumental study, *Totem and Taboo Among the Giant Centipedes of Mercury*.'

Was the Martian wildly wrong, or fantastically right?

Joy Davidman, **Smoke on the Mountain**

155 The Genies of Today

Once there was a boy named James Watt, and he had an old kettle that belonged to his mother. And one day, behold a great hissing cloud, and a vague shape that said, 'I am the Genie Steam; and I serve the owner of the kettle. What is your will, O Master?'

And the boy said, 'Make us all rich. Bring us miles of woven cloth, and piles of food, and acres of diamonds; let us have houses that touch the sky and coaches that run swifter than the wind, and let all this be done without our having to strain ourselves with overwork.'

'To hear is to obey, Master' answered the genie. And in the twinkling of an eye all men were rich and happy, neither did they study war any more, but spent their time contentedly enjoying the flow of good things provided by the genie of the kettle . . .

Or so the dream ran, for its first dreamers. Since then we have extended it somewhat. We have sent the genie for his swifter brother Petroleum, and then for his tall, glittering sister Electricity, and we have put all three to work turning out riches for us, until every man of us has become entirely happy and peaceful . . . Well, perhaps not quite. But now we have learned to call up the great-granddaddy of all genies, the towering cloud-and-fire shape named Atomic Power, and by his efforts we are certain to content all our desires at last . . .

Well, perhaps not quite.

Joy Davidman

6 SERIES OF EXTRACTS

Assemblies

1 *Mister God, This is Anna*, Fynn, **156–161**

a)   Glad that I live am I
     Reading **156**: *Coming Home*
     Prayer **77**

b)   Gracious spirit, Holy Ghost
     Reading **157**: *Mister God*
     Prayers **82** and **93**

c)   For the beauty of the earth/All creatures of our God and
         King
     Reading **158**: *God's World*
     Prayers **9** and **12**

d)   God is love; his the care
     Reading **159**: *The Fourth Dimension*
     Prayer **80**

e)   We ask that we live and we labour in peace/I belong to a
         family, the biggest on earth
     Reading **160**: *Unity* (2 readings)
     Prayers **59–62**

f)   O brother Man, fold to thy heart thy brother/When in His
         own image/Love divine, all loves excelling
     Reading **161**: *Mister God* (2 readings)
     Prayers **71**, **75**, **80** and **91**

(e) and (f) are suitable for ecumenical or inter-religious readings;
(f) for the ten commandments, love of God and community.

2 *Don Camillo*, Giovanni Guareschi, **162–165**

a)   God is love; his the care
     Reading **162**: *Forgiving Others*
     Prayer **72**

b)   Fight the good fight with all thy might
     Reading **163**: *Justice*
     Prayer **79**

c)   Eternal ruler of the ceaseless round
Reading **164**: *What's in a Name?*
Prayers **70** and **73**

d)   He who would valiant be
Reading **165**: *A Baptism*
Prayer **83**

3 *Emma and I* (story of a guide dog), Sheila Hocken, **166–168**

a)   New every morning is the love
Reading **166**: *The Decision*
Prayer **71**

b)   For the beauty of the earth
Reading **167**: *Training*
Prayer **79**

c)   Now thank we all our God
Reading **168**: *At Home – Travelling*
Prayers **82** and **83**

Suitable for community, courage, disabilities, animals

4 *The Water Babies*, Charles Kingsley, **169–171**

a)   Help us to help each other, Lord/Be thou my guardian and my guide
Reading **169**: *Mrs. Bedonebyasyoudid*
Prayer **82**

b)   Dear Lord and Father of Mankind/Love divine, all loves excelling
Reading **170**: *Mrs. Doasyouwouldbedoneby*
Prayer **81**

c)   Father hear the prayer we offer
Reading **171**: *The Nation of Doasyoulikes*
Prayer **79**

Suitable for family, community and use of talents

5 *The Screwtape Letters*, C. S. Lewis, **172–174**

a)   Soldiers of Christ arise
Reading **172**: *Friends*
Prayers **75** and **76**

b) Gracious spirit, Holy Ghost
Reading **173**: *Self*
Prayer **78**

c) Fight the good fight with all thy might
Reading **174**: *Gluttony*
Prayer **83**

These readings need careful introductions. They can also be used singly in connection with virtues and vices, the commandments, etc.

6 *Epistles to the Apostle*, Colin Morris, **175–178**

a) Now join we, to praise the Creator/Life could be good and rich and whole
Reading **175**: *Andrew alias Plutus alias Simeon to Paul*
Prayers **71** and **83**

b) He who would valiant be
Reading **176**: *Pilgrim's Regress*
Prayers **84** and **86**

c) O Jesus I have promised
Reading **177**: *Timothy to Paul*
Prayers **69**, **70** and **74**

d) Soldiers of Christ arise
Reading **178**: *Titus to Paul*
Prayers **70** and **85**

Readings

MISTER GOD, THIS IS ANNA, FYNN

156 Coming Home

'The diffrense from a person and an angel is easy. Most of an angel is in the inside and most of a person is on the outside.' These are the words of six-year-old Anna, sometimes called Mouse, Hum or Joy. At five years Anna knew absolutely the purpose of being, knew the meaning of love and was a personal friend and helper of Mister God. At six Anna was a theologian, mathematician, philosopher, poet and gardener. If you asked her a question you would always get an answer – in due course. On some occasions the answer would be delayed for weeks or months; but eventually, in her own good time, the answer would come: direct, simple and much to the point.

She never made eight years, she died by an accident. She died with a grin on her beautiful face. She died saying, 'I bet Mister God let me get into heaven for this', and I bet he did, too.

My name is Fynn. Well that's not quite true; my real name doesn't matter all that much since my friends all called me Fynn and it stuck. If you know your Irish mythology you will know that Fynn was pretty big; me too. Standing about six foot two, weighing some sixteen stone odd, close to being a fanatic on physical culture, the son of an Irish mother and a Welsh father, with a passion for hot saveloys and chocolate raisins – not all together, I may add. My great delight was to roam about dockland in the night-time, particularly if it was foggy.

My life with Anna began on such a night. I was nineteen at the time, prowling the streets and alleys with my usual supply of hot dogs, the street lights with their foggy haloes showing dark formless shapes moving out from the darkness of the fog and disappearing again. Down the street a little way a baker's shop-window softened and warmed the raw night with its gas-lamps. Sitting on the grating under the window was a little girl. In those days children wandering the streets at night were no uncommon sight. I had seen such things before, but on this occasion it was different. I sat down beside her on the grating, my back against the shop-front. We stayed there about three hours.

About ten-thirty that evening, whilst she was sitting between my knees having an earnest conversation with Maggie, her rag doll, I said 'Come on Tich, it's about time you were in bed. Where do you live?'

In a flat matter-of-fact voice she exclaimed 'I don't live nowhere. I have runned away.'

'What about your Mum and Dad?' I asked.

She might have said the grass is green and the sky is blue. What she did say was just as factual and effortless. 'Oh, she's a cow and he's a sod. And I ain't going to no bleeding cop shop. I'm going to live with you.'

That was no request but an order. What could you do? I merely accepted the fact.

'Right, I agree. You can come home with me and then we will have to see.' At that point my education began in earnest. I'd got myself a large doll, but not an imitation doll, a real live one and, from what I could make out, a bomb with legs on. Going home that night was like coming home from Hampstead Heath, slightly tiddled, a little dizzy from the merry-go-round I'd been on, and not a little bewildered that the beautiful doll I'd won on the shooting range had come to life and was walking beside me.

'What's your name, Tich?' I asked her.

'Anna. What's yours?'

'Fynn', I said. 'Where do you come from?'

I didn't get an answer to this question, and that was the first and last time she didn't answer a question – I gathered later the reason for this. It was because she was afraid that I might have taken her back.

'When did you run away?'

'Oh, three days ago, I think.'

We took the short way home by climbing over the 'cut' bridge and crossing over the railway yards. This was always my way in because we lived next to the railway and it was convenient, to say nothing of the fact that it meant I didn't have to get Mum out of bed to open the front-door.

157 Mister God

Mum and Anna shared many likes and dislikes; perhaps the simplest and the most beautiful sharing was their attitude towards Mister God. Most people I knew used God as an excuse for their failure, 'He should have done this', or 'Why has God done this to me?', but with Mum and Anna difficulties and adversities were merely occasions for doing something. Ugliness was the chance to make beautiful. Sadness was the chance to make glad. Mister God was always available to them. A stranger would have been excused for believing that Mister God lived with us, but then Mum and Anna believed he did. Very rarely did any conversation exclude Mister God in some way or other.

After the evening meal was finished and all bits and pieces put away Anna and I would settle down to some activity, generally of her choosing. Fairy stories were dismissed as mere pretend stories; living was real and living was interesting and by and large, fun. Reading the Bible wasn't a great success. She tended to regard it as a primer, strictly for infants. The message of the Bible was simple and any half-wit could grasp it in thirty minutes flat! Religion was for doing things, not for reading about doing things. Once you had got the message there wasn't much point in going over and over the same old ground. Our local parson was taken aback when he asked her about God. The conversation went as follows:

'Do you believe in God?'

'Yes.'

'Do you know what God is?'

'Yes.'

'What is God then?'

'He's God.'

'Do you go to church?'

'No.'

'Why not?'

'Because I know it all!'

'What do you know?'

'I know to love Mister God and to love people and cats and dogs and spiders and flowers and trees,' and the catalogue went on, 'with all of me.'

Carol grinned at me and Stan made a face and I hurriedly put a cigarette in my mouth and indulged in a bout of coughing. There's nothing much you can do in the face of that kind of accusation, for that's what it amounted to. (Out of the mouths of babes . . .) Anna had bypassed all the non-essentials and distilled centuries of learning into one sentence – 'And God said love me, love them, and love it, and don't forget to love yourself.'

158 God's World

Mum always said that she pitied the girl I married, for she would
have to put up with my three mistresses – Mathematics, Physics
and Electrical Gadgetry. I would rather read and practise these
subjects than eat or sleep. I never bought myself a wrist-watch or
a fountain-pen, and very rarely did I buy new clothes, but I never
went anywhere without a slide-rule. This device fascinated Anna
and soon she had to have a slip-stick of her own. Having mastered
the whole business of counting numbers, she was soon extracting
roots with the aid of her slip-stick before she could add two
numbers together. . . .

Some evenings were given over to piano-playing. I play a fairly
good honky-tonk piano, a bit of Mozart, a bit of Chopin, and a
few pieces like 'Anitra's Dance' just for good measure. On the top
of the piano were several electronic devices. One device, the
oscilloscope, held all the magic of a fairy wand for Anna. We'd sit
in this room for hours on end playing single notes, watching the
green spot on the 'scope do its glowing dance. The whole exercise
of relating sounds that one heard with the ears to the visual shape
of those sounds actively seen on the little tube's face was a source
of never-ending delight.

What sounds we captured, Anna and I. A caterpillar chewing a
leaf was like a hungry lion, a fly in a jam-jar sounded like an
airship, a match being struck sounded like an explosion. All these
sounds and a thousand more were amplified and made available,
both in sound and visual form. Anna had found a brand new
world to explore. How much meaning it had for her I didn't
know, perhaps it was only an elaborate plaything for her, but her
squeals of delight were enough for me.

It was only some time during the next summer that I began to
realize that the concepts of frequency and wavelength were
meaningful to her, that she did, in fact, know and understand
what she was hearing and looking at. One summer afternoon all
the kids were playing in the street when a large bumble-bee
appeared on the scene.

One of the kids said, 'How many times does it flap its wings in a
minute?'

'Must be millions', said another kid.

Anna dashed indoors humming a low-pitched hum. I was sitting
on the doorstep. With a few quick prods at the piano she had
identified the note, her hum and the drone of the bee. Coming to
the door again, she said 'Can I have your slip-stick?' In a moment
or two she shouted out 'A bee flaps its wings such-and-such times

a second.' Nobody believed her, but she was only a few counts out.

Every sound that could be captured was captured. Meals began to be punctuated with such remarks as 'Do you know a mosquito flaps its wings so many times a second? or a fly so many times a second?' . . .

Another of Anna's magic carpets was the microscope. It revealed a little world made big. A world of intricate shape and patterns, a world of creatures too small to see with the naked eye; even the very dirt itself was wonderful.

159 The Fourth Dimension

Before all this adventuring into these hidden worlds, Mister God had been Anna's friend and companion, but now, well this was going a bit too far. If Mister God had done all this, he was something larger than Anna had bargained for. It needed a bit of thinking about. . . .

'Mister God made everything, didn't he?'

There was no point in saying that I didn't really know. I said 'Yes'.

'Even the dirt and the stars and the animals and the people and the trees and everything, and the pollywogs?' The pollywogs were those little creatures that we had seen under the microscope.

I said, 'Yes, he made everything'.

She nodded her agreement. 'Does Mister God love us truly?'

'Sure thing', I said. 'Mister God loves everything.'

'Oh', she said. 'Well then, why does he let things get hurt and dead?' Her voice sounded as if she felt she had betrayed a sacred trust, but the question had been thought and it had to be spoken.

'I don't know', I replied. 'There's a great many things about Mister God that we don't know about.' . . .

'Fynn, you can love better than any people that ever was, and so can I, can't I? But Mister God is different. You see, Fynn, people can only love outside and can only kiss outside, but Mister God can love you right inside, and Mister God can kiss you right inside, so it's different. Mister God ain't like us; we are a little bit like Mister God, but not much yet.' . . .

'There's another way that Mister God is different.' We obviously hadn't finished yet. 'Mister God can know things and people from the inside too. We only know them from the outside, don't we? So you see, Fynn, people can't talk about Mister God from the outside; you can only talk about Mister God from the inside of him.' . . .

'Fynn, you know that book about four dimensions?'

'Yes, what about it?'

'I know where number four is; it goes inside me.'

'I'd had enough for that night and said with all the firmness and authority I could muster 'Go to sleep now, that's enough talking for tonight.'

160 Unity

Anna searched for Mister God and her desire was for a better understanding of him. Anna's search for Mister God was serious but gay, earnest but light-hearted, reverent but impudent, and single-minded and multi-tracked. That one and two made three was for Anna a sign that God existed. Not that she doubted God's existence for a moment, but it was for some time a sign that he did exist. By the same token a bus or a flower was also a sign that he existed. How she came by this vision of the pearl of great price I do not know. Certainly it was with her before I met her. It was just my luck that I happened to be with her when she was doing her 'working out'. To listen to her was exhilarating, like flying on one's own; to watch her was to be startled into seeing. Evidence for Mister God? Why, there was nowhere you could look where there wasn't evidence for Mister God; it was everywhere. Everything was evidence of Mister God and it was at this point that things tended to get out of hand.

The evidence could be arranged in too many ways. People who accepted one sort of arrangement were called by one particular name. Arrange the evidence in a new way and you were called by a different name. Anna reckoned that the number of possible arrangements of the available evidence might easily run into 'squillions' of names. The problem was further complicated by the fact of synagogues, mosques, temples, churches, and all the other places of worship, and scientific laboratories were not excluded from the list. By any reasonable standards of thinking and behaviour nobody could, with their hand on their heart, honestly say that these other people were not worshipping and loving God, even if they did call him by some other name like 'Truth'. She could not and would not say that Ali's God was a lesser kind of God than the Mister God she knew so well nor was she able to say that her Mister God was greater or more important than Kathie's God. It didn't make sense to talk about different Gods; that kind of talk inevitably leads to madness. No, for Anna it was all or nothing, there could only be one Mister God. This being so, then the different places of worship, the different kinds of names given to those worshippers, the different kinds of ritual performed by these worshippers could be due to one thing, and to one thing only, the different arrangements of the evidence for Mister God.

Anna solved this problem to her own satisfaction, or better still resolved it, on the piano. I've played the piano for as long as I can remember, but I can't read a note of music. I can listen to music and make a reasonable copy of it by ear, but if I attempt to play the same piece of music by reading the score, I turn it into a dirge. Those little black dots throw me into a flat spin. Whatever I've managed on the piano stems from the popular sheet-music of pre-war, the little frets with their constellation of dots which showed you how to finger the ukulele – or was it guitar? – and those cryptic symbols underneath the lines of music such as 'Am7' or the chord of A minor seventh. This was the kind of music that I learnt, limited perhaps, but it did have one great advantage. Given a suitable handful of notes, you could call it a 'this' chord or a 'that' chord, or perhaps any one of half a dozen names, it all depended on something else.

This then was the method I used to teach Anna something about the piano. Soon she was romping through major chords, relative minor chords, minor sevenths, diminished sevenths, and inversions. She knew their names and how to call them, more than that, she knew that the name given to a sprinkling of notes depended on where you were and what you were doing. Of course, the question of why a group of notes was called a 'chord' had to be gone into. Mr. Weekley's dictionary was called into service. We were informed that 'chord' and 'accord' were more or less one and the same word. One more flip through the dictionary to find out how the word 'accord' was used and we ended up with the word 'consent' and there we stopped.

It wasn't many hours later that day when I was confronted with the open-eyed, open-mouthed look of astonishment on Anna's face. She suddenly stopped playing hop-scotch with the rest of the kids and walked slowly towards me.

'Fynn,' her voice was a squeak of amazement, 'Fynn, we're all playing the same chord.'

'I'm not surprised,' I said. 'What are we talking about?'

'Fynn, it's all them different names for Churches.'

'So what's that got to do with chords?' I asked.

'We're all playing the same chord to Mister God but with different names.'

It was this kind of thing that was so exciting about talking to

Anna. She had this capacity for taking a statement of fact in one subject, teasing it until she discovered its pattern, then looking around for a similar pattern in another subject. Anna had a high regard for facts, but the importance of a fact did not lie in its uniqueness but in its ability to do service in diverse subjects. Had Anna ever been given a convincing argument in favour of atheism she'd have teased it about until she had got a firm hold of the pattern, viewed it from all sides and then shown you that the whole argument was a necessary ingredient in the existence of God.

The chord of atheism might be a discord, but then discords were in Anna's estimation 'thrilly', but definitely 'thrilly'.

'Fynn, them names of them chords', she began.

'What about them?' I asked.

'The home note can't be Mister God because then we couldn't call them different names. They would all be the same name', she said.

'I guess you're right at that. What is the home note then?'

'It's me or you or Ali. Fynn, it's everybody. That's why it's all different names. That's why it's all different churches. That's what it is.'

It makes sense, doesn't it? We're all playing the same chord, but it seems we don't know it. You call your chord a C major while I call the same notes A minor seventh. I call myself a Christian, what do you call yourself? I reckon Mister God must be pretty good at music, he knows all the names of the chord. Perhaps he doesn't mind what you call it, as long as you play it.

161 Mister God

'Will you make me two paddle-wheels this morning?' she asked.

'Could be', I answered. 'Where are you paddling off to?'

'Nowhere. I want to do an experiment', she replied.

'What size paddle-wheels and what are they in aid of?' I questioned.

'Little ones like this', and her hands measured about three inches apart. 'And it's for finding out about Mister God.'

Requests like that I took in my stride these days. After all, if it was possible to read sermons in stones and things, why not in paddle-wheels?

'And can I have the big bath, and some hosepipe, and a tin

with a hole in it? I might want something else but I don't know yet.'

While I made the paddle-wheels, Anna assembled her experiment. The paddle-wheels were mounted on axles. A large cylindrical tin had a half-inch hole drilled in its side near the bottom of the tin. One of the paddle-wheels was soldered inside the tin across the newly drilled hole. After about an hour of hectic activity I was called into the yard to see the Mister God experiment in action.

A hose from the tap was filling the large bath. The tin with its paddle-wheel sat in the middle of the bath, weighted down with stones. As the water poured in through the hole, the paddle-wheel was turning. More hosepipe was doing service as a siphon, taking the water out of the tin, falling onto and spinning the second paddle-wheel and ending up going down the drain. I walked around the experiment and raised my eyebrows.

'Do you like it, Fynn?' asked Anna.

'I like it. But what is it?' I asked.

'That's you', she said, pointing to the tin with its paddle-wheel.

'Bound to be. What am I doing?'

'The water is Mister God.'

'Gotcha.'

'The water comes out of the tap into the bath.'

'I'm still with you.'

'It goes into the tin, that's you, through the hole and makes you work', she said, pointing to the spinning wheel, 'like a heart.'

'Ah.'

'When you work, it comes out of this tube', she pointed to the siphon, 'and that makes the other wheel work.'

'What about the drain?'

'Well, she hesitated, 'if I had a little pump like Mister God's heart, I could pump it all back into the bath. Then I wouldn't need the tap. It would just go round and round.'

So there you are, then. How to make a model of Mister God, with a couple of paddle-wheels. No home should be without one. I sat on the wall and smoked a fag while I watched Mister God and me spinning paddle-wheels.

'Ain't it good, Fynn?'

'Sure is good. We'd better take it to church on Sunday. It might give somebody some ideas.'

'Oh no, we couldn't do that. That would be bad.'

'How's that?' I asked.

'Well, it isn't Mister God, but it's a little bit like him.'

'So what? If it works for you and it works for me, that's fine. It might work for someone else.'

'It works because me and you is full up.'

'And what might that mean?'

'Well, if you are full up, you can use anything to see Mister God. You can't if you're not full up.'

'Why's that? Give me a for instance.'

She never hesitated.

'The cross! If you're full up, you don't need it 'cos the cross is inside you. If you're not full up, you have the cross outside you and then you make it a magic thing.'

She tugged at my arm and our eyes met. She spoke quietly and slowly. 'If you're not full up inside you, then you can make anything a magic thing, and then it becomes an outside bit of you.'

'Is it that bad?'

She nodded. 'If you do that, then you can't do what Mister God wants you to do.'

'Oh! What's he want me to do then?'

'Love everybody like you love yourself, and you've got to be full up with you to love yourself properly first.'

'Like most of a person is outside', I said.

'She smiled. 'Fynn, there ain't no different churches in heaven 'cos everybody in heaven is inside themselves.'

Then she went on:

'It's the outside bits that make all the different churches and synagogues and temples and things like that. Fynn, Mister God said "I am", and that's what he wants us all to say – that's the hard bit.'

THE LITTLE WORLD OF DON CAMILLO, GIOVANNI GUARESCHI

162 Forgiving Others

The little world of Don Camillo is to be found somewhere in the valley of the Po river. I want you to understand that, in the Little World between the river and the mountains, many things can happen that cannot happen anywhere else. Here, the deep, eternal breathing of the river freshens the air, for both the living and the dead, and even the dogs, have souls. If you keep this in mind, you will easily come to know the village priest, Don Camillo, and his adversary, Peppone, the Communist Mayor.

You will not be surprised that Christ watches the goings-on from a big cross in the village church and not infrequently talks, and that one man beats the other over the head, but fairly – that is, without hatred – and that in the end the two enemies find they agree about essentials.

And one final word of explanation before I begin my story. If there is a priest anywhere who feels offended by my treatment of Don Camillo, he is welcome to break the biggest candle available over my head. And if there is a Communist who feels offended by Peppone, he is welcome to break a hammer and sickle on my back. But if there is anyone who is offended by the conversations of Christ, I can't help it; for the one who speaks in this story is not Christ, but my Christ – that is, the voice of my conscience. . .

When the time of the elections drew near, Don Camillo had naturally been explicit in his allusions to the local leftists. Thus there came a fine evening when, as he was going home at dusk, an individual muffled in a cloak sprang out of a hedge as he passed by and, taking advantage of the fact that Don Camillo was handicapped by his bicycle and by a large parcel containing seventy eggs attached to its handlebars, belaboured him with a heavy stick and promptly vanished as though the earth had swallowed him.

Don Camillo had kept his own counsel. Having arrived at the presbytery and deposited the eggs in safety, he had gone into the church to discuss the matter with the Lord, as was his invariable habit in moments of perplexity.

'What should I do?' Don Camillo had inquired.

'Anoint your back with a little oil beaten up in water and hold your tongue,' The Lord had replied from above the altar. 'We must forgive those who offend us. That is the rule.'

'Very true, Lord,' agreed Don Camillo, 'but on this occasion we are discussing blows, not offences.'

'And what do you mean by that? Surely you are not trying to tell me that injuries done to the body are more painful than those aimed at the spirit?'

'I see your point, Lord. But You should also bear in mind that in the beating of me, who am Your minister, an injury has been done to Yourself also. I am really more concerned on Your behalf than on my own.'

'And was I not a greater minister of God than you are? And did I not forgive those who nailed me to the Cross?'

'There is never any use in arguing with You!' Don Camillo had exclaimed. 'You are always in the right. Your will be done. We must forgive. All the same, don't forget that if these ruffians, encouraged by my silence, should crack my skull, the responsibility will lie with You. I could cite several passages from the Old Testament . . . '

'Don Camillo, are you proposing to instruct me in the Old Testament? As for this business, I assume full responsibility. Moreover, strictly between Ourselves, the beating has done you no harm. It may teach you to let politics alone in my house.'

Don Camillo had duly forgiven. But nevertheless one thing had stuck in his gullet like a fish bone: curiosity as to the identity of his assailant.

163 Justice

Time passed. Late one evening, while he sat in the confessional, Don Camillo discerned through the grille the countenance of the local leader of the extreme leftists, Peppone.

That Peppone should come to confession at all was a sensational event, and Don Camillo was proportionately gratified.

'God be with you, brother; with you who, more than any other man, have need of His holy blessing. It is a long time since you last went to confession?'

'Not since 1918', replied Peppone.

'You must have committed a great number of sins in the course of those twenty-eight years, with your head so crammed with crazy notions . . . '

'A good few, undoubtedly', sighed Peppone.

'For example?'

'For example, two months ago I gave you a hiding.'

'That was serious indeed', replied Don Camillo, 'since in assaulting a minister of God, you have attacked God Himself.'

'But I have repented', exclaimed Peppone. 'And, moreover, it was not as God's minister that I beat you, but as my political adversary. In any case, I did it in a moment of weakness.'

'Apart from this and from your membership of your accursed Party, have you any other grave sins on your conscience?'

Peppone spilled all the beans.

Taken as a whole, his offences were not very serious, and Don Camillo let him off with a score of Paters and Aves. Then, while Peppone was kneeling at the altar rails performing his penance, Don Camillo went and knelt before the crucifix.

'Lord', he said. 'You must forgive me, but I am going to beat him up for You.'

'You are going to do nothing of the kind', replied the Lord. 'I have forgiven him and you must forgive him also. All things considered, he is not a bad soul.'

'Lord, you can never trust a Red! They live by lies. Only look at him; Barabbas incarnate!'

'It's as good a face as most, Don Camillo; it is your heart that is venomous!'

'Lord, if I have ever served You well, grant me just one small grace: let me at least break this candle on his shoulders. Dear Lord, what, after all, is a candle?'

'No', replied the Lord. 'Your hands were made for blessing, not for striking.'

Don Camillo sighed heavily.

He genuflected and left the sanctuary. As he turned to make a final sign of the cross he found himself exactly behind Peppone who, on his knees, was apparently absorbed in prayer.

'Lord', groaned Don Camillo, clasping his hands and gazing at the crucifix. 'My hands were made for blessing, but not my feet!'

'There is something in that', replied the Lord from above the altar, 'but all the same, Don Camillo, bear it in mind: only one!'

The kick landed like a thunderbolt and Peppone received it without so much as blinking an eye. Then he got to his feet and sighed with relief.

'I've been waiting for that for the last ten minutes', he remarked. 'I feel better now.'

'So do I!' exclaimed Don Camillo, whose heart was now as light and serene as a May morning.

The Lord said nothing at all, but it was easy enough to see that He, too, was pleased.

164 What's in a Name?

One day the church was unexpectedly invaded by a man and two women, one of whom was Peppone's wife.

Don Camillo, who from the top of a pair of steps was cleaning St Joseph's halo with Brasso, turned round and inquired what they wanted.

'There is something here that needs to be baptised', replied the man, and one of the women held up a bundle containing a baby.

'Whose is it?' inquired Don Camillo, coming down from his steps.

'Mine,' replied Peppone's wife.

'And your husband's?' persisted Don Camillo.

'Well, naturally! Who else do you suppose gave it to me?' retorted Peppone's wife indignantly.

'No need to be offended', observed Don Camillo on his way to the sacristy. 'Haven't I been told often enough that your Party approves of free love?'

As he passed before the high altar Don Camillo knelt down and permitted himself a discreet wink in the direction of the Lord. 'Did you hear that one?' he murmured with a joyful grin. 'One in the eye for the Godless ones!'

'Don't talk rubbish, Don Camillo', replied the Lord irritably. 'If they had no God, why should they come here to get their child baptised? If Peppone's wife had boxed your ears it would only have served you right.'

'If Peppone's wife had boxed my ears I should have taken the three of them by the scruff of their necks and . . . '

'And what?' inquired the Lord severely.

'Oh, nothing; just a figure of speech', Don Camillo hastened to assure Him, rising to his feet.

'Don Camillo, watch your step', said the Lord sternly.

Duly vested, Don Camillo approached the font. 'What do you wish to name this child?' he asked Peppone's wife.

'Lenin Libero Antonio', she replied.

'Then go and get him baptised in Russia', said Don Camillo calmly, replacing the cover on the font.

The priest's hands were as large as shovels and the three left the church without protest. But as Don Camillo was attempting to slip into the sacristy he was arrested by the voice of the Lord.

'Don Camillo, you have done a very wicked thing. Go at once and bring those people back and baptise their child.'

'But Lord', protested Don Camillo, 'You really must bear in mind that baptism is not a jest. Baptism is a very sacred matter. Baptism is . . . '

'Don Camillo', the Lord interrupted him. 'Are you attempting to teach me the nature of baptism? Did I not invent it? I tell you that you have been guilty of gross presumption, because, suppose that child were to die at this moment, it would be your fault if it failed to attain Paradise!'

'Lord, do not let us be melodramatic', retorted Don Camillo. 'Why in the name of Heaven should it die? It's as pink and white as a rose!'

'Which means exactly nothing!' the Lord admonished him.

'What if a tile should fall on its head or it should suddenly have convulsions? It was your duty to baptise it.'

Don Camillo raised protesting arms: 'But Lord, just think it over. If it were certain that the child would go to Hell, we might stretch a point; but seeing that despite being the son of that nasty piece of work he might very easily manage to slip into Paradise, how can You ask me to risk anyone going there with such a name as Lenin? I'm thinking of the reputation of Paradise.'

'The reputation of Paradise is my business', shouted the Lord angrily. 'What matters to me is that a man should be a decent fellow and I care less than nothing whether his name be Lenin or Button. At the very most, you should have pointed out to those people that saddling children with fantastic names may involve them in annoyances when they grow up.'

'Very well', replied Don Camillo. 'I am always in the wrong. I must see what I can do about it.'

165 A Baptism

Just at that moment someone came into the church. It was Peppone, alone, with the baby in his arms. He closed the church door and bolted it.

'I do not leave this church', he said, 'until my son has been baptised with the name that I have chosen.'

'Look at that', whispered Don Camillo, smiling as he turned towards the Lord. 'Now do You see what these people are? One is filled with the holiest intentions and this is how they treat you.'

'Put yourself in his place', replied the Lord. 'One may not approve his attitude, but one can understand it.'

Don Camillo shook his head.

'I have already said that I do not leave this place unless you baptise my son as I demand!' repeated Peppone. Whereupon, laying the bundle containing the baby upon a bench, he took off his coat, rolled up his sleeves and advanced threateningly.

'Lord', implored Don Camillo. 'I ask You! If You think it just that one of your priests should give way to the threats of a layman, then I must obey. But in that event, if tomorrow they should bring me a calf and compel me to baptise it You must not complain. You know very well how dangerous it is to create precedents.'

'All right', replied the Lord, 'but in this case you must try to make him understand. . . . '

'And if he hits me?'

'Then you must accept it. You must endure and suffer as I did.'
Don Camillo turned to his visitor.

'Very well, Peppone', he said. 'The baby will leave the church
baptised, but not by that accursed name.'

'Don Camillo', stuttered Peppone, 'don't forget that my
stomach has never recovered from that bullet that I stopped in the
mountains. If you hit low, I shall go for you with a bench.'

'Don't worry, Peppone. I can deal with you entirely in the
upper storeys', Don Camillo assured him, landing him a neat one
above the ear.

They were both burly men with muscles of steel, and their
blows fairly whistled through the air. After twenty minutes of
silent and furious combat, Dom Camillo distinctly heard a voice
behind him. 'Now, Don Camillo! The point of the jaw!' It came
from the Lord above the altar. Don Camillo struck hard and
Peppone crashed to the ground.

He remained where he lay for some ten minutes; then he sat up,
got to his feet, rubbed his jaw, shook himself, put on his jacket
and re-knotted his red handkerchief. Then he picked up the baby.
Fully vested, Don Camillo was waiting for him, steady as a rock,
beside the font. Peppone approached him slowly.

'What am I to name him?' asked Don Camillo.

'Camillo Libero Antonio', muttered Peppone.

Don Camillo shook his head. 'No; we will name him Libero
Camillo Lenin', he said. 'Yes, Lenin. When you have a Camillo
around, such folk as he are quite helpless.'

'Amen', muttered Peppone, gently prodding his jaw.

When all was done and Don Camillo passed before the altar the
Lord smiled and remarked: 'Don Camillo, I am bound to admit
that in politics you are My master.'

'And also in fisticuffs', replied Don Camillo with perfect
gravity, carelessly fingering a large lump on his forehead.

EMMA AND I, SHEILA HOCKEN

166 The Decision

I was, if the truth be known, ashamed of being blind. I refused to
use a white stick, and hated asking for help. After all, I was a
teenage girl, and I couldn't bear people to look at me and think I

was not like them. Looking back, I must have been a terrible danger on the roads. Motorists probably had seizures; suddenly coming across me wandering vaguely through the traffic, they would have to step rapidly on their brakes. Apart from that, there were all sorts of disasters that used to strike on the way to and from work.

On the evening that made such a difference to my life, I got off the bus just about half-way home where I had to change buses, and as usual I was walking gingerly along to the right stop. Almost immediately I bumped into something. 'I'm awfully sorry', I said and stepped forward only to collide again. When it happened a third time, I realized I had been apologising to a lamp standard. This was just one of those idiotic things that constantly happened to me, and I had long since learnt to put up with them or even to find them faintly amusing. So I carried on and found the bus stop, which was a request stop. No one else was there and I had to go through the scary business of trying to estimate when the bus arrived . . .

My home teacher was there when I finally reached home that evening. Home teachers visit the blind. They come regularly to help, to talk over any problems, and to supply various aids such as braille paper, braille clocks, egg timers that ring and so on. Mr. Brown who used to visit my family (since we were all registered as blind people) was quite a feature of life while I was growing up. Mr. Brown had been waiting for me for about an hour. I explained why I was so late, and gave all the details of my nightmare journey. He immediately asked, 'Why on earth don't you have a guide-dog?'

They were the nine most important words of my life up to that time.

[Eventually Sheila was accepted for training with a guide-dog and travelled to the training centre.]

As we went on to the dining-room, the prospect of a familiar ordeal loomed up in my mind. I hated eating meals with sighted people. It always led to some kind of embarrassment. They usually wanted to cut my meat up, and imagined it would be better if I ate with a spoon instead of a knife and fork. Or they said, 'Oh dear, if only I'd known you couldn't see, I would have made sandwiches.' I would become so demoralized and nervous I could hardly eat at all when a plate of food was eventually put in front of me. Not knowing what was on it, much less exactly where the food was, I would stab away, usually missing potatoes or meat or whatever, and ending up bringing my teeth together on the metal of an empty fork.

At the training centre it was totally different. Brian sat next to me and put a plate in front of me.

'Here we are', he said. 'Fish, chips and peas. Chips at twelve o'clock, peas at three o'clock and fish between nine and six.'

So I not only knew what I was going to eat, but where to find it.

167 Training

I owe a great deal to Brian, not only for his training, but also for matching Emma and me together. His assessment of all he knew about us resulted in an inspired pairing, as time was to prove.

One day I remember asking him where Emma came from. What I really meant was, how did the centres come by the guide-dogs? Brian explained that they came to Leamington, or one of the other centres, after being puppy-walked. The Guide-Dog Association has a big breeding and puppy-walking centre at Tollgate House, near Warwick. They own a number of brood bitches and stud dogs that are let out to people as pets, because, naturally, a permanent kennel life is not desirable, and living with a family is a much happier arrangement. At the same time the Association controls which dog should mate with which. When the litters come along, it picks the dogs and bitches required for training. At about eight weeks old, a puppy undergoes various tests to see if it is basically bold and friendly, and capable of being trained as a guide-dog. Dogs bred in this way form about sixty per cent of the total, and there are now about two thousand guide-dog owners in the country. The remaining forty per cent come to the Association either by purchase or donation from breeders or private individuals. But the rejection rate is high. Dogs are kept on approval for about three weeks to see if they are suitable. If they're not, they are returned to their owners. . . .

One of the centre's ingenious ways of familiarizing us with the day's programme was by using tactile maps. Pavements, buildings, and so on were raised on a wooden map of Leamington, so we could feel our way over the routes beforehand, right down to the zebra crossings and the bus stops. Emma would find these things for me, but I had to be in the right road, and the map helped enormously to make sure we did not miss our way. Our walks became more and more complicated, and Brian would try to find places where there were road works, to ensure we had mastered the business of getting round them, as well as other obstacles. Bus trips and shopping expeditions were also in the curriculum, and I really enjoyed shopping with Emma. She would not only find the shop, but also take me up to the counter. I began to forget I was blind. No one fussed round me any longer. They were all too interested in Emma.

Brian told us we were going to the railway station as a final test. Emma took me through the doors, down a couple of flights of steps, in and out between people on the platform and sat down. I had no idea where I was. I just stood and waited for Brian. He was there within a couple of minutes. 'Right', he said, 'Emma's sitting bang on the edge of the platform. There's about a six-foot drop in front of you to the railway line. Now tell her to go forward.'

I was petrified, and could feel my spine tingle.

'You must be joking', I said.

'No, go on. Tell her to go forward.'

I stood there, not knowing what to do. This really was a terrible test. Dare I do it? I was so scared. I felt sick. In that moment I really did not want a guide-dog. Everything I had heard about them, all the training we had done, all I felt about Emma flashed through my mind, and it meant nothing. I just wanted, there and then, to lay the harness handle on Emma's back, and leave, get out, escape, anything. But, in a sort of hoarse whisper, I heard myself saying 'Forward'.

Immediately, up she got, and almost in the same motion pushed herself in front of my legs. Then she started pushing me back, right away from the edge of the platform. . . .

So that was it. We had made it. The sense of freedom was incredible.

168 At Home – Travelling

Emma and I started to go to work together as soon as we were settled again. At that time I lived in Carlton, on one side of Nottingham, and I worked right over the other side, the Bulwell side, of the city. I had to catch two buses, with a walk across the Market Square in the middle of Nottingham in between. The terminus for the first bus was at the bottom of our road, so that part was easy. Emma trotted down the road with her tail in the air – I could feel it brushing my hand as we went along – and, at the same time, I began to learn how sensitive it was possible to be, via the harness, to what she was doing. Through it I could tell whether her ears were up or down, whether she was turning her head left or right, and all sorts of little movements.

We found the stop, and from that moment Emma loved going on buses. It was not just the bus itself, however. One important factor was the admiration she received that morning, and every time we got on a bus henceforth. 'Oh, what a lovely dog. Oh, what a beautiful colour.' And so on. I could sense Emma basking in the glory. She had picked the second seat on the right for me. For some reason, this was the place she always chose on this particular bus. I sat down, and Emma went under the seat. Strangely, this was the only bus on which she had such a preference: it always had to be the same one. After we had been going to work for about three weeks, we were nearing the bus one morning when I began to pick up the sound of a great commotion going on inside it. As we came alongside I could hear a woman's muffled shout: 'You'll have to get up you know. You can't sit there, I tell you it's Emma's seat. Come on – they'll be here in a minute.'

On other buses, Emma simply went for any empty seat, preferably – in the winter at least – one near the heaters. But since we normally travelled in the rush hour the buses, apart from our first one, were very often full, so she had to use a different technique. She would drag me along the aisle, nosing everyone else out of the way if there were standing passengers, decide on where she wanted us to sit, then stare at whoever was sitting there until they gave way. To be fair, they normally gave up the seat very quickly, and before the bus was in an uproar. This, of course, appealed to the exhibitionist in Emma. When she was sure she had got her audience, she would turn to me, lay her head across my knee, looking, I imagined, specially devoted and possibly a little pathetic. By this time the entire bus was hers.

THE WATER BABIES, CHARLES KINGSLEY, WRITTEN 1863

169 Mrs. Bedonebyasyoudid

[Tom had been apprenticed to a chimney sweep who made him climb up the chimneys to sweep them with his brush. One day he climbed down the wrong chimney, landed in a small girl's bedroom and was so frightened by all the fuss that he ran away. Eventually he waded into a river and there he turned into a water baby, although the people chasing him thought he had been drowned.

As a water baby he was very happy and played all day long,

with no work to do. However, he soon started to tease all the sea creatures . . .]

The other children warned him, and said, 'Take care what you are at. Mrs. Bedonebyasyoudid is coming.' But Tom never heeded them, being quite riotous with high spirits and good luck, till, one Friday morning early, Mrs. Bedonebyasyoudid came indeed.

A very tremendous lady she was; and when the children saw her they all stood in a row, very upright indeed, and smoothed down their bathing dresses, and put their hands behind them, just as if they were going to be examined by the inspector. And she had on a black bonnet, and a black shawl, and no crinoline at all; and a pair of large green spectacles, and a great hooked nose, hooked so much that the bridge of it stood quite up above her eye-brows; and under her arm she carried a great birch rod. Indeed she was so ugly that Tom was tempted to make faces at her, but did not, for he did not admire the look of the birch rod under her arm.

And she looked at the children one by one, and seemed very much pleased with them, though she never asked them one question about how they were behaving; and then began giving them all sorts of nice sea-things, – sea-cakes, sea-apples, sea-oranges, sea-bullseyes, sea-toffee; and to the very best of all she gave sea-ices, made out of sea-cow's cream, which never melt under water. . . .

Now little Tom watched all these sweet things given away till his mouth watered, and his eyes grew as round as an owl's. For he hoped that his turn would come at last; and so it did. For the lady called him up, and held out her fingers with something in them, and popped it into his mouth; and, lo! and behold, it was a nasty, cold, hard pebble.

'You are a very cruel woman', said he, and began to whimper. 'And you are a very cruel boy who puts pebbles into sea-anemones' mouths to take them in, and make them fancy that they had caught a good dinner! – As you did to them, so I must do to you.' . . . 'And now do you be a good boy and do as you would be done by; and then, when my sister, Madame Doasyouwouldbedoneby, comes on Sunday, perhaps she will take notice of you, and teach you how to behave. She understands that better than I do.'

And so she went.

170 Mrs. Doasyouwouldbedoneby

Tom determined to be a very good boy all Saturday; and he was; for he never frightened one crab, nor tickled any live corals, nor put stones into the sea-anemones' mouths to make them fancy they had got a dinner: and when Sunday morning came, sure enough, Mrs. Doasyouwouldbedoneby came too. Whereat all the little children began dancing and clapping their hands, and Tom danced too with all his might.

And as for the pretty lady, I cannot tell you what the colour of her hair was, or of her eyes: no more could Tom; for, when anyone looks at her, all they can think of is, that she has the sweetest, kindest, tenderest, funniest, merriest face they ever saw, or want to see. But Tom saw that she was a very tall woman, as tall as her sister: but instead of being gnarly, and horny, and scaly, and prickly, like her, she was the most nice, soft, fat, smooth, pussy, cuddly, delicious creature who ever nursed a baby . . . And therefore when the children saw her, they naturally all caught hold of her and pulled her till she sat down on a stone, and climbed into her lap, and clung round her neck, and caught hold of her hands . . . and Tom stood staring at them; for he could not understand what it all was about.

'And who are you, you little darling?' she said. 'Oh, that is the new baby!' they all cried . . . 'and he never had any mother', and they all put their thumbs back again.

'Then I will be his mother, and he shall have the very best place; so get out, all of you, this moment.'

And she took up two great armfuls of babies – nine hundred under one arm, and thirteen hundred under the other – and threw them away, right and left, into the water. But they minded it no more than the naughty boys in Strewelpeter minded when St. Nicholas dipped them in his inkstand; and did not even take their thumbs out of their mouths, but came paddling and wriggling back to her like so many tadpoles, till you could see nothing of her from head to foot for the swarm of little babies.

But she took Tom in her arms, and laid him in the softest place of all, and kissed him, and patted him, and talked to him, tenderly and low, such things as he had never heard before in his life; and Tom looked up into her eyes, and loved her, and loved, till he fell fast asleep from pure love.

[When he woke the fairy was nursing him still.]

'Now', said the fairy to Tom, 'Will you be a good boy for my sake and torment no more sea-creatures till I come back?'

'And you will cuddle me again?' said poor little Tom.

'Of course I will, you little duck.' And away she went.

So Tom really tried to be a good boy, and tormented no sea-beasts after that as long as he lived; and he is quite alive, I assure you still.

171 The Nation of Doasyoulikes

[After seven years Tom was told that before he could go to the most beautiful place in the world he must first go where he did not like, and do what he did not like and help somebody he did not like. Before he rather reluctantly set out, Mrs. Bedonebyasyoudid showed him the most wonderful waterproof book, full of such photographs as never were seen . . .]

And on the title page was written: 'The history of the great and famous nation of the Doasyoulikes who came away from the country of Hardwork because they wanted to play on the Jews' harp all day long.'

In the first picture they saw these Doasyoulikes living in the land of Readymade, at the foot of the Happy-go-lucky Mountains, where flapdoodle grows wild . . . They were very fond of music but it was too much trouble to learn to play the piano or the violin; and, as for dancing, that would have been too great an exertion. So they sat on ant-hills all day long, and played on the Jews' harp; and if the ants bit them, why, they just got up and went to the next ant-hill, till they were bitten there likewise.

And they sat under the flapdoodle trees, and the flapdoodle dropped into their mouths; and under the vines, and squeezed the grape-juice down their throats; and if any little pigs ran about ready roasted, crying 'Come and eat me', as was their fashion in that country, they waited till the pigs ran against their mouths, and then took a bite, and were content, just as so many oysters would have been. And so on, and so on, and so on, till there were never such comfortable, easy-going, happy-go-lucky people in the world.

[He turned over the next 500 years.] And behold, the mountain had blown up like a barrel of gunpowder, and then boiled over like a kettle; whereby one-third of the Doasyoulikes were blown into the air, and another third were smothered in ashes, so that there was only one-third left . . .

And then she turned over the next five hundred years, and there were the remnants of the Doasyoulikes, doing as they liked, as before. They were too lazy to move away from the mountain; so they said, 'If it has blown up once, that is all the more reason that it should not blow up again.' And they were few in number; but they only said, 'The more the merrier, but the fewer the better the fare.' However, that was not quite true, for all the flapdoodle trees were killed by the volcano, and they had eaten all the roast pigs, who, of course, could not be expected to have little ones. So they had to live very hard, on nuts and roots, which they scratched out of the ground with sticks. Some of them talked of sowing corn, as their ancestors used to do before they came into the land of Readymade; but they had forgotten how to make ploughs (they had forgotten even how to make Jews' harps by this time), and had eaten all the seed-corn which they brought out of the land of Hardwork years since; and, of course, it was too much trouble to go away and find more. So they lived miserably on roots and nuts, and all the weakly little children had great stomachs, and then died. . . .

And she turned over the next five hundred years. And there they were all living up in trees, and making nests to keep off the rain. And underneath the trees lions were prowling about . . .

And she turned over the next five hundred years. And in that they were fewer still, and stronger and fiercer; but their feet had changed shape very oddly, for they laid hold of the branches with their great toes, as if they had been thumbs . . .

And in the next five hundred years they were all dead and gone, by bad food and wild beasts and hunters! And that was the end of the great and jolly nation of Doasyoulikes.

Other suitable instalments can be found, such as:
>How Tom helped the lobster out of the trap;
>How Tom stole some sea-sweets and what happened;
>The Caucus of the scaul-crows;
>The Isle of Tomtoddies and their idol Examination.

THE SCREWTAPE LETTERS, C. S. LEWIS

172 Friends

My dear Wormwood,

I was delighted to hear from Triptweeze that your patient has made some very desirable new acquaintances and that you seem to have used this event in a really promising manner.

I gather that the middle-aged married couple who called at his office are just the sort of people we want him to know – rich,

smart, superficially intellectual and brightly sceptical. I gather
they are vaguely pacifist, not on moral grounds but from an
ingrained habit of belittling anything that concerns the great mass
of their fellow men and from a dash of purely fashionable and
literary communism. This is excellent. . . .

No doubt he must very soon realise that his own faith is in
direct opposition to the assumptions on which all the conversation
of his new friends is based. I don't think that matters much
provided that you can persuade him to postpone any open
acknowledgement of the fact, and this, with the aid of shame,
pride, modesty and vanity, will be easy to do. As long as the
postponement lasts he will be in a false position. He will be silent
when he ought to speak and laugh when he ought to be silent. He
will assume, at first only by his manner, but presently by his
words, all sorts of cynical and sceptical attitudes which are not
really his. But if you play him well, they may become his. All
mortals tend to turn into the thing they are pretending to be. This
is elementary. The real question is how to prepare for the Enemy's
counter attack. . . .

Sooner or later, however, the real nature of his new friends
must become clear to him, and then your tactics must depend on
the patient's intelligence. If he is a big enough fool you can get
him to realize the character of the friends only while they are
absent; their presence can be made to sweep away all criticism. If
this succeeds, he can be induced to live, as I have known many
humans to live, for quite long periods, two parallel lives; he will
not only appear to be, but actually be, a different man in each of
the circles he frequents. Failing this, there is a subtler and more
entertaining method. He can be made to take a positive pleasure
in the perception that the two sides of his life are inconsistent.
This is done by exploiting his vanity. He can be taught to enjoy
kneeling beside the grocer on Sunday just because he remembers
that the grocer could not possibly understand the urbane and
mocking world which he inhabited on Saturday evening; and
contrariwise to enjoy the bawdy and blasphemy over the coffee
with these admirable friends all the more because he is aware of a
'deeper', 'spiritual' world within him which they cannot
understand. . . .

Thus, while being permanently treacherous to at least two sets
of people, he will feel, instead of shame, a continual undercurrent
of self-satisfaction. . . .

Meanwhile you will of course take the obvious precaution of
seeing that this new development induces him to spend more than
he can afford and to neglect his work and his mother. Her

jealousy, and alarm, and his increasing evasiveness or rudeness, will be invaluable for the aggravation of the domestic tension.
Your affectionate uncle,
Screwtape

173 Self

My dear Wormwood,
The most alarming thing in your last account of the patient is that he is making none of those confident resolutions which marked his original conversion. . . .

I see only one thing to do at the moment. Your patient has become humble; have you drawn his attention to the fact? All virtues are less formidable to us once the man is aware he has them, but this is specially true of humility. Catch him at the moment when he is really poor in spirit and smuggle into his mind the gratifying reflection, 'By jove! I'm being humble', and almost immediately pride – pride at his own humility – will appear. If he awakes to the danger and tries to smother this new form of pride, make him proud of his attempt – and so on, through as many stages as you please. But don't try this too long, for fear you awake his sense of humour and proportion, in which case he will merely laugh at you and go to bed . . .

You must therefore conceal from the patient the true end of Humility. Let him think of it not as self-forgetfulness but as a certain kind of opinion (namely a low opinion) of his own talents and character. . . . By this method thousands of humans have been brought to think that humility means pretty women trying to believe they are ugly and clever men trying to believe they are fools. And since what they are trying to believe may, in some cases, be manifest nonsense, they cannot succeed in believing it and we have the chance of keeping their minds endlessly revolving on themselves in an effort to achieve the impossible. . . .

For we must never forget what is the most repellent and inexplicable trait in our Enemy: He really loves the hairless bipeds He has created and always gives back to them with His right hand what He has taken away with His left.

The Enemy's whole effort, therefore, will be to get the man's mind off the subject of his own value altogether. He would rather the man thought himself a great architect or a great poet and then forgot about it, than he should spend much time and pains trying to think himself a bad one. Even of his sins the Enemy does not want him to think too much; once they are repented, the sooner

the man turns his attention outward, the better the Enemy is
pleased.
Your affectionate uncle,
Screwtape.

174 Gluttony

My dear Wormwood,
The contemptuous way in which you spoke of gluttony as a means
of catching souls, in your last letter, only shows your ignorance.
One of the great achievements of the last hundred years has been
to deaden the human conscience on that subject, so that by now
you will hardly find a sermon preached or a conscience troubled
about it in the whole length and breadth of Europe. This has
largely been effected by concentrating all our efforts on gluttony
of Delicacy not gluttony of Excess. Your patient's mother, as I
learn from the dossier and you might have learned from Glubose,
is a good example. She would be astonished – one day, I hope, will
be – to learn that her whole life is enslaved to this kind of
sensuality, which is quite concealed from her by the fact that the
quantities involved are small. But what do quantities matter,
provided we can use a human belly and palate to produce
querulousness, impatience, uncharitableness, and self-concern?
Glubose has this old woman well in hand. She is a positive terror
to hostesses and friends. She is always turning from what has been
offered her to say with a demure little sigh and a smile 'Oh please,
please . . . all I want is a cup of tea, weak but not too weak, and
the teeniest, weeniest bit of really crisp toast.' You see? Because
what she wants is smaller and less costly than what has been set
before her, she never recognises as gluttony her determination to
get what she wants, however troublesome it may be to others. At
the very moment of indulging her appetite she believes that she is
practising temperance. In a crowded restaurant she gives a little
scream at the plate which some overworked waitress has set before
and says 'Oh, that's far, far too much! Take it away and bring me
about a quarter of it.' If challenged, she would say she was doing
this to avoid waste; in reality she does it because the particular
shade of delicacy to which we have enslaved her is offended by the
sight of more food than she happens to want.

The real value of the quiet, unobtrusive work which Glubose
has been doing for years on this old woman can be gauged by the
way in which her belly now dominates her whole life. The woman
is in what may be called the 'All-I-want' state of mind. All she

wants is a cup of tea properly made, or an egg properly boiled, or a slice of bread properly toasted. But she can never find anyone who can do these simple things 'properly' – because her 'properly' conceals an insatiable demand for the exact, and almost impossible, palatal pleasures which she imagines she remembers from the past. . . . Meanwhile, the daily disappointment produces daily ill temper.

EPISTLES TO THE APOSTLE, COLIN MORRIS

175 Andrew alias Plutus alias Simeon to Paul

Reverend and Dear Sir,

You may remember I had cause to correspond with you when I was Secretary of the Burglar's Guild concerning the question of the Return of Our Lord and the social implications of this belief insofar as and for as much as my own profession is concerned. Whether you did me the honour of replying to my letter I have no way of knowing as I took a rather long holiday shortly after I had written to you; well, to tell no lie and shame the Devil, I did a spell at sea, in the galleys. However, I have now returned and have been most moved to hear how the poor in Jerusalem have no food and you are raising a fund to help them.

At a meeting of our Guild on the 15th inst. this matter was discussed in some detail and the following resolution was passed nem. con. – that 10% (ten per cent) of our net earnings, before the shareout and after necessary overheads have been paid, should be handed over to you for the benefit of all those poor people in Jerusalem who must be so weak and hungry that they haven't the strength to nick the purses of some of those big, fat merchants of whom there is no shortage (so we are given to understand by our colleagues in that area).

I shall be most happy to meet you – preferably after dark in some suitable place – to hand over our first contribution. We ask nothing in return, except your prayers that nothing should prevent us from carrying on our profession, such as police, big dogs or those new-fangled locks the rich are importing from Rome.

Yours most honestly,

Andrew alias Plutus

How about helping the poor by the wages of honest work?

If you used to be a thief you must not only give up stealing, but you must learn to make an honest living, so that you may be able to give to those in need.

Let there be no more foul language, but good words instead. Live your lives in love – the same sort of love which Christ gives us. But as for sexual immorality in all its forms, and the itch to get your hands on what belongs to other people – don't even talk about such things. The keynote of your conversation should not be nastiness or silliness or flippancy, but a sense of all we owe to God. For of this much you can be quite certain: that neither the immoral nor the covetous man (which latter is, in effect, worshipping a false god) has any inheritance in the Kingdom of Christ and of God. Let your lives be living proofs of the things which please God. Steer clear of the activities of darkness, you know the sort of things I mean!

176 Pilgrim's Regress

Demas and Luke are my fellow-workers for God.
Luke and Demas send you their best wishes.
Demas has left me, having loved this present world.
Only Luke is with me now.

Demas to Paul

My dear Paul,
By the time you receive this letter I shall be with wife and family in Thessalonica. I'm afraid I can take no more. Unlike Luke and yourself I am weary to the marrow of my bones with all the persecution and torment we have endured these past years. In spite of your handicap, you seem to be made of iron – prison, torture, hardship, constant harassment seem only to strengthen your resolve and make your faith burn all the brighter. I'm not made of any metal that is refined by fire; I warp, and melt.

I wish with all my heart I could have stayed by your side, but you demanded too much of me, even though you were probably unaware of the fact. I am not the stuff of which missionary martyrs are made. I am only capable of a little love, of a small sacrifice, of moderate hardship. Luke will care for you. In his gentle way he has your steadfastness. Pray for me because I am afraid of death and pain and loneliness. I ask your pardon and the forgiveness of Christ. I am not worthy to be an apostle, but I shall continue to follow from a distance. But no more prison! No more controversy! No more endless journeys! I have come home, and here I want to stay.

Please don't think too badly of me. I have deserted you, but I hope I have not deserted Christ. It is just that my strength and endurance have deserted me. Possibly in time I shall regain them. Meanwhile, God grant you the companionship you deserve and which I was not able to give you.
Yours penitently,
Demas

177 Timothy to Paul

Dearest Father in God,
I was frankly terrified when you put me in charge of the Christian community here in Ephesus. I started badly and things have got steadily worse. I'll never make a preacher; never! No matter how carefully I prepare my sermons, the moment I see all those faces staring up at me, my legs turn to water and I stammer and stutter, losing my place in the manuscript and repeating myself over and over again. I'm afraid I'm not much credit to you. Ephesus, as you know well, is not short of cunning orators who know every trick of the trade and draw the crowds. I'm no match for them in argument. They just run rings round me. And there are times when I am silent in the face of evil. It's not that I am afraid. I just can't think of anything to say until it is too late, so I'm scorned as either a fool or a coward.

The elders of the congregation are fully justified in their criticism of me, though in all charity, I do feel that some of them scorn me because I am of mixed race; and that cannot be right, for as you yourself have written, 'In Christ there is neither Jew nor Gentile; all are one in Him.' There is the usual bickering and quarrelling in the congregation that we experienced so often when I was travelling with you. But whereas you have the authority to rebuke and reprove I just flounder, and I'm sure the followers of the Goddess, Diana, who are everywhere in this city, must think the Ambassador of King Jesus is a wooden donkey!

I am truly ashamed to send you such a dismal report of my progress whilst you are in prison. God works in a strange way. How much better it would be if I were in chains and you were free to preach the Gospel! I might make a tolerable job of being a prisoner instead of being an utter failure as a minister. I fear constantly for your life, and I dearly wish our roles could be reversed. I'm sure I should find it easier to die for Christ than live for Him.

Yours abysmally,

Timothy

Stick at it, Timothy

My son, be strong in the grace that Jesus Christ gives. Everything that you have heard me teach in public you should in turn entrust to reliable men who will be able to pass it on to others.

I urge you, Timothy, as we live in the sight of God and of Christ Jesus (Whose coming in power will judge the living and the dead) to preach the Word of God. Never lose your sense of urgency, in season or out of season.

Stand fast in all that you are doing, meeting whatever suffering this may involve. Go on steadily preaching the Gospel and carry out to the full the commission that God gave you.

I rely on this saying: If we died with Him we shall also live with Him: If we suffer with Him we shall also reign with Him. If we deny Him He will also deny us: yet if we are faithless He always remains faithful. He cannot deny his own nature.

Set your heart not on riches, but on goodness, Christlikeness, faith, love, patience and humility. Fight the worth-while battle of the Faith, keep your grip on that life eternal to which you have been called, and to which you boldly professed your loyalty before many witnesses. Grace be with you.

178 Titus to Paul

Paul sent Titus on difficult missions to Corinth and then left him behind in Crete to organise the church there. Titus, whom Paul called 'my true son in the common faith', had a much more difficult task than that of Timothy, who had been entrusted with imposing some kind of order on the church at Ephesus. The Christian community in Crete was scattered to such a degree that it is stretching language to call the Cretan Christians a 'church' at all. Equally, the opposition from Jews in Crete seems to have been particularly intense.

Revered Sir,

How much longer must I stay in this God-forsaken spot? This place is a howling bedlam of argumentative, uncharitable ranters. I have known no place like it. When the so-called church gathers for worship, it is more like a market-place with a multitude of self-styled teachers peddling their conflicting ideas, none of which seem to me to have much to do with the Christian faith. The Jews are the most vicious and divisive. They tell people that they ought not to listen to me because I have not been circumcised and so am an outsider – a semi-pagan who cannot be in the true tradition of Jesus, who was circumcised on the eighth day. They also spend hours reciting the genealogies of the Jewish faith, arguing about who begat who and in what order and claiming their own place in the true succession of the sons of Abraham. And their legends! Fanciful stories that have no spiritual value and recount the most weird and miraculous happenings which seem to me to have more in common with the mystery religions than with our common Faith.

I am at my wit's end. I have tried to impose some order on our gatherings but they shout me down and hurl abuse so vile that I truly believe that they are disciples of Satan rather than servants of Christ.

What am I to do? Please advise me.
Your son in Christ,
Titus

I know exactly what you are up against

Mind you steer clear of stupid arguments, genealogies, controversies and quarrels over the Law. They settle nothing and lead nowhere. There are many amongst the Jews who will not recognise authority, who talk nonsense and yet in so doing have managed to deceive men's minds. They must be silenced, for they have upset the faith of whole households, teaching what they have no business to teach for the sake of what they can get. One of them, yes, one of their prophets, has said: 'Men of Crete are always liars, evil and beastly, lazy and greedy.' There is truth in this testimonal of theirs! Don't hesitate to reprimand them sharply, for you want them to be sound and healthy Christians, with a proper contempt for Jewish fairy tales and orders issued by men who have forsaken the path of truth.

Let your own life stand as a pattern of good living. In all your teaching show the strictest regard for truth and show you appreciate the seriousness of the matters you are dealing with. Your speech should be unaffected and logical, so that your opponent may feel ashamed at finding nothing in which to pick holes.

As soon as I send Artemas to you (or perhaps it will be

Tychicus), do your best to come to me at Nicopolis, for I have made up my mind to spend the winter there.

Titus, again to Paul

Father,
Artemas or Tychicus can't arrive quick enough for me! I honestly feel I am wasting my time here. I have, since the first day you introduced me to Jesus, wished to be a missionary. But this is not missionary work; it is one long argument against men who are more cunning and fluent than I am. Nothing is sacred to these cynical debaters. Now they are questioning the Resurrection and claiming that the raising from the dead of Jesus by God is a past event and that the only way in which we shall also rise from the dead is by living on through our children and their children. Perhaps I lack the pastoral heart, but I long for nothing more than to move on, possibly to Dalmatia, where, God willing, people will be prepared to hear the Good News and live as those who know and follow the Risen Lord.

I feel so defenceless.
A thoroughly demoralised
Titus

You are not defenceless: these are your weapons!

Put on God's complete armour so that you can successfully resist all the Devil's methods of attack. For, as I expect you have learned by now, our fight is not against any physical enemy: it is against organisations and powers that are spiritual. We are up against the unseen power that controls this dark world, and spiritual agents from the very headquarters of evil. Therefore you must wear the whole armour of God that you may be able to resist evil in its day of power, and that even when you have fought to a standstill you may still stand your ground. Take your stand then with the Truth as your belt, Righteousness your breastplate, the Gospel of Peace firmly on your feet, Salvation as your helmet and in your hand the Sword of the Spirit, the Word of God. Above all be sure you take Faith as your shield, for it can quench every burning missile the enemy hurls at you. Pray at all times with every kind of spiritual prayer, keeping alert and persistent as you pray for all Christ's men and women. And pray for me, too, that I may be able to speak freely here, to make known the secret of the Gospel for which I am, so to speak, an ambassador in chains.

Index of Authors and Titles

References to prayers are preceded by 'P'. References to readings give the number of the reading.

Index of Readings

In some cases the titles given here differ from the titles used for the pieces in this book. The title used in this book is given in the numerical list of readings.

Numerical List of Readings

The original title of the work has not always been used but this is given in the text at the end of each piece.

49 *Judas*: Rex Chapman
50 *Indifference*: G. A. Studdert Kennedy
51 *Father to the Man*: John Knight
52 *Ecce Homo*: David Gascoyne
53 *Christ is Risen*: Leslie Newbigin
54 *Calvary*: Peter Casey
55 *It is Accomplished*: William Temple
56 *Ballad of the Bread Man*: Charles Causley
57 *The Lion, the Witch and the Wardrobe*: C. S. Lewis
58 *Three Assemblies for Remembrance Day*: Wilfred Owen, Vera Brittain, Rupert Brooke and Edward Thomas
59 *The Armistice*: Vera Brittain
60 *Disabled*: Wilfred Owen
61 *Ecclesiasticus XLIV*
62 *Micah IV*
63 *Preamble to the Charter of the United Nations, 1945*
64 *The White Flag*: Spike Milligan
65 *Feed My Little Ones*: C. Day Lewis
66 *Alf*: Colin Morris
67 *Statistics*: C. Rajendra
68 *The Arithmetic of Poverty*: D. Appadurai
69 *1941*: Yevgeny Yevtushenko
70 *Fishers of Men*: Joan Brockelsby
71 *The Story of Taizé*: J. L. G. Balado
72 *Space Between the Bars*: Donald Swann
73 *Unity*: Carolyn Scott
74 a) *Watch Your Tongue*
   b) *The Royal Chatterbox*
75 *Taking the Donkey to Market*: based on Aesop
76 *The Smuggler*
77 *Treasure in the Basket*
78 *A Pig Named Percy*
79 *The Quail*
80 *The Magic Mirror*
81 *What's in a Name?*
82 *Spoilt Broth*: H. L. Gee

83 Extracts from *The Rock*: T. S. Eliot
84 *Over the Great City*: Edward Carpenter
85 *The Brick*: Michel Quoist
86 *Chopsticks*: John R. Hogan
87 *Good Fruit Salad*
88 *Adolescence*: Doris Odlum
89 *The Need to be Nasty*: P. Okeden
90 *Maternity*: Bernadine Bishop
91 *Coping with Grandpa*: Joy Davidman
92 *Old Age*: Anon.
93 *Love*: Michel Quoist
94 From *The Velveteen Rabbit*: M. Williams Bianco
95 *Love*: Ken Walsh
96 *These I have Loved*: Rupert Brooke
97 *Ahimsa or the Way of Non-violence*: Mahatma Gandhi
98 *Which Half?*: Ken Walsh
99 *November Third*: Miyazawa Kenji
100 *Purple Papers*: John Ward
101 *Common Assault*: Joan Brockelsby
102 *The Refrigeration of Silas Hunt*: C. Astle
103 *St. George's Day*: W. H. Elliott
104 a) *Mary Verghese*
    b) *Androcles and the Lion*
105 *Mr. Mandragon*: G. K. Chesterton
106 *Four Freedoms*: Franklin D. Roosevelt
107 *Freedom and My Neighbour*: Jim Bates
108 *Freedom*: Kahlil Gibran
109 *How to be Happy*: Thomas Merton
110 *Happiness and Vision*: William Blake
111 *Canoe Story*: Geoffrey Summerfield
112 *On a Bicycle*: Yevgeny Yevtushenko

Index of Topics

Indexed topics are mainly additional to those in the main sections although these are included, in some cases with extra references. References are to the numbers of readings, prayers and hymns (in the list on page xiv. References can be quickly checked by using the 'Numerical List of Readings' (on page 266).

Bibliography

Hardened assembly-compilers will instantly recognise my main sources, and I have already acknowledged my debt to the established collections. I have found the following indispensable: C. Campling and M. Davis, *Words for Worship* (Edward Arnold); H. Elfick, *Folk and Vision* (Granada Publishing) and D. Thompson, *Readings* (C.U.P.). Of the more recent compilations I have found some useful material in: Tony Castle, *Assemble Together* (Geoffrey Chapman) and David Self, *Anthology for Assembly* (Hutchinson), particularly his modern parables. Of the less specifically assembly-oriented collections I would recommend: Elfrida Vipont, *The Highway* (O.U.P.) and Elfrida Vipont, *The Bridge* (O.U.P.). The only collection of suitable poetry I have found is *Let There be God* compiled by T. H. Parker and F. J. Teskey (Religious Education Press) but the following books of poetry/prose seem to keep their freshness: Rex Chapman, *A Kind of Praying* (S.C.M. Press); Michel Quoist, *Prayers of Life* (Gill and Son, Logos Books) and Joan Brockelsby, *Step into Joy* (Belton Books). Otherwise one has to keep an assortment of the works of individual poets of whom I have a sample in this collection.

Successful assemblies can be compiled by serialising or taking extracts from good or 'relevant' modern writing. Sheila Hocken's *Emma and I* is an example of this – other stories of personal achievement used include: James Copeland, *For the Love of Ann* (Arrow), the story of an autistic girl; Elizabeth Quinn, *Listen to Me*, the story of the deaf actress; Leonard Cheshire, *The Hidden World* (Collins, Fontana), about the Cheshire Homes. There are also excellent accounts of achievements like the ascent of Everest and Fiennes trans-globe expedition.

With younger children Paul Gallico's *The Small Miracle*, set in Assisi, is well received, while David Kossoff's *Bible Stories* (Collins, Fontana) give a painless and entertaining introduction to the Old Testament. Incidentally, his moving account of his son Paul who died of drug addiction is to be found in *You Have a Minute, Lord?* (Pan) and his *A Small Town Is a World* (Pan) gives an entertaining insight into a Jewish community. This is a good foil to Guareschi's Don Camillo stories and to the Sufi stories to be found for instance in Idries Shah, *The Way of the Sufi* (Penguin).

'Popular' theological works also have a place, particularly those with anecdotes or personal experiences. Roughly in this category are: Joy Davidman, *Smoke on the Mountain* (Hodder Christian Paperbacks); Colin Morris, *Hammer of the Lord* (Epworth Press) and also by Colin Morris, *Include Me Out* (Collins, Fontana).

Biographies and autobiographies are of course a fertile source of material – special mention to Donald Swann's *Space between the Bars* (Hodder) – and a good D.I.Y. kit can be built up from extracts noted in one's own general reading and, if they are willing, in that of friends and colleagues.